My Neighbor's Faith

My Neighbor's Faith

*Stories of Interreligious Encounter,
Growth, and Transformation*

Edited by

Jennifer Howe Peace, Or N. Rose, and Gregory Mobley

ORBIS BOOKS
Maryknoll, New York 10545

Thirteenth Printing, June 2020

Founded in 1970, Orbis Books endeavors to publish works that enlighten the mind, nourish the spirit, and challenge the conscience. The publishing arm of the Maryknoll Fathers and Brothers, Orbis seeks to explore the global dimensions of the Christian faith and mission, to invite dialogue with diverse cultures and religious traditions, and to serve the cause of reconciliation and peace. The books published reflect the views of their authors and do not represent the official position of the Maryknoll Society. To learn more about Maryknoll and Orbis Books, please visit our website at http://www.maryknollsociety.org.

Library of Congress Cataloging-in-Publication Data

My neighbor's faith : stories of interreligious encounter, growth, and
    transformation / edited by Jennifer Howe Peace, Or N. Rose, and
    Gregory Mobley.
          p. cm.
    Includes bibliographical references.
    ISBN 978-1-57075-958-1 (pbk.); eISBN 978-1-60833-117-8
    1. Religions—Relations.   I. Peace, Jennifer Howe.   II. Rose, Or N.
    III. Mobley, Gregory.
    BL410.M9 2012
    201'.5—dc23

                                                                    2011040734

To Edie Crary Howe

A Woman of Valor—
"With the fruit of her hands she plants a vineyard."
(Proverbs 31:16)

Founding member of the student interfaith community
at Hebrew College and Andover Newton Theological School

In loving memory and gratitude

Contents

Part V: Stepping across the Line

Part VI: Finding Fellow Travelers

Part VII: Repairing Our Shared World

Foreword

My first struggle with Scripture came early. The Sister who taught second grade made it a practice to read bible stories to us as part of our daily recess period. I went to school every day barely able to wait for the moment to come. I loved the telling of them. I loved the surprises in every single one of them. But one day one of them threatened my faith in ways no child can plumb. If truth were told, the story of the Tower of Babel plagued me with troubling questions for years.

The story tells of a group of people who decided to build a ziggurat all the way up to heaven. They were in search of God. They were giving their lives to the process of finding the Divine. They were good people.

But, the story goes on, when God discovered the plan, God was not pleased. Instead, it seems, of being happy to see such living faith, such thirst for the Divine, such driving commitment to seek the living God, God deliberately interfered with the project. Dashed the whole endeavor, in fact. "I will confuse their language," God says.

What kind of a God was this, I thought, that would make it impossible for people to find the God they seek, as we are all meant to do.

It took me a lot of thinking to understand the situation. The arrogance of it, I began to understand as the years went by, for any one group to think that they can achieve a monopoly on God. Instead, God explains in the story, "I will confuse their language so that they can come to know one another."

Suddenly I understood: We are not meant to go to God alone, no matter who we are. We are meant to go together, enriched by one another's faith and wisdom and insights into the ways of God.

I grew up in a period of intense denominational rivalry in what was euphemistically called "a mixed marriage." My mother was Catholic, my father was Protestant. I learned one thing early: Religions taught one thing—mutual love and respect—but modeled another—that our own religions, whatever they happened to be, were the privileged ones in the process. Everyone else's was not. Like the people in the Tower of Babel, we each wanted, and assumed we could get, a monopoly on God.

This is a book that pulls deeply at my heart. In this book all the languages of God are spoken—Hindu, Buddhist, Jewish, Christian and Muslim—so that we can learn from one another.

As a result, this book is a gemstone of faith writ large.

In this book seekers from every dimension meet together and begin to talk things out. They tell of meeting someone whose very life taught them something about God, despite the fact that they were frighteningly Other. They begin to see different dimensions of their own faith that call them to learn from the Other. They see in the faith of another a facet of the God-life they have been blind to before now.

They form friendships and faith partners beyond any obstacles meant to separate them. And they enable the reader to do the same, to become a living part of the God question, a participant in the dialogical journey to God. It is, in fact, the best example I have ever seen of a book that really captures the spirit of the academic conference out of which it sprang.

In this book, I saw my own spiritual adventure into the great wide world of faith become one with persons whose spirituality seemed at first to be far different from my own.

I have been a student of interfaith dialogue—of interfaith living—for a long, long time now. It began in my home. My Irish Catholic father died when I was almost three. My Irish Catholic mother married my stepfather, a Protestant of uncertain roots but avidly anti-Catholic upbringing, soon after. It was an era when ecumenism was not even a word, let alone a virtue.

It was a strange mix. He was not church-going at all but uncompromisingly Protestant; she was not at all a rigorously practicing Catholic but defensive of it to the hilt, nevertheless. It was like growing up in a microcosm of the Wars of Religion. Somehow or other, I knew from childhood that neither of the two extremes was right. How did I know? Easy: my religion itself taught me this, even while its very actions denied it. The Jesus who cured the Canaanite woman, who blessed the daughter of the Roman Soldier, who commissioned the Samaritan woman, who called the Samaritan man Good, who saved the woman taken in adultery from the injustice of her own faith was clear model to me of a totally other world view.

Not surprisingly then, years later, I found myself teaching a course called "Women in World Religion" in a Catholic university. The course was divided into three, three-hour segments devoted to one of each of the major traditions, Hindu, Buddhist, Jewish, Christian, and Muslim.

It was my practice to open every evening session by having the class pray in the posture and with the prayers of the tradition we happened to be studying at the time. On September 11, 2001, as the Twin Towers turned to deadening smoke and white ash, as thousands of people lay dead, incinerated, at the hands of Muslim bombers in the streets of New York, we just happened to be beginning the segment on Islam.

In the midst of that moment, my class stood shoulder to shoulder as they dropped on their knees to press their foreheads to the ground in the prayer of submission to God. I remember glancing up at the window in the classroom door. What, I wondered, would be the reaction to this scene if anyone passes this door at this moment? If they were truly Catholic, I knew there would be nothing whatsoever to be concerned about; if they were simply one brand among many of the competing forms of national Christianity, there could be trouble.

But down deep, I knew it was exactly where we needed to be at that moment. The words of Jonathan Edwards rang in my heart that night: "We have just enough religion to make us hate," Edwards had written, "but not enough religion to make us love one another."

The truth is that at its roots all religion speaks of the Mystery of Life that seeded all of us into life, that holds the cosmos in Being, that is the ultimate End of all our hope. It is the Unity for which we seek, the Oneness of Life that has many faces and speaks in many tongues.

This book takes us all back into that moment in our lives when, for whatever reason, we found ourselves face to face with the other—

and saw, in the words of Genesis, that this great work of God, too, "was good."

It requires us, as it does the people whose testimonies are in this book, to confront our own struggles with our own faith as well evaluate anyone else's. We watch them discover the beauty in other traditions.

This is a gentle, personal, heart-rending gem of honesty, a study in the many shades of blessing.

It enabled me to think again about what it is that brings me to the point in life where I am still closed to the work of God in others, to the blindness in myself. It challenges me to consider whether or not I am still trying to capture God for myself as the people in the Tower of Babel planned. It examines the degree of my openness to the holiness of the unknown others, to the power of faith everywhere, to our own need to learn about God from others who seek that same God but differently. It will make you rethink your own life, too.

Read this book. Meet all the people here. Listen to them carefully. Let them speak for you—for your fears, for your surprise, for your delight in the God who is bringing you to see in one another a fresh new path to the God you both seek.

Joan Chittister, OSB
St. Scholastica Priory
355 East Ninth Street
Erie, Pa. 16503

Acknowledgments

Many people helped inspire and shape this book, and many provided the resources necessary to complete it. First and foremost we thank Lynn Szwaja and Michael Gilligan from the Henry Luce Foundation for their generous support and encouragement over the last four years. The grant from Luce established the Center for Interreligious and Communal Leadership (CIRCLE) and literally made this work possible. They are visionaries with a deep understanding of the importance of working across religious lines for the sake of a stronger civil society.

We also want to thank the Reverend Nick Carter, president of Andover Newton Theological School and Rabbi Danny Lehmann, president of Hebrew College, for their steadfast commitment to this work both personally and institutionally.

The conference held in April 2010 that first inspired this book could not have happened without the partnership of the Boston Theological Institute and many hours of work by Dr. Rodney Petersen and Dr. Marian Gh. Simion. Dr. Priscilla Deck was also instrumental, both in helping organize the conference and in her support and leadership of CIRCLE during her tenure at Andover Newton.

In addition we thank Adina Allen for her essential support as we put the manuscript together; from copyediting to gathering author bios, to creating streamlined systems to keep the process organized. We also gratefully acknowledge Kathryn Henderson and Susan Fendrick for additional copyediting.

We thank Robert Ellsberg, our editor from Orbis, for his patient encouragement and supportive suggestions from the proposal stage through publication.

For their support in the face of long days and extra hours involved in completing this project we are grateful to Joel Howe and Dr. Judith Rosenbaum.

We gratefully acknowledge each of our contributing authors for taking a vision and making it concrete through the honesty and simplicity of their stories.

Finally, we acknowledge the energy, insights, hard work, and stories of the students in our interfaith fellowships at Andover Newton Theological School and Hebrew College. They inspire us to do this work every day.

Introduction

We live in one of the most religiously diverse nation in the history of humankind. Every day, across the country, people of different religious beliefs and practices encounter one another in supermarkets, hospitals, schools, chat rooms, and family gatherings. How has this new situation of religious diversity affected the way we understand the religious "other," ourselves, or ultimate reality? Will it lead us to overcome the long history of religious intolerance, bigotry, and violence that has plagued humanity for centuries? Can we learn to live together with mutual respect, acknowledging commonalities *and* differences, working together to create a more just and compassionate world?

My Neighbor's Faith: Stories of Interreligious Encounter, Growth, and Transformation, is a collection of personal narratives about the impact of interfaith dialogue, study, and action on the lives of religious educators, community leaders, and activists. This volume is an outgrowth of a national conference on interfaith education in Jewish, Christian, and Muslim seminaries (or their equivalents) in the United States, held at Andover Newton Theological School and Hebrew College in April 2010. Even as the conference was still in session, many participants commented that the personal stories people shared about experiences of interfaith engagement was one of the most powerful aspects of the gathering. The honesty, insight, and humor that flowed through these reflections made a deep impression on the group.

As co-hosts of the conference, we felt compelled to find a way to share some of these stories with a wider audience. We invited participants from the conference as well as others working in the growing field of interfaith dialogue and action to reflect on a significant moment in their lives when they were inspired, challenged, or transformed by an encounter with another religious tradition. This encounter may have taken place with an individual or a community, through ritual, study, civic or political engagement, or in the context of a personal relationship. Alternatively, contributors were invited to share how an encounter with someone or something from their own religious tradition—positive or negative—helped shape (or reshape) their view of the religious "other."

The result of our invitation exceeded our expectations. This volume includes more than fifty personal narratives set in various times and places, involving religious interactions of a dizzying variety. Some of the authors are well-known public figures in American life, while others are scholars, clergy, or activists whom you may not know by name but who quietly go about their work helping to transform relationships across religious lines for the sake of a more peaceful planet. In many cases, the stories they share shed light on their personal histories, core beliefs, and the motivations that animate their interfaith work.

Although wide ranging, this collection is not comprehensive. We reached out to writers from many different religious communities in the United States (and a few from Canada), but there are more stories from Jewish, Christian, and Muslim practitioners since these were the traditions primarily represented at our conference. One will also quickly discover that while all of the contributors share a commitment to interreligious cooperation, they do not necessarily agree on the theoretical or practical foundations of this work. At the same time, this collection contributes to our understanding of a wide variety of challenges and possibilities that interreligious encounters offer.

We have divided the book into seven parts, each of which begins with a brief introduction. Using the metaphor of a journey—including images of home, neighbors, boundaries, and fellow travelers—the essays are grouped according to different experiential elements common to our interfaith explorers.

Although these broad thematic categories create certain tensions and resonances among the stories, there is no "right way" to read this volume. Each contributor tells a unique story. Allow your curiosity to guide you. Perhaps a particular author or title will catch your eye. In some cases, you might recognize something of your own story in these pages. In other cases, you might be surprised, challenged, or even disappointed by the actions of the storyteller or others in the narrative. We hope that these stories help you reflect on your own life story and the place of interfaith encounter in it. May these narratives inspire you to explore anew your own religious or ideological terrain and help you expand the borders of your understanding as you seek to participate more fully in the healing of humanity and the earth. We wish you well on your journey!

Jennifer Peace, Or Rose, Gregory Mobley
Newton, Massachusetts

Part I

Encountering the Neighbor

We shall not cease from exploration
And the end of all our exploring
Will be to arrive where we started
And know the place for the first time.

T. S. Eliot, *Little Gidding*

In Part I of *My Neighbor's Faith: Stories of Interreligious Encounter, Growth, and Transformation*, we hear reports from explorers about meeting new neighbors across faith lines. What happens when you find yourself in new neighborhoods, searching for meaning in somebody else's religious world? What happens when you find (or are found by) a text, a person, or an idea from this neighboring world that is so powerful that it (or he or she) cannot be denied or suppressed?

In Brian McLaren's "Entering without Knocking," it is a case of "and a little child shall lead them," as the charming humanity of an eight-year-old Iranian neighbor inspires an evangelical Christian to rethink his assumptions about Muslims. Ibrahim Abdul-Matin, author of "Water Carriers," forges an unlikely friendship with a fundamentalist Christian, with whom he finds himself doing the heavy lifting on an Outward Bound expedition.

In Irving Greenberg's "What Would Roy and Alice Do" (*WWR-and-AD*, for readers paying close attention), a Jew encounters the moral courage of the Hebrew prophets in the witness of a handful of heroic Christians willing to face the anti-Semitism of their history. In "The Hijabi Monologues" Zeenat Rahman emphasizes the importance of telling our stories as a crucial first step in recognizing the humanity of our religious neighbors. Pravrajika Vrajaprana, a Hindu nun, goes undercover in "Interfaith Incognito: What a Hindu Nun Learned from Evangelical Christians," to explore the limits of public interreligious dialogue and show the power of interfaith learning in the context of personal relationships.

Jennifer Howe Peace in "God Is Greater" describes a religious turning point in her young adulthood: a Christian experience of the numinous. However, the story is incomplete until a revelation from a Muslim classmate shifts and broadens her understanding of her brush with the divine. The initial encounter helped define her religious path; the ensuing conversation her vocation as an interfaith educator.

In "My Ever-Present Interfaith Interlocutors," Sherman A. Jackson takes us back to the neighborhood that this Muslim academic left long ago, but that has never left him. He describes his childhood home in urban Philadelphia where he first experienced the love and support of Christian friends and family that continue to sustain him long after his conversion to Islam.

The final essay in Part I is Burton Visotzky's "It Begins with a Text." For Rabbi Visotzky, true to his biblical and Talmudic training, interfaith encounter always begins with texts, with words, language, and symbols. But if it existed, the second line of his title might be "and it ends in personal relationship," as he offers us snapshots from a lifelong journey of sacred text study with an array of the teachers and writers from New York to Rome and several points in between.

1

Entering without Knocking

Brian D. McLaren

We all know the standard traditions of marriage in America: something borrowed, something blue . . . the groom doesn't see the bride before the wedding . . . processional and recessional . . . the kiss, the toast . . . the newlywed couple cutting the cake and smearing it on each other's faces, throwing rice on the departing couple. But there are also some nonstandard traditions that include a wide array of practical jokes.

My brother masterminded one on Grace and me. He and my parents kindly offered to move some furniture into our apartment while we were away on our honeymoon. After hauling in the furniture, my brother blew up a couple hundred balloons and filled our only bathroom with them. When I say filled, I mean that the room was jammed with balloons floor to ceiling. (It must have been a challenge to squeeze the last few dozen in there!)

Imagine us returning home after midnight from our honeymoon in Bermuda. Bleary-eyed and emotional about spending our first night in our apartment, we wandered around with a mix of excitement and exhaustion. But when we tried to open the bathroom door, *it wouldn't open!*

Once we diagnosed the problem, the question became how to treat it. Popping several hundred balloons after midnight would surely elicit 911 calls from our new neighbors and not make the ideal first impression: "They must have a shooting gallery down there in Apartment 101!"

Or, "Wow, that new marriage doesn't seem to be going too well. Guns already!"

So we gingerly reached in and began pulling out balloons, one at a time. After fifteen or twenty minutes, the bathroom was more or less empty, but a slow tide of balloons had spread through our apartment, covering the floor of our living room, dining room, and kitchen like a motley tide. "We'll deal with it in the morning," I told my wife.

The next morning, I stepped out on our front stoop to survey our new neighborhood as my bride slept in. There I bumped into a boy of about eight, rushing into the apartment building like a bat into a cave. He struck me as friendly and energetic, maybe precocious, maybe even brash. "You're the new guy," he said. "Gotta go!"

By his breathless pace, I suspected the unspoken end of the sentence was "to the bathroom." I sat down on the stoop to ponder what I was going to do with a couple million—more or less—balloons. A minute later, the boy returned and plopped down on the step next to me, still breathless but talkative. He was Armin, eight years old, from Iran, lived in the apartment directly above ours.

If life were a cartoon, one of those little light bulbs would have appeared above my head about three minutes into our conversation. "Hey, Armin, do you like balloons?" "Sure. You got some?" "Come with me," I replied.

We went up one flight of stairs and when I opened the door and he peered in, his eyes opened wide and he flashed me a huge smile. "I can help you, Brian. I can help you with these." But instead of grabbing even one, he raced down the stairs and out the door. I could hear his little sneakers slapping down the sidewalk. I was a little puzzled, but Armin seemed like a young man who knew what he was doing.

A few minutes later, the door opened—no knock: I learned that Armin never knocked. In came a stream of kids, seven, eight, nine, ten, eleven. Each of them took as many balloons as he or she could hold, the little ones two, the bigger ones three or four. A few minutes later, they came back for a second load, and after a few loads, all the balloons were gone.

That day earned us a heroic reputation with the neighborhood kids and a slightly less stellar reputation with their parents who had to endure the random sounds of popping balloons for days to come. But it also began a friendship with Armin. I'd have to say that Armin was my first Muslim friend.

Soon we got to know his mom, Liza (Anglicized from a Farsi name). We never succeeded in getting Armin to knock. I think we became his second family, which meant a lot to both him and his mom, for reasons that gradually became clear.

Armin's dad was a graduate student at the university where I was also studying. He had come to the United States a year before his family to get things ready for their arrival and to get acclimated to his studies in a foreign language. A few months after their arrival, Liza realized that her husband had grown close—very close—with an American student, and soon, he moved in with her, leaving Liza and Armin stuck in America with no husband, no father, no work, and no English.

We and our balloons moved in about a year after the breakup. In that time, Armin had gone to school and mastered English as only kids can. Liza got a job at a McDonald's, and her English had improved from nonexistent to broken but functional. Over the next few years, our friendship deepened, and Liza expressed that friendship in a most delicious way: Iranian dishes delivered to our door. We once hosted a party for her Iranian friends. It turned out Americans, back in those days after the Iranian Revolution and the hostage situation, weren't very welcoming to Iranians, so word spread that Liza knew some Americans who liked Iranians.

My brain was filled with the same ignorant misconceptions about Islam and Muslims that most Americans share today. Liza and Armin reeducated me. They helped me know Muslims as my neighbors, my friends, human beings who struggled with the same mice and cockroaches that we did in that grimy little apartment building.

Since then, I've been blessed with many more Muslim friends in my life. Each has brought a gift to me, but none greater than Armin. By becoming my first Muslim friend, he forever shattered my preconceptions and false assumptions.

The standard approach to Muslims from my Evangelical upbringing was to be nice to them when necessary in order to evangelize them; otherwise, see them as spiritual competitors and potential enemies. Armin was the first instrument of my conversion away from that sub-Christian attitude, and he was an ideal agent for conversion. As my neighbor, it was pretty hard to ignore Jesus' commandment to love him. As a child, he didn't pose a threat. As my benefactor—the angelic agent of post-honeymoon balloon removal—how could I not be grateful to him? And as a naturally bold and precocious child who never learned to knock before entering, he was determined to be part of my life unless I locked the door.

I'm glad I didn't. Thank God I didn't.

2

Water Carriers

Ibrahim Abdul-Matin

I forget his name. To be honest, I have forgotten all of their names. But I will never forget the twenty-two-day winter adventure we shared, hiking, climbing, and discovering ourselves in Joshua Tree National Park, and how I found an unlikely friend and confidant, and deepened my own faith along the way.

Before this trip, I had never been to a desert before. In fact, I had never been outside of the Northeast during the winter. This experience was intentional. I wanted to expand my horizons and challenge myself in every way possible through this expedition in the harsh Southern California desert with a group of strangers.

After spending a few days with extended family members along the West Coast, I made my way to the LA Greyhound bus station. I had my backpack and ticket in hand and boarded the bus to Twentynine Palms, the departure point for the trip. We had to arrive on time or else the group would simply leave without the latecomers.

And so began the adventure. Since I had assumed that Greyhound service was reliable all over the country, I was a little more than surprised when the bus driver abruptly stopped in Palm Springs saying that he would go no further. "But I bought a ticket to Twentynine Palms," I insisted.

He told me the next bus would leave in six hours. I didn't have six hours. And so, I did what any New Yorker would do when they are late—I hailed a cab and convinced the driver to take me the fifty miles to my destination. I managed to arrive at the rendezvous point on time to meet up with my fellow course members.

Twentynine Palms is exactly what you would imagine it to be: a "Wild, Wild West" desert town. I kid you not when I say that a tumbleweed bounced past the cab as we pulled into the dirt parking lot of the Pacific Crest Outward Bound School. The sun was piercing as I paid the driver and lifted my pack out of the trunk. The soles of my boots (loaned to me by an older Outward Bound instructor back East), crunched the burning sand of the Mojave. I might as well have landed on Mars!

The first thing you do on an Outward Bound expedition is prepare your gear and supplies. With help from our instructor we organized our individual and shared equipment, including cooking utensils, ropes, walking sticks, maps, tarps, and of course, water containers. The water containers were the most important of all. Since there were no naturally occurring water sources along the trail, we would essentially hike from water cache to water cache. As we traveled, the biggest and strongest hikers were responsible for carrying the extra water supply. As it turns out, on this trip there were two designated water carriers: me and a guy we will call "Christian."

I grew up around a lot of Christians. My schools in upstate New York and Brooklyn were populated by Christians from many different denominations. In fact, my mother would actually take my siblings and me to church services so that we would understand more deeply something of the spiritual lives of our friends and neighbors.

My fellow water carrier was, however, a different kind of Christian. He was from the deep backwoods of the Pacific Northwest and was deeply distrustful of people different from him. You can imagine how he felt about me. Early on in our trip, he shared with the group that the end of the world was near. He also told the non-Christians among us that we were, unfortunately, doomed to suffer in hell. While sharing all of this "good news" with us, he added that Muslims, according to the teachings of his church, were the scourge of the earth.

The first few days of the trip were not easy for me and Christian, to say the least. We were both young, testosterone-filled, and the biggest guys on the course. It could have been a disaster. But slowly, we managed to forge a bond. One very basic factor that allowed us to avoid some of the obvious pitfalls was that we shared a mutual burden: we knew we were the two people who were going to be stuck carrying the heavy water containers for the next three weeks. This common enemy created just enough of a connection for a real relationship to grow.

And then there was the whole sleeping thing. On Outward Bound trips, participants sleep under the stars. When the weather was bad, we used our walking sticks and tarps to fashion temporary shelters. At night, when the temperature dropped, we would arrange our sleeping area so that we could huddle together and use our body heat to keep us warm. Since Christian and I were the biggest of the bunch, we had to sleep close to each other in order not to freeze.

Christian and I were also the only people on the course who were vocal about our faith. When I would wake up early to pray, often he would already be praying. As we hiked under the blazing hot sun, we talked for hours about our differences *and* our similarities. We never tried to proselytize the other and came to really support each other in our practices. We would encourage each other to make sure we said our prayers, read our holy books, and took the time to reflect on the meaning of this experience in the light of our beliefs.

I will never forget the night of the first of January. We settled into our sleeping bags, watched the stars and constellations, and talked about what we wanted to do with our lives and the kinds of families we wanted to create. We talked about God and how awesome God is as we looked out at the dazzling night sky. We saw planes zoom past in the distance, and in the bed of a dry spring creek we fell asleep just after midnight swearing we had both just seen a UFO!

Outward Bound expeditions are broken into phases. Initially the instructor guides the group very carefully before gradually handing off the reins to the crew. Each member learns different tasks—cooking, cleaning, arranging a campsite, navigating, etc.—rotating through the circuit until by time of the final expedition, the people who are best at a chosen job take it on. During this final leg of the trip the instructors are nowhere to be seen (they observe us from a distance). For the final expedition the crew had to choose two navigators. They chose Christian and me, since we were the most adept at using the compass and the contour maps, and because, as it turns out, by this point in the trip we worked very well together.

On January 17, 2001, we finished our expedition, left Joshua Tree, and rolled into the Outward Bound headquarters with the latest U2 hit "Beautiful Day" serendipitously playing on the radio. We all said our good-byes and promised to stay in touch. I connected with a few folks afterwards, but mostly, I cannot even recall their names. At this point they are all part of the hazy memory of a powerful moment in young adulthood. Over time, the faces and names have blended into the desert scenery with its hot sun, awesome mountains, and beautiful cholla cactus gardens.

Interestingly, Christian and I never allowed ourselves the false comfort of sentimental promises. Like the tough guys we were, we looked each other square in the eye, hugged, and said "God Bless," knowing that we would never see each other again in this world.

"I hope we see each other in heaven," I remember him saying to me.

"God willing," I said. "*InshAllah*."

3

What Would Roy and Alice Do?

Irving (Yitz) Greenberg

I first learned about dialogue from reading Martin Buber. From him, I understood that religious dialogue was all about meeting the other in an I-Thou encounter. Certainly there should be no intention to change the other or make him/her over in my image. But I confess that I did not enter the Jewish-Christian conversation in a very dialogic frame of mind. I was driven by a shocking life-changing encounter with the Holocaust in 1961 that tore apart my devout, believing relationship with the God of Israel and shattered my religious equilibrium as a fulfilled modern Orthodox Jew. I could not understand how the Nazis could single out the Jews for total extermination while the whole modern civilized world stood by. Nor could I accept that God had not intervened to save God's people from this fate.

As I read and studied, I came to believe that the Jews were set up to be victims of genocide by almost two thousand years of Christian "teaching of contempt"—a horrifying typology of Jews and their religion that proposes a malicious narrative: the Jews grew self-satisfied and spiritually blind having been besotted by pride in being chosen. Their faith turned into a religion with no soul or compassion. They arrogantly rejected God who in the person of Jesus Christ walked among them, and they became cruel murderers who mocked and tormented the mild, loving Lamb of God and condemned him to death. Thus they forfeited their election and brought down an eternal curse from God on themselves.

These teachings intensified as time went on. It was said that, having lost their connection to the living God, Jews bought a (dead) life by selling their soul to the devil. They became the synagogue of Satan—and behaved like devils. By the Middle Ages, the portrait grew even worse. Jews were afflicted with pestilent diseases—and horns—that betrayed their pact with the Arch Fiend. They poisoned wells and spread plagues to decimate their neighbors. They kidnapped innocent children, cut their throats, drew their blood and baked it into the matzah, their ritual bread. Thus Christianity injected deep into Western culture the image of Jews as uncanny and demonic, beyond the pale of humanity.

By the nineteenth century, this profile had mutated into racial anti-Semitism. In religious anti-Semitism, the evil characteristics of being Jewish could be shucked off by becoming Christian; racial anti-Semitism held that Jews were incorrigibly subhuman. Hitler and many Nazi leaders were not faithful Christians—indeed they were enemies of Christianity—but they seized upon the group already designated by Christianity as unworthy of life to be their scapegoat; by the elimination and death of the Jews, the world would be made whole.

Desperate and looking for allies, my wife and I joined the Jewish-Christian dialogue to persuade Christians to root out anti-Semitism before it struck again. Christians would have to recognize the good truth about Jews so they could reject the vicious stereotyping embedded in their tradition. My goal in "dialogue" was not to learn about Christianity, but to teach Christians about Christianity's deeply embedded anti-Semitism.

Continued circulation of these images would make these themes available for reuse in future generations. My children and grandchildren would be at risk. I realized that for Christians to shake off the incubus of supersessionism, demonization, and "justified" hatred, an active program of positive affirmation of Judaism by Christians was essential. It would take a wrenching acknowledgment of past guilt and a determined repentance, including confronting the New Testament itself. It would take unblinking self-criticism and heroic efforts to neutralize the Church Fathers' and various saints' teachings about "the Jews." Protestants would have to repudiate the violent, eliminationist anti-Semitism of Martin Luther—the very man who gave them so much spiritual nurture and understanding of faith. Could a religion with such a bad record generate such a noble and selfless reformation in order to stop inflicting pain on others? It did not seem very promising.

My initial efforts to educate Christians about anti-Semitism were met with some classic responses: Christianity may have been anti-Jewish but not anti-Semitic because anti-Semitism is hate, and Christianity is a religion of love; the New Testament is sacred, and a divine text by definition cannot be besmirched with hatred so if there is anti-Semitism in Christianity it was injected later.[1]

Had all the Christians I met responded defensively, my entry into dialogue would have been futile, if not disastrous. However, by the grace of God, I met a most remarkable group of Christians including Roy and Alice Eckardt, who became soulmates.[2] These people got it. They understood the Christian problem, because they had studied it themselves. They did not need me to teach them; they taught me. They were able to offer a critique from within that was not airbrushed in any way. As faithful Christians, they were determined to erase the blot of anti-Semitism from the religion they loved.

Roy and Alice Eckardt spoke out in their community. They wrote a searing article, "Again, Silence in the Churches" in the weeks before the outbreak of the Six-Day War in 1967.[3] They grasped that certain classic Christian beliefs were deeply implicated in the worst Christian behaviors. They critiqued leading contemporary Christian theologians of their

---

[1] I remember, thirty years later, having such an exchange with the Reverend Jerry Falwell. Since our paths had crossed at a conference in a hotel, I pulled out a Bible and asked him to read Matthew 27:25 ("The people cried: 'His blood be on us, and on our children.") and some of the classic passages in John. He was obviously shaken up, fell silent for a moment and then said: "You know my mother read me these passages starting from my childhood. My mother loved the Jews and there was not a drop of hatred in these verses as she read them." (I am not recalling his exact words, but the gist of them.) In a way, I believed him, but in the early days, such responses evoked righteous indignation in me, if not scorn.

[2] I met many other wonderful conversation partners, including Franklin Littell, Gerald Sloyan, Paul Van Buren, John Palikowski, J. Coert Rylersdaam, Clark Williamson —and especially Sister Rose Thering—and many more too numerous to name.

[3] Roy Eckardt and Alice Eckardt, "Again, Silence in the Churches," *Christian Century*, 74, no. 30 (July 26, 1967): 970–80, and no. 31 (August 2, 1967): 992–95.

time for false witness about Judaism's claims as well as unselfconscious, self-flattering triumphalism expressed in statements like, "Through the cross of Jesus, the Jewish legal tradition as a whole has been set aside in its claim to contain the eternal will of God in its final formulation."

They even understood how the Christian focus on Jesus' infinite suffering in the crucifixion could lead to a dismissal of the suffering of others, including the enormity of the Holocaust itself. This led them to write *A Long Night's Journey into Day*.[4] In it, they quoted the account of the Nazis in Auschwitz burning Jewish children and described it "as an evil that is more terrible than other evils [including the crucifixion of Jesus who was a mature person on a mission who knew what he was dying for]. This is the evil of little children witnessing the murder of other little children . . . being aware absolutely that they face the identical fate." By this standard, "The Godforsakenness of Jesus has proved to be non-absolute—for there is now a Godforsakenness that is worse by an infinity of infinity—that Godforsakenness of Jewish children which is a final horror."[5]

I began to reflect on the apparent paradox that these prophets were people shaped by and suffused with Christian faith, which surely deserved some credit for raising such people. Clearly, I had not paid sufficient attention to the total substance of the religion and its effects on its adherents. The real turning point came for me in 1975 when I broke my boycott of Germany to participate in a conference on the Holocaust in Hamburg. The German participants were noble Christians, headed by Gertrud Luckner, who had been sent to the concentration camps for her resistance to the Nazis.

In one session, Roy Eckardt presented. As he began, the murmurings from the audience grew. People were embarrassed by the uncensored dissection of Christianity's sins against the Jews (a feeling no doubt intensified by the presence of Jews). They were offended by the reduction of Christian claims—even though Eckardt explained that this was the only way to break the vicious cycle of Christian triumphalism. The group literally silenced him. I felt that we were inches away from some kind of excommunication.

---

[4] A. Roy Eckardt and Alice Eckardt, *A Long Night's Journey into Day: Life and Faith after the Holocaust* (Detroit: Wayne State University Press, 1982).

[5] Ibid., 104.

Then it struck me that I had to speak up. I testified that as I heard Roy, I experienced Christianity's moral grandeur in that it could raise up such prophetic voices. I had not heard such penetrating words of unsparing self-criticism since the prophets of Israel had chastised the people. Although many prophetic words have been misused by Christians to degrade the Jews, in actual fact the prophets' critique was testimony to the ethical stature of Jewry and the high standards by which Judaism was being judged. Now I understood that Jews would have to make a herculean effort to match such a standard of self-purification from sins against others.

In this moment, I came to see the profound moral force in Christianity. I was also deeply moved by meeting other people who out of faithfulness to Christianity devoted their lives, in sacrificial ways, to help and heal human beings in great need. This set me on a long journey to reconceive the Jewish relationship to Christianity. I tried to understand what vision for the world and message to the Jews God wanted to convey in extending the covenant to a vast segment of humanity through Jesus and Christianity. This went beyond rethinking Christianity from a Jewish perspective.

The power of the Eckardts for me was that they had no axe to grind against Christianity. They were seeking truth, and they would speak it even to God. They would show no favoritism to humans or God; they refused to soften the failures, responsibilities, and obligations that they uncovered. Therefore, their critique implicitly challenged all religious people—and inevitably, extended to Judaism as well.

Here was their final impact on my life: The Eckardts' approach forced me to ask myself, "What in my tradition teaches contempt for other traditions or for the full dignity of other human beings?" Prodded by their example, I spoke out. I had been increasingly in tension with my own Orthodox Jewish community due to my theological journey under the impact of the Holocaust. In the eyes of my community's leadership, my offenses were many: restoring the fullest possible image of God as a response to the systematic degradation of the image in the camps meant affirming black liberation, women's liberation, gay liberation. The Shoah revealed the unity of our fate and the inadequacy of all positions, which led me to affirm internal Jewish pluralism; reconceptualizing the relationship with Christianity to recognize it as a covenantal partner in *tikkun olam* meant a grave departure from past consensus. I felt that all these teachings were desperately needed in a post-Holocaust world, but I knew that I was straining my own ties to their breaking point.

Time and again I hesitated or tried to soften my positions to narrow the distance between me and my community. In truth, I wanted to sell out more than once. But the compelling moral example of the Eckardts rose before my eyes and stopped me. I asked myself: What would Roy and Alice do? I could do no less. I got into trouble; relationships were ruptured. But I learned the final lesson of dialogue: It made me into a better—and certainly a changed—member of my own faith.

4

The Hijabi Monologues

Zeenat Rahman

Several summers ago, I found myself in a dimly lit auditorium in southern Florida. The room was packed, and the air was buzzing with anticipation. The play that I created with colleagues in graduate school, *The Hijabi Monologues,* was about to begin. The play was a labor of love that grew out of a close friendship with two of my peers, Sahar and Dan. Sahar is a highly intelligent, vivacious, fiercely loyal friend who wears the veil and is a great storyteller. Dan, a fellow Middle East Studies major, is a secular person with great curiosity and confidence, and a penchant for asking good questions. Over the course of many stolen study breaks and car drives around campus, we became good friends who gained a deep understanding of one another. One day, when Sahar was telling us a particularly hilarious story involving a stranger's reaction to her veil, Dan had an epiphany, "Other people need to hear these stories! They need to know about Muslim American women and their real experiences. We should create a play, and it should be called *The Hijabi Monologues.*" With that, our play was born.

Five years later, we had performed in countless venues, from our campus at the University of Chicago to the Kennedy Center in Washington, D.C. But this night in Miami was different. Sahar was from Miami, and tonight we were performing for an audience full of people from her community, with a very special guest front and center—her mom.

The lights went down and the play began. A series of short monologues, our play tells the stories of Muslim American women who veil; not simply why they veil, but who they are. The stories are sad and funny, representing the experiences of older and younger women alike. We don't seek to represent all Muslim women but to give audiences a glimpse of the diversity that exists within our community. Our goal has always been that people leave with more questions than when they walked in.

Jamarah began with a monologue called "I'm Tired." It's a story that expresses the frustration of feeling that one is constantly called upon to represent all of her coreligionists and the pressure of having to always be a model citizen. Sahar then told the "The Football Story": a tale of two young women in college, one with *niqab* (http://en.wikipedia.org/wiki/Cloth), a cloth that covers the face), who attended a major college football game and ended up praying in the ABC sports news trailer (you really have to hear the whole story!). Sahar then told a second story called "My Son's Wedding Feast." It is a heartbreaking account of a mother who lost her son in a car accident, and in her grief imagined that the funeral attendees were actually guests at her son's wedding. We ended with a sweet story about a young hijabi girl in high school whose friends from different religious backgrounds protect her from taunting bullies.

As the lights came up in the theater, I headed up to the stage with the performers. Although I don't perform in the play, I often moderate the discussion between the audience and the cast members following the show. That night, the audience was a mix of men and women, Muslim and non-Muslim, old and young. We felt fortunate to have a diverse and packed house; Sahar's mom was beaming with pride!

As I began the dialogue and invited questions, many hands went up throughout the hall. I noticed an African American man sitting in the back of the room, vigorously waving his arm back and forth. "Yes," I called on him, "you, Sir, in the back."

He cleared his throat and said, "I just wanted to say thank you. I have to admit that before watching this play, when I saw an Arab-looking man in the airport, I would be watching him instead of reading my newspaper. When I saw a Muslim woman in a veil, I would be worried that she had a bomb under there. Now, I'm an African

American man in my fifties and I should know better, but I have to admit, I was scared. So thank you."

"What changed for you in watching this play?" I asked him.

"Oh," he responded, "I realized that y'all are just normal people."

Many years and countless performances later, that comment still moves me. It was a simple yet profound reminder. As someone who has worked in the field of interfaith cooperation for the last five years, I believe that sharing our stories is the most important thing we can do to get to know one another. I can spend hours explaining the "Five Pillars of Islam," but until someone knows and trusts me, they cannot understand how and why I live my Islam. It is a powerful practice to tell our stories and to hear the stories of others. It helps us see our common humanity, to notice differences in our life journeys, and it invites conversation. To extend the lesson I learned from my teacher from Florida, "Normal" is a good first step.

5

Interfaith Incognito:
What a Hindu Nun Learned from
Evangelical Christians

Pravrajika Vrajaprana

Although I have attended any number of interfaith events and have found them interesting, even engrossing, experiences, one could argue that these gatherings have limited value. I say this not from any lack of respect for interfaith dialogue. Indeed, the monastic order to which I belong, the Ramakrishna Order of India (whose Western branches are known as Vedanta Societies), has long been in the forefront of interreligious dialogue. Ramakrishna, a Hindu saint of nineteenth-century India, practiced not only the various spiritual disciplines within the Hindu tradition, he also practiced spiritual disciplines in the Islamic and Christian traditions. He achieved mystic union with the divine by following each path, and thus it was from his own experience that he taught that every religion is a valid and true entryway to the ultimate Reality. That Reality is called by various names since it seen through different lenses, interpreted through various minds, and refracted through various cultures, but that one Reality is the same.

This outlook gained greater currency when Ramakrishna's disciple Swami Vivekananda spoke as the Hindu representative at the World's Parliament of Religions in Chicago in 1893. The parliament was the first genuinely representative interfaith event in Western history. Vivekananda's appearance there also marked the first real introduction of Hinduism to the Western world. In his address, presciently delivered on September 11th of 1893, Vivekananda noted that he was "proud to belong to a religion which has taught the world both tolerance and universal acceptance. We believe not only in universal toleration, but we accept all religions as true." He concluded:

> I fervently hope that the bell that tolled this morning in honor of this convention may be the death-knell of all fanaticism, of all persecutions with the sword or with the pen, and of all uncharitable feelings between persons wending their way to the same goal.

One hundred and eight years later in New York City, the significance of Vivekananda's words became more poignant than ever. Given that, why would I suggest that the importance of interfaith gatherings is overstated? One reason is that the learning that occurs in these gatherings typically flows in one direction: I speak; you listen. Then you listen; I speak. There is no two-way traffic here; thus the knowledge that is gained, while worthy, tends to be superficial.

The deeper, more intractable problem is that those of us who attend these gatherings are those most likely to be open-minded about other religious traditions in the first place. Preaching to the choir can be a satisfying experience because we all enjoy getting positive feedback: we all get to agree, we can all get along, we pat each other on the back, and we feel good about ourselves and our enlightened motives. But I do not think that these kinds of gatherings are the best way to fundamentally change anyone—let alone the world.

Having been in the back-patting position often enough myself, I would propose that what works more effectively as far as genuine interreligious dialogue is what I call "interfaith incognito." By this I mean interfaith dialogue that is not initiated for the sake of public consumption. It is spontaneous, unrehearsed, and often completely unexpected. This kind of encounter—chanced upon without our official garbs, without our sonorous voices chanting our Sanskrit chants or Koranic surahs or Psalms of David, without our made-for-the-public explanation of our traditions—can be much more genuine, contain much more truth, and can be much more transformative. There are no speeches, just real human interaction. This kind of genuine two-way traffic *can* effect change, but the change is quiet, incremental, and without fanfare. We are not dealing with auditoriums of hundreds or thousands of people, we are addressing one human being at a time, and we are also *being* changed as we change others who encounter us.

I may be the only Hindu nun in the world who is also an enthusiastic choral singer. I love my Sanskrit chants, but I also love my Bach B-Minor Mass. I've sung in a choral group for over fifteen years, and it was during a choral rehearsal that an incognito interfaith event took place. Every rehearsal during break, I have a cup of Lemon Lift tea. One of our baritones, a kindly looking gentleman by the name of Will, liked the same tea, and after some time, he began saving me a teabag, knowing I'd be looking for that vocal-clearing brew. One evening as we were sipping tea, Will said: "You know, I've been singing with you so long, but I have no idea what you do for a living." The question made me smile because I knew he would be surprised by my response. I have never attended a rehearsal in the official saffron colors of my monastic order. I wore jeans and pullovers like everyone else.

In response to Will's question I said: "Of *all* the people in this choir, I am the one with the strangest occupation." A soft-spoken and careful man, Will said, "No, I can't believe that! What do you do?" OK, I thought, I might as well go for it. "Will, I'm a Hindu nun." I saw the color drain from his face. "You're a *what?*" "A Hindu nun." "I didn't know there *was* such a thing." He was clearly perturbed. "Yes, not only *is* there such a thing, I *am* one." He stared at me in disbelief. I reached for a tenor walking by, one who had visited our temple: "Denny, am I a Hindu nun?" "Yeah, she's a Hindu nun all right!" Looking at me seriously, Will said: "I'm in Campus Crusade for Christ. I go to India every year and do free heart surgeries."

Now *I* was the one who was taken aback. Will wasn't the only one with something to learn. "Will," I said, "I'm so happy to learn that. The monastic order to which I belong, the Ramakrishna Order of India, is one of India's largest social service organizations. We have many hospitals and educational facilities—from preschool to university level. We have schools for the blind and for the physically and mentally disabled. We do relief and rehabilitation work for victims of famine, flood, epidemics, and community disturbances. We believe that in serving humanity we are worshipping God in the same way that we worship God in the temple."

Will listened gravely then finally said: "I see that I need to learn more about your religion." The truth is, I could have said the same thing myself, although I knew well the tenets of popular Christianity. Will listened with complete attention to every word I said. You can always tell when someone isn't listening to what you say; they may be looking at you with glazed eyes, but their minds are preoccupied as they prepare their counterresponse. Will was not doing that. To my surprise, he did not attempt to dissuade me from my tradition, nor did he speak slightingly of it. His humility, his humane and respectful response, his willingness to listen and learn instead of preach, taught me more than I taught him. I had attended many an interfaith gathering with Christians, but no one spoke more powerfully to his faith than Will.

And, truth be told, if I had known that Will belonged to Campus Crusade for Christ *before* we had shared that cup of Lemon Lift tea, I doubt that I would have looked forward to a conversation with him. If he had negative preconceptions about Hinduism, I have to admit that I also had plenty of misconceptions—and prejudices—about Evangelical Christians. It is shameful to be involved in interreligious dialogue and still expect narrow-mindedness in others when, in fact, it is lodged in oneself. Had my own unexamined prejudices not unexpectedly been put under the light of Will's open-hearted response, I wouldn't have known they were there.

Was Will's reaction a cosmetic response? Was he merely being polite? Nothing indicates that. We spoke more often during breaks; he was always there, saving me a teabag. His kindness, his goodness, his unselfish character came through whatever he did and said, no matter what or with whom he was discussing.

A cardiologist, Will developed serious heart problems himself, and illness compelled him to leave the choir. After some months elapsed, he called to see how I was doing. I told him that I was praying for him, and he was genuinely grateful—just as I was grateful when he told me that I was included in his prayers. In our telephone conversations today he thanks me for my prayers. I have been on various interfaith panels with high-profile Christians, but no one has broadened my mind more than Will, no one has made me appreciate Christianity more, and no one else has given me a sense of how transformative Evangelical Christianity can be. And for that, I can only be grateful.

Not everyone is interested in interreligious events. By and large the world is populated by people who either don't care or whose beliefs allow no place for interfaith dialogue—attitudes we can find in every one of our faith traditions. How we reach *them* is our challenge. How we change *ourselves* and remove our own unexamined prejudices is also the challenge. Interfaith gatherings lack the means to solve these challenges. They, like wrongly prescribed drugs, often serve to mask the symptoms without curing the illness. For, after our gatherings have ended, our good-byes have been said and the kumbaya moments have dissipated, what has changed? The only way to genuinely effect change—change in ourselves and change in others—is to *be* what each of our religions tells us that we should be. To be a Hindu in the best way possible is to be a human being in the best way possible. It works with every faith tradition. By *being* our religion we do much more for interfaith work than all the speeches we've ever made put together. Do it, and make it a lifetime commitment. And try doing it incognito. You may be surprised by what you discover.

6

God Is Greater

Jennifer Howe Peace

The first time I met Mohammed he was sitting behind a flimsy card table in the back of the School of Oriental and African Studies (SOAS) coffee shop. It was orientation week, and student groups were set up to advertise their activities. "Do you like poetry?" he asked me as I wandered by his table. Mohammed had a mop of black hair that begged for a cut and dark brown eyes. He looked at me with an earnest expression. "Sure, I like poetry," I answered. I was eager to meet new students and explore new topics. What I didn't realize when I signed up for his Sufi poetry group was how meeting Mohammed would change my theology and expand my understanding of God.

I was here on a junior year abroad studying the history, religion, politics, and music of India. I had come to SOAS because I was outgrowing the comfortable college in Connecticut where I entered thinking I would be a child development major. Taking my first course on the history of India, I was fascinated to discover a whole subcontinent where people seemed to function perfectly well (and for thousands of years) without the assumptions I inherited growing up in the United States in a middle-class Christian family.

The coffee shop was the central gathering place for the diverse student body who attended this commuter school in the University of London network. The main floor was littered with paper and lively conversations. While sipping tea with biscuits, students discussed the day's news with the enthusiasm of budding politicians or future revolutionaries. I had to read three different newspapers just to keep up with the flow of casual conversation. The lower level of the coffee shop was darker, and the atmosphere was suitably more subdued. This was where I gathered with classmates to listen to music, talk about what we were reading, and compare notes about "back home." The bustling, cosmopolitan ethos in London was a long way from the small homogeneous New England town where I spent most of my childhood. But I thrived in this mix and fell in love with city life. Conversant in this multivocal landscape, Mohammed and the other students in my classes were happy to share what they knew with me as my social, political, and intellectual horizons expanded.

While at SOAS, I rented a bedroom in the family home of a couple my parents knew. Reverend Cooke was a vicar; Mrs. Cooke was a budding historian; and together they were raising two lively children. Living with a priest's family meant that the weekends were organized around church—not an unfamiliar pattern for me as a minister's daughter who spent my first five years in South Africa as a missionary kid. I attended two services each Sunday—in the morning, a traditional Anglican service with the Cookes, and in the evening, a youth-oriented service at Holy Trinity, Brompton (HTB). HTB, while still Anglican, was a charismatic, unpredictable place that featured rock bands and rowdy shouts of praise.

Although I enjoyed the community aspect of church and the familiarity of the routine, I began to notice that the biblical texts I was listening to no longer moved me. The faith of my childhood did not feel like a living faith; the words had become empty. At the same time it struck me that faith cannot be inherited or bequeathed. It has to be chosen. In London I found myself choosing Sufi poetry and Indian ragas in the company of my new international friends over the practices of my past.

The trajectory of my faith life might have been very different had it not been for an invitation to attend a weekend retreat with the HTB youth group. I started the retreat with a bad attitude and an ultimatum. Essentially, I thought of it as God's last chance to convince me that there was something to this whole religion business. The retreat was held in a lovely house in the English countryside. I was moved by the initial gathering and wrote in my journal, "What a relief to say, all right, God, you created me. You wanted me here. So now, what are you going to do with me? I'm here and I'm honestly asking; how does your existence translate into my experience?"

By the morning, I was nursing my skepticism again. "Religion isn't for me after all. I am being a fool," I confessed to my journal. During the morning session I jotted down sarcastic notes while listening to a sincere young man read passages about love from the Bible. Once the reading stopped and the singing began, the atmosphere changed. Some people stood and swayed with their arms spread wide over their heads, palms up. Some spoke softly in unintelligible words. Some were weeping. I kept writing in my journal—my buffer against the inexplicable. "What are all these people crying about? What a bunch of emotional wrecks."

As the singing continued, I began to feel surges of emotion as though I might cry myself. I dismissed the feelings as quickly as they arose. But singing has always been a good way to get the agitated, judgmental parts of myself to be still. It was taking all my willpower to resist the palpable energy I could feel in the room. When a friend walked over to ask how I was doing, my resistance broke and I was undone. I cried and cried and cried, no longer concerned that I could think of no good reason to cry.

Different than regular crying where the tears start from just behind the eyes, this was more like overflowing. It was as if there had been a wall holding back the water, and once it came down, water filled me up and spilled out. The first wave brought a painful awareness of my own faults and weaknesses. This was followed closely by a more existential experience of collective suffering that was hard to bear. The second wave brought joy. I felt the value of my particular life and the joy I can bring to others. I had a profound sense of being loved—of being beloved. It was unlike anything I have ever experienced—unconditional, all-encompassing love coming on the heels of a sober recognition the suffering of the world as well as my own flaws and failings.

Back at SOAS on Monday morning, I ran into Mohammed in the coffee shop. He casually asked about my weekend, and I mumbled something about a "powerful experience." We sat down on a couch against the wall, and Mohammed looked at me with what I now recognized as his trademark intensity. "Tell me what happened over the weekend," he urged.

I was shy about sharing my experience with Mohammed. The weekend still felt raw and unprocessed. But I wondered if I was now a newly minted "born-again" Christian and if perhaps this was my first call to be God's witness. So I tried to answer honestly. Mohammed listened intently. As I described what happened, he nodded but remained silent. I ended with a description of the tears and how they had felt transforming.

I paused and looked up at my friend, feeling vulnerable after sharing my experience. I wasn't sure how he would react. He looked back thoughtfully. Finally he said, "I have a very good friend who described almost the exact same experience. He cried for three days and now he is devoted to Allah."

That was not the response I expected. "I don't think it is the same at all," I said, getting up from the couch. The deepest moment in my own faith journey suddenly felt mundane or somehow diminished. Mohammed remained seated, as I stormed out of the coffee shop.

Ultimately, this conversation ended our friendship. I was simply unprepared and unequipped to understand my experience in the context of another faith claim. For many years, when I shared my "conversion" story with others, I left out the conversation with Mohammed. It simply did not fit with the paradigmatic Christian story. But I never forgot our conversation, and years later, I am still grateful for his words. They planted a seed that taught me, whether I liked it or not, that my personal experiences did not give me full knowledge or exclusive rights to God. God is greater than my experience.

I have had many significant encounters across faith lines over the last twenty years since I first began work as an interfaith organizer and educator. In the 1990s I helped write the charter for the Untied Religions Initiative, a grassroots, international organization based in San Francisco. As its youngest board member, I coordinated youth participation at a conference we hosted in 1993 where the idea for the Interfaith Youth Core was born. During my years as part of the Interfaith Youth Core leadership team I had many powerful encounters with young people from around the world. But when I think back over the varied moments of transformation and growth I've experienced in an interfaith context, I keep returning to that moment with Mohammed in the SOAS coffee shop.

Directly on the heels of my own most sacred moment—the moment when I learned there was something profound and undeniably real at the heart of my faith—I was invited to make room for the undeniably real at the heart of someone else's faith. At a moment when my religious identity could have been narrowly defined in Christian terms, it was broken open by Mohammed's story. I could have missed it or ignored it. But all these years later, it is still with me.

Christianity continues to be my spiritual home. But I cannot follow a one-track theology. For me, witnessing to my faith means sharing my experiences as honestly as possible while being equally open to listening deeply to the witness of others. The insights differ. I don't believe that all religions are fundamentally the same. People live with many different gods and with no gods at all. But the refrain, for me as a Christian is simply this—God is greater than my experience. God is greater than any of our experiences. In Arabic, as Mohammed might have expressed it, this insight is recorded in the words, *Allahu Akbar*. Recited repeatedly during each of the five daily Muslim prayer times, it is alternatively translated as God is great, God is the greatest, or, as I prefer, God is greater.

7

My Ever-Present Interfaith Interlocutors

Sherman A. Jackson

Recently, a Muslim colleague of mine visited our law school to lecture on Islamic law. I was to deliver a few introductory remarks and then share the podium with her for the question-and-answer period that followed. After the event—which went wonderfully—we went out to the local Starbucks with a group of students, where we fell into a long and juicy conversation about the state of Islamic studies. Amid the random laughter and myriad half-conversations, everyone's attention was suddenly snapped back to focus when my colleague—an SJD from Harvard—remarked about how formal and intimidating the language of much of my scholarship was. Like one of those cheap nodding puppy-figurines on the dashboard of a suddenly stopped car, the students all bobbed their heads in agreement, which almost made me feel like I had been the victim of a slick little conspiracy of sorts. But they were being honest, and I knew it.

So I decided to reciprocate in kind. "That's because it's not my language," I responded. "It's a language I learned for a specific craft: academic discourse." I went on to explain that the language I really think in is that of those smart but undereducated interlocutors of that tough but inscrutably loving neighborhood of my Philadelphia childhood. It is the language of one of America's many margins, of "Two-Pound," "Pon," and "Nana," of Mr. Green, "Turk," and Walt the barber. It is their tone, their lingering spirit of defiance and accountability, their ruthless cross-examinations, and yes, their hopes and wrenching failures that haunt my ruminations. And, increasingly as I get older, it is that strange and lingering sense of support that is the birthright of every homeboy that continues to embolden and at times even compel me to say what I otherwise might not say (if I know what's good for me). For in the end, I know that they—some now even in death—would still "have my back," even if the academy should decide to consign me back to the margin whence I came.

To a person, all of these folks who so ever-presently populate that metacognitive universe I carry around as a part of me were Christians. They were not scholars or theologians or big names. They were not all even all that religious, certainly not as we tend to think of religiosity. But as far as I know, they all believed in God; and the only God they knew—or at least the one they knew best—was the God of Christianity. And yet, none of this ever seemed to stand in the way of their wanting what was best for me, even as a Muslim. And even as the more truly religious among them invariably feared that this "Moozlim" thing might be ultimately committing me to a very warm place, they were perfectly willing to leave those "honors" to God. Here and now, their criterion was basically what Islam was doing for me as a person. And they tended to be much more at ease seeing me as a believing, practicing Muslim than they were as a nonpracticing Christian or anything else.

I remember, for example, quite vividly, a few months or so after I converted to Islam, I ran into Two-Pound over by the recreation center. Pound and I had been "cut-buddies" who got together for mainly certain types of "recreational activities." He noticed that he had not seen me for a while and probably suspected that my attitude toward our theretofore valued indulgences might have changed. So when he saw me he exclaimed, with an enthusiasm that signaled that we were still cut-buddies, "Wassup, Sherm? Where you been, man?" Then, in a calmness and sincerity that still moves me today, he said: "Look here, I heard you found yourself. I want you to know I'm happy for you, man. A lot of these cats out here ain't gonna feel that way; so don't expect it. But I just want you to know, man, you go 'head on and do your thing. I'm happy for you."

Pound understood that my conversion to Islam involved a whole new régime of discipline that many of my homeboys, friends, and associates simply would not be ready for. (In those days, incidentally, i.e., back in the late '70s, whether we are talking about the Nation of Islam or orthodox Sunni Islam—my conversion was to the latter—the very term Islam in the black community connoted discipline.) It was not so much my Islam that they might oppose but this new disciplined, critical demeanor that would put them on the defensive. He wanted to encourage me not to relax my standards in the face of this pressure and to go on and "be all that I could be" as a Muslim. At the time, I was about twenty-two years old and had barely started college. I had no idea that I would eventually leave that neighborhood and the pressures of which he spoke. Two-Pound's words of encouragement meant more to me than he (or I at the time) could probably ever know. So much for the invariably negative contributions of the religious other.

Closer to home, there was the response of my parents, especially my mother. My mother, who is still alive, is a believing, practicing Holiness Christian, who still goes to church several times a week. In theological terms, my conversion had to scare and even disappoint her, given the centrality of "very warm places" to Holiness eschatology. Socially speaking, on the other hand, it had to be an embarrassment. After all, to the members of her church, her son had just apostatized! And yet, the real meaning of my conversion for her ultimately resided, once again, in its impact on me. I remember one afternoon coming back home (I was among that last generation to fall under the "18 and out" rule) for a real home-cooked meal. I prepared a plate for myself and proceeded to sit down at the dining-room table to eat. Suddenly, my mother stormed from the kitchen and rushed over to me and snatched my fork out of my hand. Speechless, I just sort of turned to her with my mouth held open and my hands hung aimlessly waiting for someplace to fall. She quickly relieved my incredulity, however, with the words, "This is not allowed in your religion."

It turns out that the fork I had chosen was made of silver. My mother had apparently overheard one of the many conversations with my younger brother (who later also converted) about these and many other tangential matters, which we as new converts tended to take as the end-all of religious identity. Rather than gloat, however, at the sight of this little "infidel apostate" violating his little "false" religion, my mother preferred to see me keep the commitments of the religion to which I had dedicated myself. She too, it turns out, preferred to see me as a practicing Muslim than as a nonpracticing anything else.

Of course, this raises serious and unavoidable questions about reciprocity. What if my Muslim children or Muslim friends were to convert to Christianity or some other religion: How supportive would I be? Well, on the one hand, I too believe in the reality of very warm places. On the other hand, I know that these choices on their part are ultimately not up to me. As the Quran says, "Verily, you (O Muhammad) cannot guide people simply because you love them." I don't think that I could ever approve of such a choice by my Muslim friends or children (any more than my mother actually approves of mine). And this presents me with the question of whether it's better to be a nonpracticing Muslim than a practicing anything else? Although this requires a much longer answer, for the moment let me just say that, on the one hand, I would emphatically support a non-Muslim jaywalker over a Muslim axe murderer any day. On the other hand, I strongly believe in living life for God—both ethically and ritually—as God has revealed it in the sacred teachings of my religious tradition. In this light, I prefer to devote my time not so much to debating this issue but to contributing what I can to the actual likelihood that my Muslim friends and children will remain Muslims.

This means empowering my loved ones to embrace, take owner-ship of, and invest in their American heritage, including the contri-butions of Christians, Jews, and others. For me, to educate Muslims about Islam is *not* to call on them to replace a Western sociocultural identity for an essentially or emphatically Eastern one. (And one should be reminded here that Two-Pound is just as American as is Billy Graham.) It is to train their sensibilities and calibrate their ideo-logical filters so that they can let in the good and keep out the bad. As a Muslim academic, I have always been able (and counted it a blessing to do so) to read Niebuhr, Hauerwas, Barth, and others with great benefit. And this has been the rule for me rather than the exception. Indeed, my mentor and dissertation adviser in college, who had a profound and lasting impact on my intellectual and scholarly develop-ment, was a man named George Makdisi, a devout Catholic (though many mistook him from his writings to be a Hanbalite Muslim!). In short, what is exceptional in my experience is not the ability to have meaningful relationships with non-Muslim others; what is exceptional is the hate-filled, intentionally misleading Islamophobia that we have come to witness over the past ten years. Much of this is grounded in assumptions and ideological jabs that completely defy the experiences of most of the people I know.

In this context, I am reminded of something I heard the Reverend Al Sharpton say once. Shortly after 9/11, Tavis Smiley sponsored a meeting of black intellectuals, politicians, and other leaders to discuss the state of black America. At one point, Harvard's Charles Ogletree, who was moderating this particular session, posed the question of how "we" could make Muslims feel more a part of us. Almost before he could get the question out, Sharpton jumped in and said, in so many words, "Wait a minute; let's not get it twisted, 'cause ain't a person in this church who ain't got a brother, a sister, an uncle, a cousin, a mother, somebody close to them in their life who is not a Muslim. So, they are already a part of us!" For Sharpton, as with myself, Islam in the black community has been so naturally and thoroughly integrated that it is often hard to see the relevance of all this talk about "tolerance" and "pluralism" and "mutual respect" and "recognition" between Muslims and non-Muslim others.

My point in all of this is that the basic ground of my experience with the religious other has long been informed by the greatly attenuated otherness of that other. Certainly not in the most formative period of my life as a Muslim do I have any of those shocking or surprising experiences of rare and exceptional Christians who "miraculously" stretched out a hand to assist me, or who somehow actually "got me" as a Muslim, or who were ultraliberal enough to speak in terms that were so abstract and nonconfessional that I as a Muslim could actually relate to and be inspired if not empowered by their words. For me, positive, indeed, intimate interaction with Christians, was far more the norm than the exception. In fact, it might not be going too far to say that in some ways I grew to expect this dynamic rather than its opposite.

It was from the late George Makdisi that I learned the notion that big boats require big oars and a lot of oaring to navigate. I had written a paper the ideas of which he found acceptable but the language of which didn't seem to match. So he advised me (no, in fact, he ordered me!) to go out and buy a Roget's thesaurus and one of those giant-sized Webster's third international dictionaries. I complied, and almost like Malcolm X during his prison years, I proceeded to acquire the oars that would enable me to take my ship of ideas into new and challenging ports. Thus, to my colleague and those students who noted my penchant for using "big oars," I can only hope—and this is my solemn prayer—that this is less a reflection of the complexes that invariably afflict one who has come to the academy from the margin, than it is a genuine attempt to translate my experiences, insights, and sensibilities from the margins back to the center and beyond.

8

It Begins with a Text

Burton L. Visotzky

It began with a text, but for me that is always where it must begin and end. I am an exegete and have been since I first learned to decode letters on paper. As Whitman said, "I encompass worlds and volumes." Perhaps it began well before my childhood. If I search my Jewish memory, I recall standing among the myriads at Sinai, watching the thunder and hearing the lightning. God was manifest there, and we had to decide what that meant. Everyone, from the Rabbi to the water-drawer, from the Roman matron to the cleaning lady, from the Israelite to those others who joined us as we left Egypt experienced that signal moment. For each of us it meant something different, unique. But we also learned that hearing what it meant to others expanded our views of the one and only God whose sovereignty we all accepted that day under the mountain.

When I was a rabbinical student I studied Talmud with one of the great masters, Rabbi Saul Lieberman. Among his many scholarly books was a small volume called *Greek in Jewish Palestine*. Professor Lieberman did not deign to translate words from one language to the next, and so, confronted with Greek typeface, I proceeded to learn that alphabet (on the theory that if a fraternity boy could do it, so could I). But to actually understand Greek, I needed to study the language, its grammar, and its texts. To do so was remarkably easy in theory—I needed only to cross the street from the Jewish Theological

Seminary (JTS) and enroll in a Greek course at Union Theological Seminary (UTS). It was not mere coincidence that those elementary language classes were labeled "New Testament." Thus began my path in interreligious studies.

Greek at UTS in the 1970s was taught by an erudite linguist named Marcia Weinstein. She and I appreciated the humor that a Jew was instructing young MDiv's in the mysteries of the New Testament. I squirmed as I read of the "evil Pharisees," but that was less of a trial for me than conjugating the aorist. Soon I was intrigued by the New Testament as both a Jewish and a Christian document. It seemed one could do comparative work between rabbinic literature and the New Testament (a position I have grown much more cautious about in my scholarship).

It was my good fortune to find a perfect rabbi for the study of New Testament: Father Raymond Brown. Ray was a Roman Catholic teaching at Protestant Union (another miracle of ecumenism) and a beloved teacher and colleague. It was my blessing that he was also the premier New Testament scholar in the United States. It was Ray, and his Protestant colleague J. Louis Martyn, who convinced me to teach a class at UTS on "Introduction to Rabbinics for Seminarians." I first did that in 1980 and have been adjunct on Union's faculty ever since. Ray and Lou also arranged for me to teach similar classes at Princeton Theological Seminary. A final note of grace came when Father Brown wrote a recommendation enabling me to spend my first sabbatical in 1985–86 at University of Cambridge, where I studied the literature of the Church Fathers.

I spent my time on the page, reading, sifting, comparing, learning the marvels of biblical exegesis with Origen and Jerome as my guides, and with Augustine patiently teaching me Christian theology and the hermeneutics of biblical exegesis. Even as I earned my PhD in rabbinic literature, I realized that there was much Torah to be learned among the fathers of the church—and I was, and remain, an avid student. Yet for all that I studied and taught, I remained print-bound and immured in the texts of the first millennium.

Following my return from Oxbridge (where I felt I had proven my scholarly chops), I began to own the notion that I *was* a rabbi. What, then, would be my rabbinate? If my day job had me teaching rabbinical students and would-be PhDs (Jewish and Christian), how would I comport myself after hours? Was it possible to bring my expertise in Jewish-Christian engagement in the first millennium into the twentieth century? I was not at all sure, and in retrospect I see how little I knew of modern Christianity or the "interfaith dialogue movement." Wasn't it bad enough that I knew so little about modern Judaism?

A colleague at Union invited me to be the Jewish representative to the International Conference of Christians and Jews (as the ICCJ was then called). Off we went to Warsaw, to spend three hot summer days housed on the pallets of a Catholic seminary dorm. I smugly appreciated the irony of young priests serving me kosher airlines meals a mere one hundred kilometers from Treblinka, the notorious Polish death camp of the Nazis. But I was not emotionally prepared for the pall that the Holocaust still shed over European interfaith dialogue. I had been spoon-fed on the Holocaust, having grown up watching the Eichmann trial and films about concentration camps. As an adult, I had assiduously avoided crafting my Jewish identity as a victim, embracing the Hellenistic milieu of the ancient rabbis instead. Nothing in my education readied me to board the bus and ride with Germans and Poles to actually visit Treblinka.

As we stood in a circle at that awe-full site, the Jews among us recited *El Malei Rahamim*, the memorial prayer that opens with the (there bitter) words, "God full of Mercy." The Christians recited the Lord's Prayer, led by a German Lutheran minister. He intoned, *Und vergib uns unsere Schuld,* at which point he turned in the circle so he was facing us Jews directly; and he repeated, this time in English, "Forgive us our sins." That, more than any movie I had been made to watch as a child, taught me the horror of the Holocaust. But it also taught me the power of forgiveness and reconciliation; and the profound value of standing together, holding firmly to one another with tear-filled eyes. With the words of those two ancient prayers, it began with a text.

On my sabbatical in the spring of 2007, I taught "Judaism and Christianity in the First Five Centuries" at the Pontifical Gregorian University in Rome. I instructed mostly Jesuits, and the class was focused on rabbinic and church texts from those formative centuries. That I taught them Mishnah, Midrash, and Talmud was unsurprising, but that I had been invited by the venerable Gregoriana also to teach priests New Testament and Patristics was a sign of how far we have come in advancing interfaith dialogue. I was simply told that it was important that the students there learn to read these seminal texts of the church through the eyes of a Jew.

For their part, they returned the favor. My Catholic hosts literally opened the door for me to examine the otherwise closed Jewish Catacombs beneath Rome. There, guided by a priest and an electrician (who knew the catacombs well, as he maintained the derelict wiring strung there in an earlier decade), we wandered among 1,800-year-old graves, seldom visited at all, let alone by a rabbi. Among the bones of the dead and the vivid frescoes that rarely saw the light, there were inscriptions carved or graffitied by loved ones memorializing their departed. When I finally realized that these skeletons had not had a family member pay their respects in centuries, I recited the memorial prayer, *El Malei Rahamim* (no longer bitter), filling in the names of the deceased at the appropriate juncture by virtue of reading aloud the Greek, Hebrew, and Latin inscriptions. The Vatican had afforded me an opportunity to fulfill a rare *mitzvah*. Again, it began with a text, albeit underground, standing there in the dark.

In the mid-'90s I had my turn in the spotlight. Bill Moyers and I did a ten-part series on PBS. Each week for an hour we gathered Jews and Christians to read Genesis together. Our principle in choosing the colleagues with whom we studied was interreligious "balance." We decided to invite Muslims to join the show for two of the texts that the Old Testament shared with Islam: the stories of Joseph and the binding of Abraham's son. I invited Aziza al-Hibri, a lawyer and philosophy professor from Richmond, whom I had met on an interfaith panel at JTS the year before. When she asked me to speak at Richmond later that year, we mourned Yitzchak Rabin's murder together, as it had occurred in the week when I spoke. To complement her Sunni presence on the Moyer's show, we also invited Dr. Seyyed Hossein Nasr, an Iranian-born professor who writes on Shiism and Sufi philosophy.

Soon I was being invited to debates and dialogues on the Jewish-Muslim dialogue circuit, along with the Jewish-Christian round. This continued modestly until September 11, 2001, when everything accelerated to warp speed. At the first anniversary commemoration of the tragedy, at Trinity Church in lower Manhattan, standing near Ground Zero among Christians and Muslims, I spoke of Isaiah (33:18), "Who can weigh and who can count the towers?"

Often at my home at JTS, and regularly under U.S. State Department auspices, I have hosted or met with delegations of Muslim leaders. By now the list includes Muslim leaders and imams from Jordan, Egypt, Qatar, Kuwait, Palestine, Saudi Arabia, Indonesia, Turkey, India, Pakistan, Kazakhstan, Russia, Bahrain, Morocco, and even Iran. Frequently the imams stood at my side in the JTS synagogue as I read aloud from the Torah scroll in their honor. In turn, they greeted us in Arabic with words of peace from the Quran (which I am finally able to translate, sort of). Always, it begins and ends with a text.

Interfaith dialogue takes place on all levels: local, national, and international. In each venue we start with our own traditions, our own teachings, our own texts and interpretations. And in turn, we learn those of our partners. Text is a way in, a place where we can meet and study, learn, and be inspired. Like the political realities that swirl around us, there are easy texts and hard texts. There are texts that show a welcoming face and those that glower with forbidding countenances. But for me, as an exegete who studies and teaches Jewish tradition, text is my entryway, the gate through which I enter dialogue.

So I shall end this essay with a text. It comes from a ninth-century midrash on the biblical book of Proverbs. The very end of that biblical book is a paean to idealized woman. She is often allegorized by the rabbis (as she is, in fact, within Proverbs) as Wisdom herself, Torah incarnate, of whom Proverbs (31:14) sings, "She is like merchant ships, bringing sustenance from afar." The Midrash on Proverbs comments, "Rabbi Shimeon ben Halfota commented, If one does not reveal (*megaleh*) himself for the sake of learning words of Torah, he will never learn Torah." I like the required risks that this implies. To truly learn what it is that God wants of us, we must be willing to open up ourselves to those with whom we study.

But there is yet another way to read the text. The Hebrew word for self-revelation (*megaleh*) can be translated differently, rendering the phrase, "If one is not willing to exile (*megaleh*) himself for the sake of learning Torah, he will never learn Torah." Now we understand more

deeply why this is a comment on the Proverbs verse, "bringing sustenance from afar." For a Jew to learn Torah, he or she must be willing
to learn it from faraway places and sources. It might require travel to
Warsaw or Rome, to Egypt, or Qatar. It might require learning New
Testament and Patristics, or Quran and Hadith. Sometimes travel to
the other brings us home to our self. It begins with a text.

Part II

Viewing Home Anew

I never saw my hometown till I stayed away too long.

Tom Waits, "San Diego Serenade"

The authors in Part II all look back at their religious homes from the outside, gleaning the insights that this new perspective offers. In "Trouble Praying" by Nancy Fuchs Kreimer, an American Jew has a pivotal experience in post-Holocaust Germany. She hears a German Christian confess from the depths of his heart—a truth entirely subjective, personal, and contingent—and this single act of honesty has the power to inspire the author, an American rabbi, to dig beneath the surface of her tradition with comparable courage and candor. In Gregory Mobley's "What the Rabbi Taught the Preacher about the Baby Jesus," it is a Jew whose comment turns the key for a Christian, unlocking a door to reveal Jesus in a new light. Rita Nakashima Brock in "When I Get to Heaven" narrates how a frequently uprooted, Japanese-American daughter of a U.S. army medic was drawn into Christianity by the easygoing avuncularity and piety of a surrogate father, who happened to be a fundamentalist Baptist. Working to bridge the gap between her own pioneering feminist theology and his evangelical concern for the eternal state of her soul, she finds a language of the heart that can save them both.

Judith Plaskow in "An Accidental Dialoguer" is located in an intellectual neighborhood populated with fellow feminists. But as one

43

of the few Jewish feminists in this predominantly Christian field, she finds herself drawn into interfaith conversation almost by accident and reflects on how it has shaped her own religious and intellectual identity.

In Arthur Green's "A Monk's Gift," a Japanese monk unwittingly provides this Jewish author with an analogy—about marriage, no less—that helps him articulate his own unwavering allegiance to Judaism alongside his commitment to religious pluralism. Author Wendy Peterson, a Jesus-following Native Canadian, writes in "The Prayer God Could Not Answer: A Métis-Aboriginal Encounter" about hearing an Indigenous woman named Pauline talk about the great hostility she faced at the hands of the Christian church. Peterson is so moved by Pauline's story that she commits herself to work toward healing and reconciliation between these two communities that she bridges. In "How a Daoist Fire-Walking Ceremony Made Me an Episcopalian," Judith Berling travels far from home and details how watching a dramatic religious ritual in Taiwan opens her to the mysteries and sensual elements hiding in plain sight in her own more logocentric Christianity.

9

Trouble Praying

Nancy Fuchs Kreimer

"I envy you Jews," said the young German as he poured my morning coffee.

The year was 1980. I was the guest of a graduate student at Heidelberg University. My stay in his home was part of a month-long trip through Germany with Jews and Christians engaged in "post-Holocaust interfaith dialogue."

My host's statement surprised and bewildered me. I was just beginning my dissertation on the topic of anti-Judaism in Protestant "Old Testament" theology, and I thought I knew a lot about the relationship between Jews and Christians. In fact, I was planning to devote my career to helping Christians see their complicity in the suffering of the Jews and to transcend the flaws in their theology. I could understand my host feeling sorry for us Jews. I could understand him apologizing to us. But I could not understand him envying us.

"Why in the world would you envy Jews?" I asked.

His reply changed my life.

"I envy you because it is easier for you to pray. You see, we young Germans carry the weight of what our parents and grandparents did—or did not do—during the war. It is hard for us to talk to God. We feel a little embarrassed." Although the conversation took place thirty years ago, I can conjure it up in an instant: the earnestness in my fellow student's voice, the clarity in his blue eyes.

I had thought, until then, that it was we Jews, the victims, who had trouble praying! There was something about the way he said it—perhaps the phrase "a *little* embarrassed"—that made it feel completely genuine. This conversation clarified for me my core belief, a very useful thing to discover at the age of twenty-seven. After that morning, I possessed an orienting idea, a place to check in regularly to see if my plans were aligned with what I believed.

I believe that we should live our lives so that our children won't be "a little embarrassed" if they want to pray. Until that morning, I thought that meant being a good daughter, a compassionate friend, and a dutiful citizen. But now I saw something new: taking responsibility for the group from which I derive my identity, the group whose actions will lead my children to be proud or embarrassed before God. For me, that group was and is the Jewish people.

The immediate result of this revelation was that I changed my dissertation topic. Rather than looking at problematic Christian texts, I would study problematic Jewish writings. I would investigate the ways in which my own tradition misunderstands others rather than point a finger at the others for misunderstanding us.

That can be challenging. For example, today when I choose to speak out about certain policies pursued by the State of Israel, colleagues—including good friends—email me to say they disagree with my action. "You ought to be criticizing Hamas," they say. "There are enough non-Jews jumping on the bandwagon to condemn Israeli actions; we don't need rabbis doing it too!" "Besides," they often add, "however bad Israel's actions, many other countries have done much worse."

They are right, of course. But what can I do? I can learn as much as possible, consult Israelis I trust who know more than I, and try to speak with humility. My commitment to Middle East work, like the interfaith work to which I devote most of my time, grows from my core belief to which I have tried to stay true. Being part of a community means being ready to argue with it, to criticize it, to ask it to live up to its best self.

I say I do it for *tikkun olam*, to make the world more whole. But the deeper truth is that I do it for my daughters. They are now in their twenties, still figuring out their relationship to their Jewish heritage and to God. I want them to be able to pray without embarrassment.

Although there is much to lament in the way some Christians and some Muslims have treated and continue to treat Jews, that is not my issue. My job as a Jew, as a mother, is to scrutinize my own faith tradition and my own community. Given that I have uncertain knowledge and limited power, all I can do is my best. But thanks to an encounter thirty years ago, I know what I am trying to accomplish.

10

What the Rabbi Taught the Reverend about the Baby Jesus

Gregory Mobley

Rabbinic Judaism, especially as vocalized in the mystical keys of Kabbalah and Hasidism, develops the theme of a vulnerable God who enlists Israel's support in *tikkun olam*, the redemption of creation and Creator. Christian discourse is full of the former theme—moral exhortation focused on saving souls or the world—but shies away from the latter. Sure we have the magnificent Philippian hymn (Phil 2:6–11) and in the past half-century scores of portraits of a battered, suffering God who, like an earnest therapist with poor boundaries, overidentifies with creation's pain. But we don't talk much or at all in Christian circles about the church's, or humanity's, responsibility to restore and replenish the divine fullness. In most European Christian theology, developed by folks whose ethnic kin exercised a measure of control over culture, and for the theologies transplanted east and west and south of Europe by its missionaries and migrants, God is on the throne, august, omni-everything. We do not often follow up on the full implications of the analogy of the church as Christ's body, that the health and vitality of Head and Body are interrelated. That God needs us as much as we need God.

But I had become so taken with this idea in Jewish theology of the dynamic mutual interdependence of Creator and creation. It had both a poetry and a physics to it that rang true. I searched for a Christian expression of this theme, however faint. But I wasn't finding it.

48

Then I consulted with a rabbi, Rim Meirowitz of Temple Shir Tik-vah in Winchester, Massachusetts. I explained my dilemma to Rabbi Rim, that I was frustrated in my attempt to find a Christian expression of *tikkun olam*. Now Rim knows a thing or two about Christianity and Christians. Although he lives in Newton, a town in the Torah Belt just west of Brookline, his congregation in Winchester includes many interfaith families.

Rim asked me, "Don't you guys talk about the need to nurture and care for the baby Jesus?"

It had been right in front of me all my life in every crèche and in every Christmas Eve recitation of Luke's infancy narrative. It takes a village to raise a Savior. The baby Jesus required protection, nurture, and both tender and fierce loving care from a host of human characters, especially Mary and Joseph. So why then, my entire life, too much—perhaps—of it spent in church, have I never heard about our need to nurture God? There it is, right in front of us: a neglected theme of Christian theology that only emerged for me through interfaith learning. God needs our ministrations of love and liturgy, for heaven's sake, not just the world's.

Once we hear from Jewish teachers and sources about the G*d who suffered a primeval fragmentation known as the "Shattering of the Vessels" (*Shevirat Ha-Kelim*), once we hear the teachings of Isaac Luria from sixteenth-century Safed about how G*d seeks our help in mending a broken world through returning the fragments of light, one deed of virtue and worship at a time, to the Light of Lights: Can we not see this theme in our tradition?

Judaism and Christianity are siblings, each the child of Second Temple Judahite religion and a grandchild of the faith of biblical Israel. Like biological twins seeking differentiation, each community in the process of individuation preserved special configurations of a common heritage that the other group lost or de-emphasized. Amy-Jill Levine of Vanderbilt University comments on the Apostle Paul's metaphor of the olive tree and its branches in Romans 11 in her book *The Misunderstood Jew* (2006): "Had the church remained a Jewish sect, it would not have achieved its universal mission. Had Judaism given up its particularistic practices, it would have vanished from history. That the two movements eventually separated made possible the preservation of each."

Has the world changed all that much since those first centuries of the Common Era when Christians and Jews differentiated in polemical ways? When New Testament texts such as John 19:38–40 and 19:13–16 accused Jews of responsibility for crucifying Jesus? When Talmudic texts like B.T. Shabbat 104b accused Mary of infidelity and Jesus of illegitimacy? In many places, Jewish culture remains vulnerable, and productive dialogue can take place only in an environment of trust. But where we can trust each other, and the campus in Newton, Massachusetts, shared by Hebrew College and Andover Newton Theological School seems to be such a place, Jews and Christians can find the lost themes of our respective faiths by talking to each other.

Interfaith dialogue, then, is its own kind of *tikkun* as we recover the lost fragments of our respective faiths that the sibling preserved, initially for themselves, but also, as it turns out, for the Other too.

11

When I Get to Heaven

Rita Nakashima Brock

I didn't start out a Christian. For a child born and raised for six years in Japan, the hurdles that American Christians set were very high. What I was told was beyond the obstacles did not make me want to overcome them. Instead, I practiced a quiet inner resistance to becoming "saved" that I associated with loyalty to my kind and caring Japanese family.

Neuroscientists say our first language, culture, and relationships shape our epistemology and intuitions. Mine were laid down in a Japanese family in Onojo, a village on the south island of Kyushu near the city of Fukuoka, where my mother was a nurse in the U.S. occupation hospital. An absence of religious boundaries characterized the first five years of my life. I participated in daily Buddhist and Shinto rituals in my grandparents' house and in frequent village festivals.[1]

Polls put the total number of religious affiliations in Japan today at almost double the actual population. These numbers lead some researchers to conclude the Japanese are superreligious. Other researchers think the people are not very religious because there is a

---

[1] Patricia K. Kuhl, "Brain Mechanisms in Early Language Acquisition," *Neuron* 67 (September 9, 2010): 713–27. http://life-sic.org/docs/Kuhl-brainmechanisms2010.pdf.

The story of this phase of my life is found in chapter 2 of *Proverbs of Ashes: Violence, Redemptive Suffering, and the Search for What Saves Us* (Boston: Beacon Press, 2001).

fair amount of indifference to individual belief. People participate in Buddhist and Shinto rituals according to the spheres of life each administers and their social and family groups, not according to their personal faith in a deity. The emphasis is on how one behaves toward others, whatever one might believe personally.[2]

When I was five, my stepfather Roy Brock, a U.S. Army medic, got orders to report to Fort Riley, Kansas, but the Immigration and Naturalization Service would not let me enter the country. My mother and I joined him on a military base on Okinawa while he spent the year working to clear me to go with them. I switched from speaking Japanese to English while attending kindergarten during that year in limbo.

As we were preparing to leave Japan for the United States, my grandfather said to my mother, "America is a Christian country. People will expect you to become a Christian. Your mother and I want you to know that, if you decide to become a Christian, you will still be our daughter and we will still love you." It would take my mother over a decade to be baptized, after both her parents had died.

During the six years I attended grammar school in Fort Riley, various Protestant chaplains taught me about Christianity. I found it strange and dull, and I associated it with the anti-Japanese hostility I experienced from classmates. Sunday school teachers taught me about Jesus, whom they described as loving, forgiving, and kind. I read the gospels carefully, and to my Japanese sensibilities, he seemed rude, arrogant, and egocentric. I wasn't particularly interested in whether or not he loved me, as I didn't care that much for him or the kids at school who seemed to behave the same way.

I felt the pressure to convert intensely every August when my family visited Roy's family in Amory, Mississippi. I heard fiery Southern

---

[2]   Information about religion in Japan taken from the U.S. Department of State, "Diplomacy in Action," International Religious Freedom Report 2008," http:www. state.gov/g/drl/rls/irf/2008/108408.htm.

A 2006 poll found a 7 percent increase in Christian affiliation among young people and a sharp decline in overall religious affiliation, though it appears to have been slanted toward belief—i.e., toward those who claim a faith—rather than participation in rituals. "More People Claim Christian Faith in Japan: The Latest Gallup Poll Revealed a Much Higher Percentage of Christians in Japan Compared to Previous Surveys." http://www.christianpost.com/news/more-people-claim-christian-faith-in-japan-1549.".

Baptist revival sermons about sin, hell, and salvation through Jesus Christ. Many people got saved, including aunts, uncles, and cousins, with lots of weeping and confessions, but I was incapable of calling such public attention to myself. I found the blunt sermonic condemnations alienating. Such behavior was a sign of hostility or lack of intelligence in Japan, where being indirect, kind, and subtle are important as a sign of respect for others. I also didn't believe I was so bad as to deserve the punishments described in such vivid detail. I felt no terror of hell; I thought it a weird idea. However, hearing about it led me to conclude that the Christian God was cruel. I found individual salvation in heaven a cold, lonely prospect and hoped, instead, to see my Japanese family again.

I got "saved" in high school, but I don't remember having any sudden revelation about Jesus or cathartic release from sin. Instead my life was touched by the love of an extraordinary minister and his family. In 1966, the military sent my father to Fort Irwin, California, in the middle of the hot, dry Mojave Desert, to train for Vietnam, a steamy land covered with jungles. When he was home between deployments, Roy moved us to Barstow, California, rather than leave us on the base. Barstow, where I attended high school, had been an hour's bus ride from town, which made after-school activities difficult. My father served his second tour in Vietnam while we lived "on the economy," the military term for civilian life.

Whenever my American history class aced a test, our teacher let us listen to a Bill Cosby routine the next day. A girl named Joy Clark and I shared the same sense of humor; our favorite routine was "Noah." We became best friends. Her future husband Carl was away on National Guard duty and had left her his '62 Pontiac Catalina, the awesome Blue Max; it had a 400-cubic-inch engine, four-barrel carburetor and Hurst shifter with four on the floor. Joy and I cruised the Blue Max on Main Street on Friday nights, pausing to eat French dip sandwiches and banana splits at the local diner.

Soon after we met, Joy invited me to visit her father's Conservative Baptist church, a fundamentalist community. Her father, Denver, and mother, Lillian, eschewed the solemn piety of the chaplains I had known. Instead, they enjoyed life with open-hearted joy, grounded in an unshakable confidence in the love of God. They were amused by the Joy-and-Rita Blue Max adventures. They shared our delight in Bill Cosby and laughed at my silly jokes. They introduced me to Mexican food, beach life in Southern California, and prime rib dinners. Having lived in Guatemala, they loved learning about different cultures and spoke fluent Spanish. My mother fed them home-cooked suki-yaki, rice balls, sukimono, and teriyaki chicken, which they ate with relish—it was the first time I remember not being embarrassed about the foods my mother cooked for us, deemed "strange" by schoolmates.

I increasingly wanted to be a member of the church, so I asked Denver to baptize me. A few weeks later, in the church's baptismal font, he laid me under the warm waters, and I emerged a Christian. Later, in reflecting on this time in my life, I realized that the Clarks had taken care of me when Roy was absent and returned a stranger, and Denver had become my surrogate father. Beneath the success I had in high school, I felt a deep anxiety about my father and a constant feeling of having to make my way in the world alone, unassisted. Belonging to the Clark fold quelled those feelings.

Fundamentalist belief was never a good fit for me, but that didn't seem to matter. The church's behavior was quite different from the evangelical Christian conservatism advocated today. Denver disparaged the unreliable emotional enthusiasms of evangelicals. He was a fundamentalist who respected rational thinking. When I argued for evolution, Denver arranged a formal debate in the church. I was its only advocate, but I did not feel condemned for rejecting a literal interpretation of Genesis, just odd because the myths of the Bible made little sense to me. The church also had a debate about abortion; I opposed it, based on a whole life ethic. As unbelievable as it sounds now, the majority of the church thought abortion was not wrong. And they adamantly supported the separation of church and state and thought saving souls was the church's vocation, not that of politicians or legislators. On this last point, I was on the church's side.

When I was finishing my doctorate in theology, I went to visit Lillian and Denver as he was struggling with cancer. We'd stayed friends, and I went to say good-bye. At the end of our visit, he walked me out to the car. When I reached for the door, he said, "I need to ask you a question." "Of course," I said.

He began, "I know you have gone a long way from your days at Trinity Baptist Church, and you are now far better educated that I am and know a lot more. But I need to know if you still have your faith. I'm not going to be around much longer, and I want to know that the people I love will be in heaven with me."

I thought carefully about my answer. "When I was a member of your church, you gave me a solid grounding in faith. I am glad you were the one to baptize me. I want you to know that you led me to confidence in my relationship to God. I trust that relationship and always will. And I'll see you in heaven."

He gave me one of his huge, happy smiles and a big bear hug. When I drove away, we both had misty eyes.

If I'd had to encounter the kind of Christian conservatism then that dominates the media today, I doubt I would ever have become a Christian. Instead, because I knew people who trusted in the boundless love of God, I took the long journey of the last half century from Conservative Baptist to feminist theologian and licensed minister in the Christian Church (Disciples of Christ). I didn't start out a Christian, and I don't think I will ever be as good a minister as Denver Clark was to me, but I'm going to keep working on it so I can report on my progress when I see him—and introduce him to my Japanese family.

12

An Accidental Dialoguer

Judith Plaskow

I come to the issue of interfaith engagement from a somewhat un-usual perspective. On the one hand, working with Christian and post-Christian feminists has been utterly central to my career; on the other hand, it has been largely a matter of circumstance. I would call myself an accidental dialoguer.

As one of the first Jewish women to earn a doctorate in religious studies (rather than history), I was educated and have worked and taught in overwhelmingly Christian environments. I helped create the field of feminist studies in religion together with Christian and post-Christian women. I have been the only Jew, or one of very few Jews, on more panels and at more conferences and meetings than I can count, and I have taught at a Catholic college for over thirty years.

When I have worked with other feminists on images of God, women's history, attitudes toward sexuality, or numerous other top-ics, our focus has almost always been the subject matter, not the fact of conversation. I like it this way. It would have been impossible for me to have done the work I've done without this constant interaction across religious boundaries, and yet talking about talking has never especially interested me.

In 1970, when I was still a graduate student in theology at Yale, my friend Carol P. Christ and I were the only two women in a stu-dent-led seminar on the great Protestant theologians of the twentieth century. Virtually every thinker that we read had something horrible to say about women. The great Dietrich Bonheoffer wrote a letter from his prison cell in which he said that wives should be subordinate to their husbands. Karl Barth said that women were ontologically subordinate to men. Every time that Carol or I pointed out one of these comments, our fellow students responded with the equivalent of a verbal pat on the head and refused to be "distracted" from the "real" subject matter by remarks that should just be ignored.

For one of the sessions on Karl Barth, Carol brought in a two-page single-spaced paper—I can still picture it on the page—in which she connected Barth's demeaning statements about women to his larger understanding of "initiative, precedence, and authority" that shaped both his view of man's relationship to woman and God's relationship to "man." I don't think I immediately grasped the significance of Carol's argument. In fact, I remember feeling a combination of pride but also discomfort that she had made the other students angry. But over time, I came to realize the tremendous importance of what she was saying: misogynistic comments are not just verbal asides or personal opinions that can be bracketed off and forgotten; they are thoroughly intertwined with theological understandings of God and humanity. Ultimately, Carol's paper made it possible for me to write "The Right Question Is Theological," in which I argued that particular *halachot* (Jewish laws) that subordinate women are simply expressions of the profound androcentrism of Jewish understandings of Torah, God, and Israel.

I have been deeply influenced by interactions like this with colleagues from other traditions because, *on a structural level,* Jewish, Christian, and other religiously committed women face many of the same issues. Beginning in the late 1960s—as part of the larger feminist movement that was emerging at the time—we began to *notice* patterns of exclusion that we had hitherto largely taken for granted. Why weren't we being ordained? Why did the language of worship assume a male God and a male congregation?

Those of us who were graduate students began to recognize the awful things that had been said about women by key figures in our traditions. Gradually, we began to connect specific misogynistic passages with deeper patterns in Christian or Jewish thought. We began to reconstruct the history of women within our traditions, asking new questions of canonical texts and looking beyond the canon for evidence of women's status and roles. We asked how our religious histories could be reconfigured in the light of new evidence concerning women's lives. And we also undertook to transform our traditions in a wide variety of ways. I have been immensely fortunate to have come of age theologically in contexts in which large numbers of Christian (and then post-Christian) women were raising questions and striking out in new theological directions in ways that Jewish women could not for lack of both numbers and training.

At the same time, I have benefited greatly from thinking and writing in Christian contexts; however, working in such contexts has also been complicated and sometimes painful. I chose to get a doctorate in Christian theology because I wanted to be a theologian, and in the late 1960s, there was nowhere to go to study Jewish theology. My ability to fully inhabit Christian categories and to think with and through them has at some moments made it hard for me to hold onto my Jewish voice, while at others, it has very much heightened my awareness of my Jewishness, both as a positive resource and as a locus of marginalization.

As a graduate student, I was constantly engaged in the work of translation, attempting to reformulate whatever issues I was studying in Protestant thought within a Jewish framework. When I took a course on Kierkegaard, for example, I compared his interpretation of the binding of Isaac with rabbinic midrash. When I studied the question of the historicity of revelation in modern Protestant theology, I wrote a paper on the same subject in Buber. When I worked with other feminists, I was aware of the ways in which feminist issues played out differently for Jews and for Christians. I did not have to deal with the maleness of Jesus, for instance, but I had to grapple with the centrality of *halakha* and the meanings of Torah as source and key symbol of Jewish identity.

However, I lacked academic colleagues with whom to discuss the issues that were most burning in my tradition. I repeatedly found myself in situations in which "religion" was identified with Christianity in much the same way as humanity has been identified with maleness. In one emblematic moment, the facilitator of a project to establish a supposedly interfaith feminist theological institute in New York called on the women assembled to birth the baby so that we could baptize her. I had to interject that no one was going to baptize my baby! I also regularly participated as the lone Jew at events or on panels where I carried the impossible burden of representing "the" Jewish perspective.

Two important events more than two decades apart capture some of the great rewards and also considerable complexities of being a Jewish feminist theologian in a Christian-dominated academy and culture. In 1972, I had the privilege of attending the Women Exploring Theology conference at Grailville. The conference was an amazing event at which sixty women—all Christian except for me—came together not just to express our pain and anger at our marginalization within our various communities, but also to initiate new modes of thinking and acting as religiously committed women. It was a life-changing experience for me, a week during which I made formative friendships and witnessed the power of women working together to transform our respective traditions. Yet it was also an experience that had numerous, complicated layers. In the first place, I was able to be there only because my friend Carol Christ was unable to attend, and, while the organizers were happy for me to take her place, they were not about to rethink the substance of the week because a Jewish woman would be present. On one level, therefore, I was very much an outsider. The daily worship that was a central part of the week for almost all the participants was profoundly alienating for me.

On a second level, however, my facility in using Christian categories made it easy for me to simply put my Jewish self to one side and participate in the gathering. In my morning work group, which explored and analyzed consciousness-raising as a religious experience, I found myself talking about "religion" using the thoroughly Protestant vocabulary that I had acquired in the course of my graduate education. I was aware that I was using Christian terms to describe my feminist experiences, and yet they felt appropriate and familiar in ways that Jewish language did not.

But on a third level, when I sat down at the end of the week to compose a narrative that would convey the various elements of consciousness-raising that my group had discussed, I drew on the story of Lilith to convey the significance and dynamism of the consciousness-raising process. In what was one of the most powerful writing experiences of my life, I—not altogether consciously—turned to Jewish themes and modes of theological discourse to produce "The Coming of Lilith." The tremendously enthusiastic reception of the story at the end of the conference made me realize that I had brought something to the event that was unique and at the same time embodied the energy of the whole Grailville experience.

A second significant experience that reflects some of the pleasures and complications of being a Jew—and in this case, also a white person—in the white Christian academy was team-teaching a course at Union Theological Seminary in 1995 with womanist theologian Delores Williams. The title of the class was Feminist and Womanist Theologies, and Delores and I decided that we would begin planning for the semester by each producing a syllabus.

When I sat down to create a framework for the course, I was struck—certainly not for the first time—by the immensurability of Jewish and Christian categories. Where was I going to put Torah on the syllabus? Where was I going to put *halakha*? I felt that if I used these as central categories for the organizing the material, I would have nothing but Jewish readings under each heading. In this case, because I was preparing the syllabus for a Protestant seminary, I made a conscious decision to structure the course around topics central to Christian feminist theology and to include Jewish readings under each heading that would both destabilize and enrich students' understandings of the issues. Because womanist literature is largely Christian, I had no trouble incorporating it into my plan.

When I sat down with Delores, however, she pointed out that my outline placed womanist theology in the same position as Jewish theology: although both were represented on the syllabus, neither was the source of the categories around which the syllabus was structured. What was unique and most important to womanist thought—that it starts from social and political rather than "religious" issues—was thus lost. Or, to express the problem in another way, my syllabus placed white Christian feminism at the center and marginalized both Jewish feminist and womanist thought—a rather odd thing to do given that a Jew and a womanist were the professors!

In the end, we decided to divide the semester into three semi-independent units—one on Jewish feminism, one on womanism, and one on white Christian feminism—in order to allow both the particular issues and the approaches that were central to each perspective to emerge from the relevant literature. We would make the connections and draw the contrasts among them by responding to each other as part of every class and by having students represent different voices in the larger feminist conversation. The result was a rich and interesting class in which different constructions of what constitutes feminist questions were allowed to emerge in their integrity. For me, it was a very important lesson in the necessity of claiming my own voice even or perhaps especially when teaching in a Christian context.

My experience with Delores also made me realize that, although my interfaith encounters have been largely about the contexts in which I have found myself and the bonds I have forged there, they have also been something I have chosen and re-chosen in myriad, not always deliberate, ways. Such encounters have so thoroughly shaped my consciousness and so constituted the baseline from which I approach my work that I simply cannot imagine who I would have been without them.

13

A Monk's Gift

Arthur Green

The great German-Jewish philosopher Franz Rosenzweig, who himself nearly converted to Christianity as a young seeker, was quoted as saying that we lose the best and worst Jews to conversion. In the context of Germany, circa 1920, he was referring to those, like himself, who sought faith but could not find it in Judaism, and opportunist assimilationists, who thought conversion would improve their prospects for academic or professional careers, which was indeed the case in that generation.

I have always had a great concern for Rosenzweig's "best." Myself a product of the new quest for spirituality and deeper personal meaning that began to emerge in North American intellectual circles beginning around 1960, I was able to find deep satisfaction in Judaism, shaped by my own rereading of mystical and Hasidic sources that I have been studying, teaching, translating, and reflecting on over the course of the past half-century.

But I recognize that I represent a tiny minority among seekers of my generation, so many more of whom have been attracted to spiritual riches derived from other traditions. By the late 1960s the interest in meditation and eastern religion was sweeping the country, especially such hubs such as Berkeley, Cambridge, and New York's East Village. Among the many thousands of followers that the various gurus and Zen masters were accruing was a high percentage of Jews, already then the subject of familiar jokes. Some of the most interesting spiritual thought created by Jews in those years were the writings of Baba Ram Dass (aka Richard Alpert), Jack Kornford, and Joseph Goldstein (later joined by my friend Sylvia Boorstein), all of them speaking out of Buddhist and Indian wisdom traditions rather than out of the language that our shared ancestors had inherited and that no one had succeeded in passing on to them.

Of course I did not blame or condemn these good people, and in a certain way I delighted that they had found a sacred path to the same One who is the center of my own religious life (I know they will recoil at that "who"!). But I felt—and continue to feel—a great sadness about it. This large group of Jews, often calling themselves Jew-Bu's ("Jewish roots and Buddhist wings," as I've often heard them characterize it), includes many who could be my own closest Jewish soul brothers and sisters, and I feel their absence. When I pray for inner peace or Sabbath joy for "all Israel," I have these Jewish seeker-souls very much in mind.

Because I felt so richly fulfilled by Jewish symbolic language, especially blessed by the Hasidic reading of them, I never felt much need to experiment with other traditions. I understood that many of the things being written by Vedanta or Buddhist teachers (and not only the Jewish ones) were close to my own inner life experience, and I did enjoy reading them. But I never felt much need to open the door toward further involvement, beyond occasional visits. The same is true regarding post-Christian (allegedly "neutral") philosophy of religion.

People who read my books (especially my recent *Radical Judaism*) sometimes ask me if I wasn't influenced by Process Theology, especially Whitehead and Hartshorne. The truth is that I've hardly read them. My own religious thinking has been shaped over the decades by reflection on the Jewish sources, and I wanted to keep it that way. I recall having been much impressed on reading a comment by Kabbalah scholar Gershom Scholem. He said that the Kabbalists had a deeper and more lasting effect on Judaism than did the medieval Jewish philosophers in part because their teachings emerged from an inner contemplation of Jewish texts and symbols, rather than being a visible import from without, as was the case for Jewish Aristotelianism or Neoplatonism. That felt right to me.

Despite this, I have had some interesting and formative experiences over the years resulting from contact with spiritual traditions other than my own. Let me tell you about two such moments, both of them going back to many decades ago. Interestingly, both take place in Roman Catholic settings. Catholicism, with its active cultivation of a great Western mystical legacy, has always been an important religious "other" for me.

The first took place in about 1969 or 1970; I was a couple of years out of rabbinical school and in the early years of Havurat Shalom, a Jewish fellowship and "counterseminary" that I had taken a leading role in creating in Boston. Fordham University, a Catholic university in New York City, invited me to participate in a "day of spiritual teaching." The topic was to be "The Traditions and the Seasons of the Year." The speakers were Brother David Steindl-Rast, a Benedictine monk very much in the Merton tradition, Swami Sattchadinanda, founder of Integral Yoga, a well-known and much-revered figure, the head of the New York Zen center, and this young rabbi, touted as someone who spoke out of the Jewish mystical tradition.

Perhaps three quarters of the large audience were the Swami's disciples, dressed in uniform white baggy garments. Their master simply ignored the topic and shared a few words of basic teaching, followed by chants, smiles, and silence. The Zen Center head got up and said, "I have fifteen minutes. We will sit," and sat down to do his thing. Brother David gave a lovely talk on the passage from Christmas to Easter, birth to death, rich with liturgical associations. I spoke about the two sacred seasons of the Jewish year, the spring collective experience of coming out of Egypt and standing before Sinai and the fall individual check-in on one's personal inner life and relationship with God. It went pretty well, and refined versions of it are still part of my teaching.

Why was that day so significant to me? Because of two events that happened. During the question period, a bright-faced young man, dressed in the swami's disciples' uniform, raised his hand and said, "Rabbi, what you're saying is very nice; I love the idea of standing before the mountain, of inner hearing, and all the rest. But is that really Judaism? Isn't Judaism really about how God is up there in heaven with a book, keeping score, watching the good and evil that you do, preparing to reward or punish you?"

I looked at this poor young man and said to myself, "Another Jew ruined by the Long Island Hebrew Schools! This is clearly a kid who quit after Bar Mitzvah and only sees the inside of a synagogue on Yom Kippur." So I gave him my best young-rabbi pastoral answer, about how we end our Jewish education too young and need to return to it as adults. I also said something about those people who taught many of us not knowing Judaism all that well themselves. He smiled and sat down. Afterwards he came up to me and said, "I just wanted you to know that I quit [here he named a leading New York non-Hasidic yeshiva] a year before *semikhah* [rabbinic ordination]." That was devastating to me. Here was a product of what in some circles might be called the best of inner Jewish higher education—and he was still left with an infantile level of religious faith! No wonder he looked elsewhere when he grew up. Who could blame him?

The second memorable encounter of that day was a conversation with Brother David. "How is it," I asked, "that these Eastern teachers have such an easy time getting right to the heart of things? They seem totally uninterested in conveying symbolic forms, cultural legacy, or even typical Buddhist or Hindu practices. They simply invite us to close our eyes and open our hearts. Why can't we do that?" When someone wants to study the secrets of Jewish mysticism, I told him, we first expect them to become observant, to learn Hebrew (very little was yet available in translation), and lots more.

"It's too difficult!" I inveighed. "Most people will take the easier path offered by these gurus with their smiling welcomes." His answer was a clever—and perhaps sad—one, "You think you've got problems?" he said. "We Catholics expect them to become monks and promise to remain celibate for the rest of their lives before we allow them access to our secrets!"

Steindl-Rast's answer, perhaps meant as consolation, was little help. I understood that we had to find a way to unpack the religious insights of Hasidism and make them available to a wide range of seekers, both Jewish and non-Jewish. I have spent much of my life working toward that goal, and that young man at Fordham is often on my mind.

The other encounter took place just a bit later, perhaps in the early 1970s. I was invited to take part in a seminar called "Word Out of Silence," dubbed informally as a great "holy man jam" with

representatives of all religions. It was sponsored by the very distinguished Catholic thinker Raimundo Pannikar, himself a product of
the revolutionary East-West encounter of that era and an important
figure in post-Vatican II Christian consideration of world spirituality.
The seminar was held at Mount Saviour Monastery in upstate New
York, and the brothers there were most gracious hosts. Participants
included Swami Sattchadinanda, Pier Villayat Khan, head of the Sufi
Order of the West, Archimandrate Timothy Ware, a British spokes-
man for Eastern Orthodox spirituality, Rabbi Shlomo Carlebach, and
many others.

On the second day of our deliberations, the monks hosting us
turned privately to Pannikar and challenged him (in my paraphrase, of
course), "Why are you talking with these people?" they asked. "They
are not saved; they do not have the truth of Christ. What could we
possibly have to learn from them? In the end, aren't they all going to
hell?"

Very wisely, Pannikar brought their question before the plenum.
All of us, it turned out, had such people back home in our own traditions. By the very fact of being present at such a conference, each of
us had defined ourselves as belonging to the progressive wing of our
respective faith communities. But still, what did we have to say in facing that question? Didn't Judaism have an exclusive claim regarding
revelation of religious truth? Didn't we proclaim regularly the words
of the Psalmist, "The idols of the nations are but silver and gold; eyes
gave they but they see not, ears have they but they hear not. . . . Like
them are those who make them and all who trust in them?" How
could we get away from the notion that religion was a zero-sum game?

In the midst of the heated conversation, a small Japanese monk,
head of the Mount Baldy Zen Center in California, got up to break
his silence with his first comment of the conference. "A Christian who
says 'Christ is the only God' is like a man who says, 'My wife is the
only woman.'" He then sat down as abruptly as he had gotten up to
speak.

I still remember that moment forty years later, because it broke
a bubble for me. By that time I was no longer a believer in the exclusive truth of Judaism, but I didn't know what to do about it. My
great teacher Abraham Joshua Heschel had been very involved in the

Vatican II negotiations, but remained quite cautious about validating faith-claims outside Judaism, especially those outside the shared biblical heritage. I was duly afraid of proclaiming a simple flattened-out universal spirituality, to which all the traditions and their symbols might eventually become irrelevant. I still recoil at such a thought; I am a deep Jewish loyalist, representing a tradition that has struggled so long to survive.

But this monk had in a flash made it all clear to me. Of course there is a level where all I see is my own truth. I am fully engaged in that tradition, its symbols, its liturgy, and all the rest, just as a person is fully engaged in (and hopefully fulfilled by) a single marriage. I will never know what it is like to be engaged in any other marriage. Similarly, I will never know what it is like to ingest the body and blood of Christ or to walk around the Kaaba. But I don't need to. As a married person, I am happy to know that there are other good marriages in the world. That confirms the truth of my marriage, rather than challenging it.

I have carried that monk's truth with me for a long time, and I am now happy to thank him for it.

14

The Prayer God Could Not Answer:
A Métis-Aboriginal Encounter

Wendy Peterson

Hundreds of people gathered in 1995 at Hull, Quebec—across the river from the Canadian Parliament Buildings—for the Sacred Assembly called by Elijah Harper. Elijah, an iconic Cree leader and former Member of Parliament, achieved fame—some would say notoriety—for once having blocked the passage of a constitutional change that he believed was yet another slap in the face to Canada's First Peoples. He had the courage to say "no more" by sitting stoically in a parliamentary session holding an eagle's feather in his hand.

The Sacred Assembly was inspired by a vision Elijah had while suffering from a mysterious ailment. Though not a Christian, he said that in the depths of his illness he cried out to Jesus for help. Jesus healed him, said Elijah, and gave him a vision for reconciliation with Euro-Canadians and a means of uniting Canadian Indigenous peoples—fractured by centuries of oppression and internal strife—around the concept that land is a gift from the Creator. This belief is affirmed by both Traditional and Christian believers within this diverse community; hence the call for the Sacred Assembly.

People from across the country responded in spite of short notice. They came from east and west, from north and south. They drove, flew, bused, and hitchhiked; some traveled over three thousand kilometers. Participants included First Nations chiefs, Inuit leaders, Métis leaders; politicians and the prime minister of Canada; leaders from all major Christian denominations and independent churches as well as lay people; Indigenous, immigrants, and Euro-Canadians gathered.

The Sacred Assembly provided an opportunity for Indigenous people to tell their stories, including reflections on community and personal loss. The following narrative is reconstructed from the notes I took as one elderly woman bravely spoke to the assembled group. This story has had a profound impact on me, changing my educational path and creating a new sense of purpose within me. I have titled it "The Prayer God Could Not Answer"[1]

> She was seven, almost eight, when her father told her it was her decision. For the last two years she had run away and hidden in the bush each time the man came to take her away. Unlike some of the children, she had not been tricked by his offer of candy, so that he could grab them, forcing them on to the plane. Once the plane left, she would come out of hiding and make her way home.
>
> This time, she heard the man yell angrily at her father. Later, her father spoke to her in his quiet way, telling her it was her decision. But, if she didn't go with the man, her father would be jailed. She had never seen a jail, but her father's tone told her it was a bad place. Who then would hunt and trap to feed her mother, grandmother, and little brothers and sisters?
>
> And so it happened. The next fall, when the plane arrived, the frightened little girl went with the strange white man. He terrified her, as did being in a plane so far above ground. She did not understand his language and only knew vaguely where he was taking her. She would not see her village or family for two long years, and then, only briefly every other year.
>
> Finally the plane arrived at its destination. She was led into a large building and handed over to white women, some of whom wore flowing black robes and had their heads covered. She stood frozen in place with fear and shame as one grabbed

---

[1]   Originally published as Wendy Peterson, "The Prayer God Could Not Answer," in Wendy Peterson, ed., *"Aboriginal Task Force Report on the Royal Commission for Aboriginal Peoples"* (Evangelical Fellowship of Canada, 2000).

her long black braids, chopped them off, dropping them to the floor in disgust. Next, they peeled off her clothing and rubbed a smelly liquid into her scalp. It hurt. When they were done bathing her, they dressed her in discarded white girls' clothing. She longed for the beautiful clothes she had watched her grandmother sew. Later she discovered they had been taken outside and burned.

Over the next few months she learned important life lessons. She realized the word "Pauline" meant her. For the remainder of her life she would answer to Pauline rather than her Cree name. She came to understand that the God these people honored hated her Cree language—he preferred Latin, English, or French.

Sometimes she whispered in Cree to another girl, or in a moment of excitement simply forgot the new words. And sometimes she was caught. She recounted how a nun once grabbed her, pulled her to a corner of the room, and shoved a piece of paper between her teeth. She stood facing the corner for a very long time. The paper was hard and dry, with pictures of snakes on one side and flames on the other. They were reminders of the dreadful things God would do to her for speaking Cree.

Pauline discovered that God didn't like the way her people prayed or celebrated or their music. He preferred guitar, fiddle, piano, and organ. She studied a history that began when white people arrived in the land. The only important things worth learning or worth concerning oneself with involved their people.

Pauline's days were filled with lessons on reading, writing, and arithmetic, memorizing prayers, going to church, and doing chores. Day after day the lesson was reinforced that "Indian" people, her people, were savage and uneducated; their only hope lay in becoming like white people.

But the hardest lesson for Pauline came from studying the mural that decorated a hallway she walked through several times a day. It contained three scenes. The bottom scene pictured flames with people screaming in pain—a place they called hell. She observed that all those in hell were Indians.

The middle picture also depicted people in agony, but with fewer flames. This, they said, was Purgatory where people went after death for as long as it took to purge their sins. Many of the people were white, with a few Indians. The top scene was beautiful, with smiling people, winged creatures, and a king on a throne—a scene of peace and happiness. This was heaven. Why were there no Indians in heaven?

Several times a day Pauline would pray, "God, please make me a white girl so I can go to heaven too." Every time she looked in the mirror, she eagerly expected to see that this powerful God had answered her prayer. Each time she was devastated. Her little face remained brown. "God!" she would beg. "How can I go to heaven if you won't make me white?"

But God could not answer this prayer, for how could the Holy One deny the beauty of the diversity of his creation?

Pauline eventually ran away. She spent the next forty years trying to block out the pain and the shame of being an Indian. She said in later years that she came to be the most hated drunken Indian in her town. She said it wasn't until she turned to Native Traditional religion (much of which had been outlawed) that she arrived at a measure of peace.

Pauline's family had endured five or six generations of children parented by white institutions. Pauline concluded her story by stating, "I do not hate Roman Catholics. God gave them their religion just as he has given the Indian people our religion."

I never saw Pauline again. She died two years later.

I sat transfixed that day but also transformed. I had a new respect for Indigenous traditional culture, which has often been degraded, even demonized, in my country, particularly in the church. I am a Jesus-following Métis ("mixed blood") woman, and this encounter shook me to my core. I knew that I needed to delve more deeply into the brutal effects of Euro-style colonization and of the Christian church on Indigenous peoples. I felt a new sense of urgency to help recover the lost treasures of Indigenous spirituality for myself and others. I also knew that I needed to help facilitate healing and reconciliation processes among Christians and Indigenous peoples—both of which are my communities. After my encounter with this brave elder at the Sacred Assembly I whispered to God: "Lord, I will do what you want. I will go where you lead. Help me to make some tiny difference in the lives of the Paulines of this country."

15

How a Daoist Fire-Walking Ceremony Made Me an Episcopalian

Judith Berling

I spent the fall of 1971 in Taiwan in preparation for my dissertation research in Japan. In Taiwan, I was further honing my Chinese language skills, collecting books and resources, and—most importantly—observing everything I could of Chinese religious life and practice. So naturally, when a friend told me of a fire-walking ceremony at a Daoist temple on the outskirts of Taipei, I made plans to attend. My expectations were not high. I fully expected that it would be a not overly impressive "show," a sort of popular religious theater to dramatize the ostensible powers of Daoist masters. What would be interesting to me as a religious studies scholar would be how they constructed and framed the demonstration for the "audience" of Daoists who wanted to believe. My expectations were to be profoundly challenged.

When I arrived at the temple quite early, many people were already milling around, either chatting and enjoying tea and snacks or perusing the religious tracts and items for sale at the temple. Over in a far corner, I could hear chanting and instruments, so I followed my ears in the direction of the preparatory ritual.

As I passed through the main courtyard of the temple to get to the other side, I had to scurry along the wall by a huge heap of live charcoal coals, already turning the main courtyard of the temple into an oven. It was so hot that I rushed to the far end of the courtyard before the main temple building to get out of the immediate heat.

When I came to the site of the preparatory rituals, I realized that the participants in this ritual were not seasoned Daoist masters, but young adepts in their late teens or early twenties who wished to be ordained as priests. The fire walking was one of the tests they had to pass to prove their worthiness for ordination. These adepts, quite young even to me in my late twenties, surrounded a Daoist priest who was leading them in chants of Daoist scriptures and mantras to gods who could protect them from the dangers of fire. The priest and adepts were all barefoot and in white robes, but the priest wore a black kerchief on his head. I was able to get near enough that I could see the texts of the sutra and read the prayers and charms that they were chanting, invoking various Daoist gods, dragons (water spirits), and spirit warriors.

When the preparatory chanting ended, I climbed up to the temple balcony with the other spectators, from where we would be able to see the ritual in the courtyard safely distanced from the heat of the fire. The priest and adepts proceeded to the main altars of the temple, prayed to the deities there, and then took a miniature deity (about two and a half feet high) in a sedan chair from the temple, carried by two other priests. The group, led by the main priest and the god, circumambulated the fire three times, chanting and playing instruments before running three times through the live fire of coals. The fire at the center was about eighteen inches tall, so as they ran through the center their feet and legs sank into the coals, spewing red hot coals high into the air.

After the fire walking, the feet and legs of the adepts were examined for burns, and then they were brought up to the balcony so that the viewers (family and friends of the participants, temple patrons, and even curious foreigners) could see with their own eyes that they had not been burned, that they had proven their spiritual readiness for ordination by being able to successfully invoke Daoist protective deities (to whom they had been chanting during the preparatory rites) to protect them from the dangers of fire.

It is an understatement to say that this experience stunned me. The performance itself was far more effective than I had expected. It was not that it was polished "theater." The priests and acolytes did not use costumes, sound or light effects, or a narrative designed to guide the crowd through the performance. The relatively simple ritual told its own story: the adepts had followed a Daoist deity to brave the dangers of fire and had emerged unscathed.

But the impact of the ritual on me as a post-Enlightenment Protestant Christian was far deeper. I don't "believe" in the Daoist spirit soldiers, nor in the gods of fire whom they were battling. Even more fundamentally, I do not believe in such endurance tests to prove religious vocation: fire walking and sword climbing have no part in my own understanding of spiritual discernment of a sacred calling. I can understand the theological structure of beliefs that frame and establish the ritual, but they are not part of my personal belief system. Nevertheless, I found the ritual compelling and—in a sense that I cannot label or articulate in my own categories—convincing.

I was tempted to find an explanation for what I had seen: self-hypnosis, feet prepared and calloused by going barefoot, auto- or group-suggestion. But I realized that on a certain level these explanations were irrelevant—certainly for the adepts and their families but even for the impact of the ritual. In seeking such explanations, I was seeking to resolve my own cognitive dissonance, my refusal to accept what I had witnessed.

My Protestant self was shaken because I had been theologically educated with a sense that despite certain paradoxical "mysteries of faith," for the most part one could theologically understand and articulate one's faith using reasonable categories. Yet here was something that could be described in words but neither understood nor explained in "Protestant" categories. Any explanation of the rite was embedded in a world of spiritual forces well beyond my imagination.

The power of the fire-walking ritual, I came to understand, lay precisely in its central reliance on archaic religious symbols: that cultivated spiritual power can conquer the forces of destruction (fire) and that some special individuals are called to/can cultivate such spiritual power. One didn't have to be a theologian or subscribe to a creed to appreciate the "story" of the ritual; it is the stuff of many hero legends and popular cartoons as well as of sophisticated religious orders.

The memory of the fire walking stayed with me for a number of years as I studied my way further into Chinese religious writings, life, and practice; it challenged me to open my mind and imagination to aspects of Chinese religious practice that I might otherwise have filtered out or explained away. But its real impact on my own life came years later when I returned to the United States and was contemplating my future spiritual home.

On first returning to the United States, I found that I was uncomfortable in the United Church of Christ or Presbyterian churches that had been my spiritual community before my time in Asia. In the 1970s when I returned, I found that worship in these denominations left no space for what I had experienced of Asian cultures and spiritualities. I came to realize that a major contributing factor to this was the heavy emphasis on the ministry of the Word: the weight of the service was on an extensive interpretation by the pastor of specific scriptural readings, with the preacher interpreting the symbols, the metaphors, and the cultural context and implications of the readings.

Then one year I attended the Great Vigil of Easter at an Episcopal parish, and there I met another powerful ritual structured around archaic religious messages: the power of light to overcome darkness (and by extension sin and death). The readings of the Vigil, read in near darkness, contributed to this sense of God's mysterious power. The Vigil readings were not only a summary of sacred history (as they are generally characterized), but they were also biblical stories that if carefully attended to, resist our post-Enlightenment tendency to "explain away" or "rationalize" the tremendous spiritual power proclaimed therein: the creation of the world by the power (sound) of the Word, the Flood, the re-enfleshment and resurrection of skeletons in the Valley of the Dry Bones, and culminating—of course—in Christ's resurrection and the triumph of the Light. It was a powerful service at every level: the imagery, the powerful readings, the triumphant light and music celebrating the resurrection.

Christianity, I realized, has rituals that, like some Daoist rituals, embody and enact the richly symbolic story that is at the core of their religious vision. The rich and multivalent symbols, powerful and poetic readings with many layers of meaning, and liturgical structures that keep open the many resonances and layers of meaning convey the richness, the paradox, the mystery, and the ongoing revelation of religious message. Although there may be many fine and relevant interpretations of these symbols and stories, these interpretations are never conclusive or final, for the vision "keeps on giving," as it were, and insights and meanings will continue to unfold over many contexts and throughout time.

The Great Vigil converted my interest in Episcopal worship and community into a commitment. Here was a place that I could continue to explore the implications of my religious learnings in Christianity and beyond. Of course, once my sensibilities were opened to this dimension of Christianity, I found it not only in the Vigil, but in many places; I had only to open my mind and heart to the powerful layers of meaning in the ancient stories and ritual acts.

This new openness also significantly broadened my approach to interreligious encounter and learning. I had previously thought that interreligious learning was dialogical in the literal sense: a conversation between two persons of different backgrounds. Although I still respect and honor that form of interreligious encounter, the Daoist fire walking was structured differently. It was a powerful encounter with a very different religious practice. There was no Daoist host or interpreter present; we had learned of the fire walk through a poster. There was no Daoist expert or teacher to prepare us or to help us process what we had seen. The unexpected impact of the vibrant experience was itself the teacher, and I had to process it on my own, over time, keeping my mind and imagination open to the insights that would come, not prematurely closing off the challenge of difference with a Western interpretation explaining away the discomfiting aspects of the experience. Although it is not the only effective way to encounter another religion, I have come to feel that a "dialogue" or encounter that does not include the witnessing of or participating in living religious practice is somehow thin or colorless. Practice conveys a great deal, most particularly about embodied religion.

The fire walking opened up for me a new dimension of religious sensibility that has greatly enriched my life both as a scholar and as a person of faith. It has, in other words, not only established a broader foundation for religious encounter and interreligious learning, but it has also made me more open to many dimensions of my own tradition and even—I dare say—of my relationship to God.

Part III

Redrawing Our Maps

There are no boundaries in the real Planet Earth. No United States, no Russia, no China, no Taiwan. Rivers flow unimpeded across the swaths of continents. The persistent tides, the pulse of the sea do not discriminate; they push against all the varied shores on Earth.

Jacques-Yves Cousteau

The essays in Part III, "Redrawing Our Maps," in different ways address a problem that interfaith explorers inevitably confront: the boundaries between religions that appear on maps are not always reliable or useful guides in the field. On the one hand, as the divine voice in the first person plural utters in the Quran 49:13:

We have created you from a male and a female, and made you into nations and tribes, that you might get to know one another.

That is to say, our particular identities—our homelands, families, cultures, and diversity of religious expressions—are divine gifts that impart identity and community, create appreciation for difference, and inspire the kinds of exploration this book celebrates.

Nonetheless, the boundaries we draw around religious identities are often permeable. The lines we impose on the landscape of religious experience—between one religion and another, and between religion and sect— can become blurred as our horizons expand and our perspectives shift.

Kecia Ali in "Belief-O-Matic and Me," describes her experience with an online religious matchmaking service ("Tell us your beliefs and we will hook you up with your dream religion!"), and reflects on the inadequacy, even absurdity, of generalizing schemes that reduce religions to a list of traits.

The essay written jointly by Roger Gottlieb and Bill Leonard, "Gambling on Hope: One Shared Faith," describes a bond that develops despite religious differences as the authors find support, compassion, and humor in their conversations about the joys and challenges of parenting daughters with disabilities.

In "'Never Was There a Time . . .' : Crossing Over to Hinduism from Catholicism through the Bhagavad Gita," Jeffery Long narrates how a childhood trauma creates theological challenges that he cannot find adequate answers to in his own faith tradition. Discovering powerful insights about life and death in the Bhagavad Gita leads him to find his spiritual home in Hinduism. In "Dearly Beloved," a Christian university chaplain, Janet Cooper Nelson, focuses on the controversial topic of interfaith marriage. Over the long run, as many clerics caution, mixed marriages threaten the survival of distinct traditions. Nelson points to a truth that sits uneasily beside the indisputable former one. Sometimes the love of a Romeo and Juliet, of those whom Nelson calls "lovers on the borders," cannot be denied. Nelson takes on the question of what role she, as a religious leader, should play in such contexts.

Whereas Nelson's piece invites readers to think about what happens before the wedding, Paul Raushenbush takes us inside a family after the fact. In "Why Don't You Just Convert?," Raushenbush describes growing up with a rich interfaith lineage—great-grandfathers Louis Brandeis and Walter Rauschenbusch, whose moral and intellectual courage in an earlier generation nurtured a committed pluralism in their families.

Najeeba Syeed-Miller, author of "The State of the Heart in Multifaith Relationships," tells about a trip from the Bay Area to Texas where she was the Muslim speaker at an evangelical Christian conference. Her progressive friends back home worried that she was entering "the belly of hate": she discovered instead Texas-sized hearts in persons of faith eager to learn about her religion and cooperate in good works. Richard Mouw, author of "'This War of Words and This Tumult of Opinions': The Beginning of a Dialogue with Mormons," makes an explicit appeal for courtesy, decency, and sincerity—debate with others as you would have them debate with you.

In "Oh How You've Spun Me 'Round, Darling," Homayra Ziad describes the impact of seeing Moldavian monks prostrate themselves in prayer. Encountering this quintessential Islamic act of worship in an unfamiliar setting, spins her 'round and refines her notions of prayer.

Finally, in "Theological Goosebumps: A Turning Point in My Interfaith Journey," Paul Knitter takes us behind the scenes of Vatican II where as a young priest he witnessed nothing less than what the title of this part highlights, the council's drafting of *Nostra Aetate*, "In Our Time," a statement that radically redrew the map of global religion.

16

Belief-O-Matic and Me

Kecia Ali

According to the Internet, I am 100 percent a Reform Jew. This came as something of a surprise to me since I'm a Muslim.

Let me explain. In the wake of September 11, I was invited to contribute an essay to a short book on Islam sponsored by a website forcused on religion, Beliefnet. I poked around the site and came across the Belief-o-Matic quiz, which uses twenty theological and social questions to pinpoint "what religion (if any) you practice . . . . or ought to consider practicing." I answered the questions, which included issues of theism (a-, mono-, or poly-), Christology, afterlife, and various contemporary topics, with a lot of attention to sexuality and social policy. It also inquired whether each issue was of minor, middling, or major importance to me. Since I favored a single god (no divine Christ), a single lifetime, and socially liberal stances, it judged me a perfect match for Reform Judaism. Islam appeared seventh on my list of religions to try, after Unitarian Universalism and Sikhism.

As the reference to Sikhism makes clear, the religious options are global but the quiz itself is unmistakably American in spirit. Though conversion is a worldwide phenomenon with deep historical roots, the notion of shopping for a religion rather than fitting oneself more or less comfortably into the religion one was born into is both modern and very American. The Pew Forum's 2007 U.S. Religious Landscape Survey found: "More than one-quarter of American adults (28%)

have left the faith in which they were raised in favor of another religion—or no religion at all. If change in affiliation from one type of Protestantism to another is included, 44% of adults have either switched religious affiliation, moved from being unaffiliated with any religion to being affiliated with a particular faith, or dropped any connection to a specific religious tradition altogether."

Beliefnet places the quiz in its entertainment section, but its categories (never mind its sheer existence) reveal something serious, since my combination of non-Christian monotheism with lefty social views simply does not compute. The quiz endorses and reinforces the perception that there are several kinds of Christians and two kinds of Jews (Reform and Orthodox, in the Belief-O-Matic list) but only one kind of Muslim.

In practice, though, the spectrum of views among Muslims is wide. Progressive voices and practices coexist, sometimes uneasily, with conservative discourses and norms. A few mosques have fractured over issues of doctrine and ritual, but many, perhaps most, serve theologically and politically heterogeneous congregations. In the last decade or two, some people have debated whether there ought to be denominations among (American) Muslims. Rhetoric about unity—which you especially need if you are a community under siege—coexists with divisive stances: if you're not our kind of Muslim, then you're not a Muslim at all. Though intolerance is not new, and a minority has always been concerned with border patrol, these exclusivist voices are perhaps louder than they have been historically, in part because petrodollars buy a lot of (metaphorical) megaphones, subsidizing pamphlets, and glitzy websites.

In some ways the borders between Islam and other traditions are less fraught than the boundaries between Muslim groups and tendencies and cliques. As someone who studies Islamic law, my most obvious conversation partners are scholars studying rabbinic tradition. My conversations with Jewish feminists are productive and exciting. And these interfaith conversations (I cannot think of a single colleague in Jewish studies who is not, in one way or another, Jewish) are invariably illuminating. Disagreements are expected, inevitable, and do not cause consternation. But when normative issues are at stake, intrafaith conversation can be tricky, especially for Sunni Muslims. Observant

Shi'i Muslims are, for the most part, very clear about the authority structures that govern their religious lives. If they are Twelvers (the most populous of the Shi'i groups), they identify themselves as followers of a particular scholar whose guidance they have chosen to accept. Nizari Ismailis have only one Aga Khan. Among Sunnis, the situation is profoundly different. Theologian Amina Wadud once aptly described the interpretive chaos that prevails as a "Sunni free-for-all." Who gets to decide? On what basis? For whom?

This, of course, leads me to think about what it means that this interpretive diversity coexists with a certainty on the part of Beliefnet's programmers that they *know* what makes a Muslim. The same problem of choosing a "representative Muslim" affects invitations to interreligious dialogues and media roundtables. Who shall give the Muslim perspective? (This, of course, assumes that there is *a* Muslim perspective.) There are gendered dimensions to the problem: when clergy and clergy-equivalents are invited, women are not usually among them. There are also racial dimensions: it's usually brown rather than black Muslims who are called upon. But even more basically, the premise of interreligious conversation—that there are bounded entities called religions—masks the internal diversity of each tradition.

Of course, this internal diversity is not unique to Muslims, nor is the existence of a gap (sometimes a chasm) between traditional doctrine and individual belief and practice. The Belief-O-Matic (which, by the way, asks nothing about ritual performance: do I pray? fast? tithe?) cannot capture it. Life, including religious life, is messy and resists categorization. And even when categories exist, they often hide more than they reveal. Though the Belief-O-Matic has been revised at least once since I first took it (my distant-second match was most recently Liberal Quaker), I am still closer to Sikh than Muslim according to its reading, and I remain, stubbornly, perfectly a Reform Jew.

17

Gambling on Hope: One Shared Faith

Roger S. Gottlieb and Bill J. Leonard

Roger:

He was a smallish, dapper, well-dressed academic. Very accomplished, I found out later, in the history of the Baptists. He had an open, intelligent face, a slight drawl indicating he'd spent a lot of time in the South, and an easy confidence that told me we'd both spent a lot of time giving talks at academic meetings. The references to experiences in church and his explicit Christianity, the carefully pressed jacket and tie, the fact that his academic area was far from my own mix of radical politics, environmentalism, Judaism, and eclectic spirituality—all these really didn't make much difference as I listened to him deliver his paper. And I suspect the same was true for him as he heard me begin my comment, his eyes widening first in shock and then in delighted recognition. For despite my casual clothes, my obviously culturally Jewish mannerisms and (now not so new anymore) New Left politics, there was a profound fact that joined us together: we were both fathers of seriously handicapped daughters and both heavily involved in their care.

Soon after we had lunch and talked two hours nonstop, often finishing each other's sentences as we shared our experiences about doctor's appointments, unusual treatments that don't work, the effects of our daughters on our marriages, and how we feel about other people's more or less normal children. Acquaintances who knew us both could never figure out what two such different people were doing together, having dinner in some conference hotel and laughing.

And that is how I got to know Bill Leonard. We very rarely discussed religion, though I do remember once asking him why he was a Christian, and he began an answer by saying he was fascinated by the spiritual character of Jesus. But the conversation got interrupted and we never pursued it. He did send me two of his sermons to read—eloquent, morally clear, emotionally powerful, and filled with love. Were the insights necessarily *Christian* more than they might have been Jewish, Islamic, or Buddhist? I'm not sure.

So what have I learned about Christianity, about "interfaith" relations, from my American Baptist friend?

It is perhaps ironic that we have the same religion. Well, neither of us has converted, of course. He still goes to church, I to temple (and to the yoga mat, the mediation cushion, and places where I can talk to the trees). It is that the religious differences between us are really far less important than what we have in common. We each have our own names for God, religious holidays, precious spiritual teachers, and particular hymns or *niggunim* that move our hearts. But all these things, while important, are not the heart of the matter. For me, and I believe for him as well, the heart of the matter is a life of love, a sacrifice of public accomplishment to the slow, repetitive, often painful, occasionally delightful, lifelong task of parenting our daughters, and a hope that somehow global society can turn toward a modicum of care and reason and away from cruelty, collective greed, and environmental lunacy.

I suppose one could say that we have different religions but similar moral, perhaps even political, outlooks. But I think it is more than that. It is that the very *meaning* of our religious beliefs—his in the Gospels, mine in the moral ideas of the Prophets and biblical injunctions to justice and care—center on the degree to which two highly imperfect men can realize these commands to love our neighbors, see all people as made in the image of God, and replace secular injustice with a moral community. If that is the essential meaning of faith, if the differences in metaphysics or choice of holy book are real but comparatively unimportant—comparable, for instance, to the particular melody to which the words of a psalm might be put—then in just that sense we are co-religionists. There is no interfaith learning here, for there is just one faith.

There are Buddhists and Hindus, Sikhs and Native Americans, Evangelicals and Catholics with whom we share this faith. But we do not share it with the fundamentalists on either (or any) side who are attached to their metaphysics, their particular religious script, their moral arrogance and exclusivity. Religiously I have more in common with Leonard than with the Orthodox Jews who have no sense of the rights of Palestinians; and he has far more in common with me than with Christians who would cheerfully shoot abortion providers or think that 9/11 is a punishment for homosexuality.

In the end, perhaps, there are only two religions in the world. Ours, and the one that makes creed more important than love, being right more crucial than staying in touch with other people.

Bill:

"Roger Gottlieb understands." That's what I have said almost from the first moment we met years ago at a session of the Religion and Disability group at the American Academy of Religion (AAR). We started talking to each other that day and we have not stopped, gathering at each November's AAR for an uncommon meal, part Passover, part Eucharist, part Bacchanal—conversations at once disarmingly cynical and unashamedly spiritual. The process of parenting persons with special needs requires responses (it would be premature to say skills) that no one anticipates acquiring until that moment when a medical professional says something like: "I'm afraid we'll need to keep your newborn for a few days, there are some problems."

And your life is changed forever.

There are multiple stages related to physicians, therapists, teachers, schools, friends, schedules, family life, personhood, and medication, medication, medication. Friends and extended family are at once helpful, frustrating, frustrated, and often easily exhausted. To find someone who understands as Roger understands is simply a gift of grace. He is correct. Each November I say to colleagues: "I'm going to the AAR where I will have dinner with Roger Gottlieb, and once again we will finish each other's sentences." In those moments, as we debrief I know I can whine, rant, confess, weep, laugh, live, and die a little—and Roger will understand. I hope I can do the same for him.

Our journeys are profoundly distinct, yet hauntingly parallel. We both came of age in the 1960s, Roger with a strong engagement in the counterculture, I with a strong engagement in Southern culture, contexts that were strangely radicalizing for each of us. Our professional and personal identities are shaped by academia, research, writing, students, and a love for the classroom. We are married to two brilliant and fiercely independent women, creative intellectuals in their own right, who carry us with patience and wonder into the intense realities of parenting our beloved daughters. Our daughters are delightful and demanding individuals who continue to discover themselves as they move through the stages of their own lives, with us and apart from us. Turns out we are also both people of faith, at times coloring outside the canons of our respective Jewish and Christian traditions, but stuck with and in them nonetheless. As one of us (I can't remember which one) remarked after a particularly impassioned conversation, "We still believe some of this stuff, damn it!"

The traditions, at least pieces of them, still galvanize and energize. I remember the day Roger described his daughter's bat mitzvah, noting that he especially loved being Jewish at those moments when a bunch of adults have to sit down and listen to a thirteen-year-old teach them something about God. After years of quoting this comment of his in sermons and lectures it finally dawned on me that Roger Gottlieb knows something of Jesus' context and tradition—who he was and where he came from—that I may never know. They are both Jewish, aren't they? (Studies show!)

At its best, I hope our friendship mirrors Roger's superb phrase (and book) the "spirituality of resistance," a sense of the sacred that centers us separately and together while freeing us to explore the margins of our own traditions and the world we inhabit. Enlightened and ornery, by grace.

Roger:

It's not hard to say what one loses by having a severely handicapped child. The least important include time, money, and sleep. More deeply, sometimes so deep that (as Bill once said) one cannot even think about it, are personal freedom, dreams of watching a child move into a normally fulfilling life, grandchildren, and a marriage that is not shaped by endless care for a child that never grows up.

But there are also gifts. I sometimes say that with my first child, who was born brain damaged and died after two months, God picked me up by the scruff of the neck and tossed me into a very different room. With Esther, who thankfully is alive and flourishing, God slammed the door, insuring that my life would be forever and continuously different.

As difficult as it is, there are also precious lessons to be learned here.

The first is about Esther. She embodies the power of Spirit in a way I have never encountered in another human being. Physically fragile, cognitively impaired, riddled with anxieties, she remains the bravest person I know. She taught herself to shoot baskets by shooting—and missing—her first thousand shots. She gives talks about her life at local elementary schools, even though she is very nervous beforehand. She sits and meditates at a local peace center, goes to Torah study at the temple with me, and in both contexts shares her often insightful thoughts even though she understands perhaps one word out of three of what the "adults" are discussing. Regardless, she is still willing to share the truth as she knows it. For her work she socializes with residents at a nursing home—watching them age and age and then drop from sight into death. She sings to them, helps with the board games and the snacks, even though she will have nightmares when she sees them hooked up to oxygen machines or taken away in an ambulance.

"Hear O Israel, the Lord our God, the Lord is One," says the single most important Jewish prayer. And what is it to believe that God is One? For me, it is to believe that One is God—that this life, with all its sorrows and cruelties and imperfections, is a mystery and a miracle. Faith for me is not a confidence that Something Really Nice will happen later, because Someone I can't see is taking care of things. It is about finding the ability to give love now, in this life, no matter how much darkness there is and how much it all hurts. To the extent that I have faith, much of it I've learned from Esther.

And then there is a lesson about myself. For as I come to love, and cherish, and see the wondrous beauty of my handicapped child, I have also learned (at least sometimes, and usually with great difficulty) to see the same thing in myself. For am not I, like the rest of us, slow to learn? Don't I forget what I've said I should always remember? Don't my petty, and not so petty, foibles prove that I, no less than Esther, have a basic cognitive impairment?

And yet . . . if Esther is worthy of love, well then so am I. If Esther can be insightful, courageous, and compassionate despite her disability, then I too don't have to be perfect or blameless to do the same. Realizing this has been deeply healing for my own particular brand of neurotic masculinity, which took as its goal always being the best and smartest and most in control person in the room. It has made me, I believe, not only happier and more peaceful but also a lot more fun to be around. This is a gift from Esther's heart to mine. It makes me more able to treasure the One, to care for the widow, the stranger, the orphan, and the earth, and to accept the disabilities that mark the life of every human being I will ever encounter.

In that religion that Bill Leonard and I share, it has brought me closer to God.

Is that not a precious gift?

Bill:

"Nobody works a room like Stephanie." "She never meets a stranger." "Were it not for her special needs, she would surely be running for office!" Across the years, more friends than I can count have offered such descriptions of our daughter after observing her in multiple social settings. Indeed, Stephanie's social skills and networking abilities are truly amazing. They reflect both her determination and her vulnerability, signs of life that at once energize and exhaust, form and inform her way in the world. In a sense Stephanie's social abilities represent a powerful coping mechanism, allowing her to respond to situations familiar and unfamiliar; claim a setting as her own even as she fears it. Even daily transitions do not come easily for her. At the same time, her response to others lies at the heart of her personhood and spirituality, a way of declaring who she is and where she fits in the society around her. Sometimes religious communities have nurtured those skills; sometimes they have inadvertently inhibited them.

Preparing her for those moments takes great energy from us as parents as well as from other formal and informal teachers and caregivers who have known and worked with Stephanie throughout her life. Sometime she "takes a room by storm" in order to deal with the storm that surely rages within her in almost every new or transitional situation. And therein lies the vulnerability: solid moments when she recognizes what she wants to do even as she is continuously forced to come to terms with inevitable boundaries.

Celebration comes readily, from Advent through Pentecost in the church year, with elves, bunnies, bears, and leprechauns thrown in for good measure. Festivities for her late April birthday begin shortly after Christmas and are so all encompassing that one friend calls April "the festival of Stephanie," a description she appropriates gladly.

All this is to say that Stephanie helps me confront my own determination and vulnerability, qualities I can more readily nuance, indeed disguise, but that are no less present in my own social coping mechanisms and fragile spirituality. And perhaps I should stop right there, since Stephanie's life is a constant reminder of the dangers and difficulties of generalizing about who she is and what she means in the church, the world, and of course to God. Her life demands ways of parenting that we could never have anticipated thirty-six years ago. But isn't that the case with all parenting? As time passes and mortality looms large, the thought of someday leaving Stephanie alone in the world may be the greatest reality I have ever confronted. Determination and vulnerability endures to the end.

So in the religion that Roger and I share, we are at once sustained by and gambling on hope.

18

"Never Was There a Time . . . ":
Crossing Over to Hinduism from
Catholicism through the Bhagavad Gita

Jeffery D. Long

The interfaith encounter that eventually led to my conversion to Hinduism from Roman Catholicism took place in the parking lot of the Methodist church in my home town of Montgomery City, Missouri, when I was fourteen years old.[1]

To understand this moment in the parking lot I need to back up to when I was eleven years old, the year my father was injured in a truck accident that left him quadriplegic. My father was paralyzed from the shoulders down, though this paralysis did not leave him completely without sensation (which would have been more merciful). He was tormented by strange pains in his limbs, which he described as feeling as if they had been twisted tightly around each other, though this was not the case at all. Early in his ordeal he had to wear a device called

---

[1] At the time of this writing—the summer of 2011—I have been formally affiliated with the Hindu Dharma, or religion, for a little over sixteen years. Hinduism is, of course, not just one thing. There are no generic Hindus any more than there are generic Jews, Christians, or Muslims. Hinduism is made up of many often overlapping subtraditions or systems of practice and belief. I have been formally affiliated to the Vedanta tradition established by the nineteenth-century Bengali sage and saint, Sri Ramakrishna Paramahamsa, and his famous disciple, Swami Vivekananda, for six years.

a cervical halo, which was held in place by four screws that had to be driven into his skull without any anesthetic.

All of his physical pain paled in comparison with the frequent bouts of depression that accompanied his overall condition. Before the accident, he had always been a very physically active person. He enjoyed carpentry and was a brilliant musician, who could pick up and play practically any instrument he came across. The accident robbed him of all of that—as well as his will to live.

As a Vietnam War veteran, my father received a number of benefits after he was injured, including a mouth-controlled electric wheelchair. The wheelchair was a blessing that gave him a level of independence that he had thought he might never have again. He began to venture outdoors, at first with either my mother or myself accompanying him, but eventually on his own, as he became more proficient with the use of his chair, and more insistent that he was "not a baby" and could get around perfectly well without our help.

One summer evening, my father placed his wheelchair into the path of a speeding freight train. He was killed instantly. He had lived as a quadriplegic for about a year and a half and could endure it no longer.

I have come to think of that year and a half as the axis around which my life has turned. Just as Christians measure history based on the life of Christ, with years marked BC or AD, I continue to think of my life in relation to those months, and to discover new ways in which my father's experiences have shaped me, and continue to shape me.

To say that this set of experiences was both traumatic and transformative is, of course, not surprising. More surprising, perhaps, is the impact on my religious identity. I was raised in a Catholic family and was always a fairly devout if independent-minded child. The tragic circumstances that surrounded my father's death were, as one might expect, a wrenching test of faith.

How could a loving and merciful God allow such suffering to happen in the life of one man and his family? None of us were perfect. Far from it! But we certainly did not deserve the kind of ordeal that we experienced in the year and a half after my father's initial injury or in the subsequent months and years of mourning and coping with our loss.

But while these questions arose, far more powerful at the time—certainly for me—was a sentiment shared with my family by a priest who was a chaplain at one of the institutions where my father was hospitalized. "God," he told us, "never gives us any more suffering than we can endure." I also found comfort in the famous—and now clichéd—poem, "Footprints in the Sand,"[2] which affirms the idea of God, not as the one who gives or allows our suffering, but who carries us through it.

I had a definite sense, throughout this period and in the years that followed, of a loving and sustaining presence that helped me maintain my sanity and start to find meaning in all the sad, difficult experiences my family had endured. So my "faith," and by this I refer to a generalized sense of a meaningful and life-affirming connection to a transcendent reality, was never really in doubt.

God, for me, has never been the inflictor of suffering, but rather the comforter and fellow sufferer. To the question of why God inflicted or allowed the accident that destroyed my father's life. I respond that it was Dad's choices that led to all that happened to him—not in the sense that he "deserved" what happened, but in more of a cause-and-effect, matter-of-fact, naturalistic sense (which I would later come to associate with the doctrine of karma—the results of our actions—in contrast with *karuna*—divine grace or compassion).

However, a more specific doubt began to gnaw at me almost from the moment I was informed of my father's death. My grandparents gave my mother and me the news of what happened the evening my father was killed. As the initial moments of shock and disbelief passed, and the tears began to flow, my grandmother held me close and said, "It's okay, Honey. Your Dad's in heaven with Jesus now."

At the time, I accepted my grandmother's words as the expression of love and comfort that they were intended to be. But something bothered me about the idea that my father was already in heaven with Jesus, having just left his broken body behind hours ago.

The problem, for me, was not with the idea of the afterlife as such. The comforting presence of God was an irrefutable fact of my experience—an experience I felt in prayer and in quiet moments of openness to the divine that I would later come to call meditation. I also had no doubt about the reality of the soul; even before my father's

---

[2] Written by Mary Stevenson in 1936.

death, it was very clear to me that he was not that broken piece of flesh imprisoned in a wheelchair. The true essence—the reality—of my father was what sang through his music when he played his guitar or spoke through his woodwork. I never did blame him for taking his own life. I believed, and still believe, that he was freeing himself from the prison that his body had become. The idea that he had not ceased to exist, but had gone . . . *somewhere*, rang deeply true to me then, as it continues to do today.

But was he already in heaven with Jesus? The problem, as I began to understand it, was the idea that there were only two possible afterlife destinations—heaven and hell—each of which would be experienced forever by their inhabitants. But heaven, an eternal paradise, and hell, an eternal torment, both seemed deeply illogical to me, because no one I knew, and almost no one I knew of, seemed to be either good enough to go to heaven or bad enough to go to hell. Although I loved my father deeply, I was also aware of his flaws—no one is perfect. But I could not imagine him in hell. It seemed to me that he had been through a kind of hell already. But heaven also seemed like a bit of a stretch.

The Catholic tradition's response to this problem is the doctrine of purgatory. Purgatory is the destination of those souls who are in a state of grace, and ultimately destined for heaven, but who have not yet achieved the kind of perfection that would merit instant admission into eternal paradise—the kind of perfection exhibited, for example, by martyrs or those who give their lives to save others. If Dad was anywhere, I thought, he was probably in purgatory.

This, however, troubled me as well. Had he not already gone through a kind of purgatory while still alive? Indeed, hadn't we all? And if, even after all this, he had not attained the level of perfection required for heaven, and purgatory was needed to ensure total purification, then what was the point of all of the suffering he had undergone while still in his body?

For that matter, what was the point of this life at all? If one human lifetime is not enough to give final shape to one's eternal destiny—and indeed, to think otherwise seems mathematically implausible, if not impossible—then why do we have such a lifetime? In other words, why should we not just start out in purgatory? And given the purgatory-like nature of this lifetime—and this was, for me the most fateful question of all—what if we are *already* in purgatory?

It was in the midst of such reflections that I first encountered Hinduism. This was not through meeting actual, living Hindus, but through the medium of popular culture. In particular, I saw the film *Gandhi* when it premiered in 1982 (I was thirteen at the time). I also became intrigued by the Hindu themes in the music of the Beatles. Through my subsequent reading and exploration, I became aware of a Hindu scripture called the Bhagavad Gita, a book that I knew was a great inspiration to both Gandhi and George Harrison.

But copies of the Bhagavad Gita were not easy to come by in Montgomery City, Missouri. I could not seem to find it anywhere. Our local public library did not have a copy, nor did the school library. I became filled with a burning need to read this text.

Then, one day, when I was fourteen, I attended a flea market with my grandmother, held in the parking lot of the local Methodist church. I liked to go to flea markets and garage sales with my grandmother, where I often found cheap copies of old paperback sci-fi novels and comic books. I wandered over to a table that looked promising. On top of a pile of miscellaneous paperback books and magazines, was a copy of the Bhagavad Gita, as if it had been placed there just for me to find it.

I opened the book and came upon these words: "Those who are wise lament neither for the living nor the dead. Never was there a time when I did not exist, nor you, nor all these kings; nor in the future shall any of us cease to be. As the embodied soul continually passes, in this body, from boyhood to youth, and then to old age, the soul similarly passes into another body at death. The self-realized soul is not bewildered by such a change."[3]

In this part of the Bhagavad Gita, Lord Krishna is reassuring his friend, the heroic warrior, Arjuna, that death is only a provisional reality. It pertains only to the body. But the body is not what we really are. It is but a temporary vehicle through which we draw nearer to God. I found this understanding to fit perfectly with my reflections

---

[3] *Bhagavad Gita: As It Is*, with translation and commentary by A. C. Bhaktivedanta Swami Prabhupada (Los Angeles: Bhaktivedanta Book Trust, 1972), 21–24. The original verses are Bhagavad Gita 2:11b–13.

following my father's death. This life is neither the first nor the last that we shall experience. We are passing through a gradual process of spiritual purification and self-realization that takes many lifetimes to come to fruition—hence the many and varied levels of spiritual realization that we find among living beings. This explained to me the fact that so few of us are either good enough for "heaven" or evil enough for "hell." Most of us are somewhere in the middle—pilgrims on an ongoing journey of multiple lifetimes toward the highest goal of all.

What profound reassurance that the true essence of my father's being had not ceased to exist!

> That which pervades the entire body is indestructible. No one is able to destroy the imperishable soul. . . . For the soul there is never birth nor death. Nor, having once been, does he ever cease to be. He is unborn, eternal, ever-existing, undying and primeval. He is not slain when the body is slain. . . . As a person puts on new garments, giving up old ones, similarly the soul accepts new material bodies, giving up the old and useless ones. . . . Knowing this, you should not grieve for the body.[4]

Reading these words in the Methodist church parking lot, I found the answer to my problem. I felt that the reassuring presence that had been my comforter and fellow sufferer was speaking directly to me through this colorful text from a wise and ancient civilization from the other side of the world. My journey to Hinduism had begun.

Although I sometimes jokingly say that this was the moment I became a "born-again Hindu," this event did not immediately lead to a change in my religious identity. I simply felt that I had found a deep truth not fully disclosed in the tradition in which I was raised—a truth that could supplement and deepen what I had already learned in the church. It is likely that, had I chosen a different career path, I might have remained a devout but unconventional Catholic, believing in reincarnation and that God had revealed deep truths through many traditions. But my desire to become a theologian—to reflect publicly rather than privately upon these truths—eventually led me to

---

[4]   Ibid., 26–29; original verses 2:17, 20, 22, and 25b.

part company with the church and to embrace formally, twelve years after that encounter in the Methodist church parking lot, the tradition whose teachings most closely reflected my own understanding of reality. But that is a story for another day.

19

Dearly Beloved

Janet M. Cooper Nelson

Your absence has gone through me, like thread through a needle.
Everything I do is stitched with its color.

W. S. Merwin

Called to be chaplain by a secular university, I find that my work is continually on the border, often with young lovers who have come together across every possible line of devotion, culture, and prayer. My duty at these borders requires agility, to keep up, to understand what I am being asked, to come to some clearness about what rite or task to perform, to advocate, to accompany, to bless. Work at the border is always personal, and often political, but if it is the chaplain's, it must also be sacred somehow.

Universities freely interrogate nearly everything, but the idea of interrogating lovers—especially those on the verge of crossing difficult borders—is awkward at its best and at worst can be pain filled. So these moments require gentle *investigation*—a long-used name for an inventory taken by the church with betrothed couples. But at these borders, no established inventory will suffice. My inquiry as the chaplain seeks simply to discern whether I can be of use.

I promised in ordination to cherish a theology that hopes to bear witness to God's deeds—deeds that are visible to mere earthlings as *ordinances*—acts that strengthen the human condition, marriage, for example. But this promise is not upheld by *permitting* or *forbidding*, rather it *obliges* us as clergy to serve people and faiths outside our own circle. For instance, if a couple who are free and suited to marry invite me to officiate for their ceremony where prayer is central, if only for one member of the couple, I am not *permitted* to marry them, I am actually *obliged* to marry them—an obligation that I take very seriously.

Meeting this sacred obligation carries me well beyond my comfort zone and the customs of my beloved tradition. Thankfully, my denomination authorizes me to do this work, and strong strands of my family's long history underscore this calling. Equipped with these bright filaments of love and need, I strive to stitch silence into speech, to embroider shame with dignity, to bind radiant lovers for life with blessings.

My work to cut and sew new rites is modest in comparison to what these couples often undertake in beginning these marriages. But, in literally hundreds of these ceremonies, I glimpse, if only for a few hours, the transformational power of sacred extravagant hospitality where none was anticipated. "That was lovely—I did not know you were allowed to do this," guests often say as they shake my hand. I reply truthfully that it was a privilege to officiate. It's true. These rites rehearse God's welcome to all of us who, finding ourselves prodigal, yearn for a home community. But the work to make durable communities of belief and support of these momentary circles that gather joyfully around couples at weddings, is a work-in-progress. It will finally require and develop a new order of "clergy." For now, I stitch, as do many others, using the threads of history and belief.

Stitching, suturing, I do try to secure those with vast loss against despair without tearing the injured tissue through which the thread travels. I sew to effect the ancient claim that we are God's *Dearly Beloved* and that those whom *God has joined, let no one put asunder.* As I stitch new rites to honor the offices of life, my greeting is always the time-honored one: *Dearly Beloved.* A phrase to honor and bless, it affirms that a light shines still through the world's kitchen window, perennially awaiting our return. *Dearly beloved,* the greeting for which we yearn is also the best greeting for those who never imagined being together or being beloved.

But *dearly* is rarely *simply* beloved. People find one another across such varied lines of identity. Their compatibility cannot erase the differences that frequently spawn storms of family conflict. So they frequently stitch from their separate traditions a quilt of shared patches of conviction to present their newly formed coverlet of theology. Although God remains silent, their creations routinely evoke family surprise at best and fury at worst.

In just such a way, two young students invited me to officiate at their Muslim Christian marriage in early 1983. Late one afternoon the bride-to-be kept an appointment in my office. Our places, hers and mine, were the same and different. The staff "newbie," my ordination identity as a Congregationalist spanned only five years. She, by contrast, was a "lifer" born to a family of Congregationalists who farmed the Connecticut River valley of New Hampshire before the American Revolution. I was just back from maternity leave; she was newly engaged. Ostensibly, we met to discuss my officiating at her marriage later that summer, but her story was a request for something more than my prayer and signature on the wedding license.

She met her fiancé nearly seven years earlier—as he began his graduate studies. Immediately, their voltage together was special. Simply delighted with one another, their talk was patient, intrigued, passionate. At dinner, coffee, or after long workdays, their hours together flew effortlessly. Devotion to faith, family, unembarrassed idealism, bold dreams, were woven through their words. Absent in earlier relationships, they found deep sympathies in each other despite striking cultural differences.

His mother's response from Karachi, Pakistan, was resolutely opposed. Widowed, she told him that marriage to his university girlfriend would render him dead to her, a suicide. Never again would they share meals, visits, letters, family. Without his fiancé's conversion to Islam her son's death to them was inevitable. No discourse, no compromise was possible: these absolutes were God's. His brother in Chicago simply said: "Mom will get over it."

In her parents' Yankee kitchen *acceptance* was intoned: obligatory, frozen, as though incurable illness had been diagnosed. Religious conversion afforded no relief. Matters of race and class were pivotal, and their social standing weighed heavily.

Her appointment with me was an experiment—a kind of phased clinical trial conducted first, among friends, then with family, and finally, with authority figures, namely clergy. They tested three discrete concerns: whether any circle of "dearly beloved" could truly support their marriage; whether their future would be nourished by only a subsistence diet of strained acceptance and grief-filled tolerance and whether they could secure something more meaningful than a merely legal marriage.

What is the role I play when standing with such couples at these difficult thresholds? By what authority do I oblige their proposal and extend blessing? In whose name do I rename these outcasts "Dearly Beloved"? Is the unspoken accusation true: that Protestant clergy preside in these moments because our tradition lacks the rigor to preclude it?

In my own family, another pair of lovers married across Muslim Christian borders—my great-grandparents. Mohammed Ben Ayad, my paternal great-grandfather, was born in 1825 in Algiers. Muslim, black, he was serving as an officer in the French colonial military, in the year of his marriage. Marie Wardecka, my great grandmother, a white Roman Catholic woman, of French Polish heritage, was born in 1839 into an affluent Paris that was quickly devastated by penury and hunger in the aftermath of the revolutions of 1848. Her observant Catholic family deployed their seventeen-year-old, unmarried, educated daughter to serve the church by teaching music at a mission school in Algiers. A license in 1858 registers her Parisian marriage to Mohammed.

Their unfolding lives included the birth of three daughters— Mathilde, their youngest, my father's mother, was born in Blackpool, Lancashire, England, a seaside town to which they had fled from Paris. Mohammed traded in Victoriana until his business burned to the ground. In the 1880 census, he is recorded as sixty years old, a grocer's assistant, living in Leicester. After his burial in the cemetery in Groby Road, Mohammed's wife, Marie, aged seventy-nine, booked steerage to Philadelphia to live with her youngest daughter until she died a decade later. In her American sojourn even her surname became disguised. Beloved Grandmother "Bernardi" left our family large albums of unlabeled photographs and letters from a never-seen cousin—scant clues to these forebears. No stories of their lives as border-crossing lovers survive. The stitches of their commitment are strong but silent.

The marriage of Marie and Mohammed's youngest daughter, my grandmother Mathilde, required her conversion by adult baptism into the community of Christadelphians, a tiny separatist, pacifist, and British sect. Failure to comply would result in my grandfather's being removed from fellowship, extruded from a community his family helped to establish. Her immersion transformed Mathilde Ben Ayad into "Sister Cooper," erasing her name and forgiving her sin. She died when I was a toddler; and no memories seem to remain of her childhood or of her parent's pioneering marriage.

My grandparents' story evokes Merwin's lines: I am convinced that everything I do is stitched with *their* color. Their voices resound in my office when anyone arrives who is not sure they have a right to be there. Expressing affirmation carries me outside the boundaries of my credentials; it proposes rather than observes customs.

In that 1983 appointment we addressed prayer, especially the couple's list of thanksgivings. We named their beloved dead and the sacred texts to be read. I learned their core theology, a doctrine of God derived of Islam and Christianity, and the theology they would teach their children. Our conversation was expansive, and we planned a beautiful wedding—clearly intended to span gracefully, seriously the content of their faiths and families.

Our conversation's pulse generated from deep within—through layers of living tissue—whisperings, syllables, constant and yet not easily heard; uttered plainly but not at any volume; shimmering, costly, honest, with primordial sounds of hope, regret, shame, illegitimacy, radicality; just out of earshot, but absolutely audible. This sound is best heard on the *border*—at *thresholds*. It carries content that other languages cannot articulate. It is elusive. When turmoil, grief, suffering, fear abound, its grammar and vocabulary emerge in phrases, gestures, prayer, poetry, and ritual. Shouted by women in labor, sobbed by fathers in grief, barely audible. Rosetta Stone cannot yet render us fluent; our sacred traditions can nearly drown it out; but it beats steadily.

This pulse surely accompanied my great-grandparents' vows. Their lineage protrudes through history. In the mirror I see with their eyes.

Beyond their Parisian license, holy writ unseen launched a process to reverse their undocumented, illegal status. My calling and authority derive from profound obligation to complete this sacred process for them, for many.

Liberal Protestant clergy are often those who officiate at interfaith marriages. Couples, gay and straight, frequently begin these conversations asserting that they cannot "go home" to be blessed. Sometimes they are not right. When these couples can be reunited with traditions of their families, I meet my clerical obligation to God's ordinances with no need to sign a license, smash crystal, bless ducks, or duck rice.

But where couples lack spiritual formation and/or when they truly cannot go home, then my promise, my obligation, to serve all of God's dearly beloved is the authority to which I resort. This is the blessing I extend. It is not mine. It is not authority devoid of religious content. This sacred obligation observed is the ancient voice of my tradition at its best. It may speak through me and my colleagues to ensure that my great-grandparents and many more will no longer engage life's ordinances alone, devoid of any spoken blessing but the prayers of their own loving hearts.

In reverie, I position my great-grandparents in that 1983 wedding I performed— standing on a gorgeous day at the sunny end of a vine-covered porch surrounded by a bevy of guests in full finery. I intoned the words, *Dearly Beloved,* addressing them, fragmented families being joined in marriage against their better judgment and heard again his family's loud wailing. Disorienting, blunt—the kind of honesty prized by real Yankees, I persevered; the Imam did as well. I signed the license—he had no legal authority to do so. Our words ended.

My family's once embarrassing and too silent border narrative confirms and confers on me a debt and a calling. Absent a way to speak to or for them, I strive to redeem their suffering by declaring in their honor that those who proceed as they did are no less God's *dearly beloved* and may in fact, be more so. I suture.

20

Why Don't You Just Convert?

Paul Raushenbush

"Oh Paul, why don't you just convert to Judaism?"

This invitation was extended to me after a book talk in Washington, D.C., and I have to admit it took me by surprise. First, I had always heard that Jews aren't supposed to proselytize. Second, I'm not just a blank slate; I'm a Christian minister by profession, and the book talk I had just given was about a Christian book. And the third reason for my surprise is that two people who posed the question were my cousins.

Let me back up a bit and tell you how I arrived at this moment. I'm from an interfaith family. My side of the family is Christian, and my cousins are Jewish. The reason my family went to church at all was because of my mother, Marylu Raushenbush. Every Sunday she would wake up her four resentful children by snapping up the rolled shades and greeting us with a pointedly bright voice, "Good morning!" This was not a casual "good morning," this good morning meant that if you were not up in five minutes the next greeting would be much less pleasant. So up we would go from our Frank Lloyd Wright–inspired home our Frank Lloyd Wright–inspired church—complete with the wide open sanctuary space and stained glass that served as a great distraction during the services.

My father, Walter Raushenbush, was a deacon in the Presbyterian Church, which is surprising to people who know his background. Dad's mother, Elizabeth, was the daughter of Jewish Supreme Court Justice

Louis D. Brandeis. So, according to Jewish law, my dad was Jewish. However, my dad's father, Paul, was the son of the social gospel pastor, Walter Rauschenbusch, and my grandfather was raised Christian. While my grandparents' professions were influenced by the prophetic and justice elements of their respective traditions, neither felt strongly about their religion. So, like many such couples, they briefly tried to raise my dad as a Unitarian, which also failed to stick. I once asked my dad, who is judicious and agnostic by nature, if he had ever had what he would describe as a "religious experience." He told me that the only moment he might be tempted to describe as religious was the first time he saw my mother and, in his words, "I immediately knew I wanted to spend my life with her." Which is exactly what he has done.

By contrast, my mother was a conservative Presbyterian when she met my dad. Before she would marry him, she insisted he be baptized because she wanted not only to spend the rest of her life with him, but also the rest of life after life. My mother has since expressed embarrassment about asking him to undergo what Oscar Wilde might describe as "this terrible ordeal." But my father has never expressed regret. And so our family went to church on Sunday mornings—if not always joyfully, at least consistently—and my parents were leaders in the church.

There is a history to all interfaith families that involves some kind of negotiation of how religion will function within the family. My family is Christian because one of my parents felt strongly about their religious commitments. Now that I am a minister, I occasionally counsel couples that do not share a religious tradition and who are considering marriage. I never downplay the difficulty. You have to decide either to try to honor both religions, to ignore religion all together, or to concentrate on the religion of one of the parents, which is what my family did and how we became Christian.

However, the cousins my siblings and I spent the most time with were from the Jewish side of the family. Louis Brandeis had two daughters: my grandmother Elizabeth, and her older sister Susan, who married another Jew and raised her family in that tradition. The sisters inherited adjoining properties in Cape Cod and each summer we would spend weeks with our cousins who are essentially our own age. Although we were competitive with them in some areas of sports and academics, our religious differences were never brought up. I never once heard that it would be better if our Jewish cousins were Christian or that we might be better off as Jews.

This was made easier by the fact that our family as a whole had a particular approach to religion. Religion was meant to be a positive force in our personal and communal lives by instilling moral values and a vision of social justice, a sense of gratitude and duty, and an openness to the wonder and mystery of the world. It was never meant to pit "us" against "them." My family unconsciously adopted a model of interfaith cooperation that continues to influence my understanding of interreligious engagement as a religious person and leader.

When we were in our late twenties one of my Jewish cousins began a spiritual search and came to me for advice. My response was for her to start by going to synagogue. My approach leaves some of my co-religionists wondering if I truly believe Jesus is the only way to God—and I have to reply that I don't. The proof is in the pudding, as they say. I know people can live full, beautiful, meaningful lives by practicing Judaism, Islam, Hinduism, and any number of other faith traditions, or none at all. I also know that professing a certain faith tradition is no guarantee of a godly or good existence. As far as the afterlife goes, I'm willing to trust in God enough to not have to make decisions about people down here. This is not to say that I don't have thoughts on the subject. To put it bluntly: if I can't hang with my Jewish cousins up in heaven, then it doesn't sound much like heaven to me.

While I was surprised that my cousins invited me to convert to Judaism, I just laughed and took their invitation the way it was meant: as a compliment. In hearing me talk about the moral imperatives of my Christian convictions they recognized those same convictions in their practice of Judaism. By inviting me to be Jewish they were basically saying that they think I might have what it takes. That said, I don't want to be Jewish, though I am proud of my ancestry and cultural identity. I am a Christian; I love Jesus' life, his teachings, and the entire Christian narrative that offers me the Way to live my life. Yet I thank God for my family that has nurtured my interfaith heart. My heart guides my work with colleagues who are Jewish, Muslim, Hindu, Buddhist, Sikh, and others. Being a religious person for me is about expressing my solidarity and love for people who do not profess what I do, yet are those whom Jesus described as my neighbors and my family.

21

The State of the Heart in Multifaith Relationships

Najeeba Syeed-Miller

I was born in Kashmir and brought by my family to the United States at the age of three. My earliest memories are of being a part of the Muslim American landscape. Both of my parents were deeply immersed in building American Muslim institutions and identities. They engendered in my siblings and me a love for our community, our religion, and our faith.

From my father, I received a deep appreciation for the intellectual tradition and history of Islam. We were regularly exposed to the poetry, philosophy, and theological reflections of many of the great Muslim thinkers from South Asian, Arab, and African contexts. My father taught us that our Muslim identity was also rooted in the stories and spiritual lineage of the ancestors of the African slave trade to the United States. We read *Roots* when we were in elementary school and watched the TV series. To me, Kunta Kinte was just as much my forebear as were my Kashmiri great-grandparents. My father believed that American soil needed to be the context for the expression of our family's Muslim faith.

From my mother I learned a love of Allah. While my father's faith was deeply rooted in the rational or *aql* path, my mother's relationship with God was all heart. She prayed daily with her six children in a ritual suffused with deep emotion. I watched her bend to God in humility. She taught me also that our heart is a gift given to serve others. She imparted to us the conviction that daily prayer is the arboreal trunk of our faith and that acts of service to others are the branches that naturally grow from the core of Muslim piety. I saw her take in one homeless person after another. I saw her build a shelter for women. Her compassion was not discriminatory. If anyone called for help, Muslim or otherwise, she answered; she always had food at the ready.

I thought of both of my parents as I walked into the 2010 Global Faith Forum organized by Pastor Bob Roberts Jr. at the NorthWood Church in the Dallas Metroplex. I had never met the man and knew only that I would be addressing hundreds of evangelical Christian pastors in Texas at the height of Islamophobia in North America. I brought along my Texan-born, Muslim convert husband and our two children. I discovered that it is true that everything is bigger in Texas, including people's hearts. What surprised me was how anxious many of my friends in the Bay Area were before I left. "Najeeba, now you are doing something incredibly brave, you are going into the belly of hate, and I commend you," they said.

I did not feel there was any reason to commend me. I had received an invitation from a person of faith to participate in a conversation about my tradition. Of course, I understood that the climate in interfaith relations, especially between the Muslim and Evangelical Christians, was white hot with anger and pain on both sides. But I had been a mediator for nearly two decades, and one of the basic precepts I live by is that I must sit with others and listen to them in order to get to know them.

Tragically, I find that far too often we talk about each other and not each other. Just as I was asking Christians not to condemn Muslims and Islam wholesale, I had to put myself in a position to meet them, hear their fears, and confront my own preconceived notions about them. I felt great sadness that it took such a rupture in the relationship between our communities to bring me to this conversation.

Some of the online previews of the Dallas conference mentioned that the conveners held conservative or exclusivist theological positions. Underlying these statements was the assumption that those who are less conservative in their beliefs are necessarily more tolerant. For me, as a Muslim with roots in other parts of the world, I was struck by how many of the conference participants immediately grasped my concerns about global issues. This was not the case, necessarily, when I had spoken to more liberal groups, where people had very little experience actually engaging cultural differences at home or abroad.

Although it is true that many of the Evangelical pastors I met adopted a global mind-set because of a missionary impulse, their concern for the physical well-being of others was also genuine. I also discovered that these pastors were willing to engage with me in real conversation about our similarities and differences (including on the subject of religious mission) in a respectful manner. In fact, I found many points of resonance with them on the importance of sacred texts, strong community ties, and our mutual struggle to be religious in a largely secular culture.

For Pastor Roberts, the starting point for interreligious dialogue, as he stated it, was love. This was deeply grounded in his conservative Christian theology; I felt welcomed to share my own life experiences and faith commitments as an equal partner in the conversation. Neither of us let go of our deeply held beliefs, but our common passion and commitment to our distinct spiritual paths allowed us to be speak with confidence, while also actively listening to and engaging the other in respectful discussion.

In the end, for me interreligious engagement is not about changing someone's theology; it is about developing the skills to engage productively across lines of differences. Can we learn to disagree on matters of faith without turning to violence? Do we recognize our common humanity? Can we cooperate on joint projects for the common good? I often tell my students that the most vibrant interfaith projects can happen between two people who avowedly believe the other is going to hell but somehow still find ways to feed the homeless in their community.

Religion is too often a source of bitter dispute and bloody conflict. However, if people of faith are also people in search of peace and justice, then perhaps we can transform our religious borders and reach a point of mutual respect and cooperation emerging from our faith commitments, and not despite them.

22

"This War of Words and This Tumult of Opinions": The Beginnings of a Dialogue with Mormons

Richard J. Mouw

I was just entering my teens when our family traveled by car to California from our home in a town near Albany, New York. On the way we stopped in Salt Lake City and did the standard tourist thing, visiting Temple Square. Our seventh-grade class had already learned a little bit about Joseph Smith and Palmyra in our required unit on New York State history, so I found the idea of a visit to the Mormon "Zion" mildly interesting. My interest turned to fascination, however, as we left Salt Lake City and headed further west.

In the back seat of our car I read "Joseph Smith Tells His Own Story," a pamphlet edition of the official version of his First Vision narrative. For me, the most intriguing part of the story was his description of his state of mind just before his account of the visitation that he claimed to have experienced. As a fifteen-year-old boy, he reported, he was so perplexed by "the confusion and strife among the different denominations" that it seemed "impossible for a person young as I was, and so unacquainted with men and things, to come to any certain conclusion who was right and who was wrong." The Baptists were arguing with the Presbyterians, and each in turn had their own debates with the Methodists. Everyone was intent on proving their own views to be the right ones and the others riddled with error.

I found especially gripping Joseph's poignant expression of despair: "In the midst of this war of words and tumult of opinions, I often said to myself, what is to be done? Who of all these parties are right; or, are they all wrong together? If any one of them be right, which is it, and how shall I know it?"

During this time of personal religious questioning, Joseph discovered the passage in the Epistle of James that says that "if any of you lack wisdom, let him ask of God, that giveth to all men liberally, and upbraideth not; and it shall be given him."

It is no exaggeration to say that I felt like I had discovered a friend. Here was someone who understood my own confusions and yearnings, ones that I had been reluctant to express to the adults in my life—and even a bit fearful of admitting to myself.

My father had experienced an evangelical conversion in his late teens, under the influence of a fundamentalist ministry. Meeting my mother, who was of solid Dutch Calvinist stock, he was exposed to Reformed Christianity. For a while he maintained his Baptist convictions, although he gradually moved in my mother's direction theologically. Eventually he studied theology and was ordained as a Reformed Church minister. Having made that move, he was fairly zealous in his defense of infant baptism, as was evident in what seemed to me as a child to be his endless (albeit always friendly) arguments on the subject with his brother, a Baptist pastor.

My impression of those debates was not unlike the experiences described by the young Joseph. My dad and my uncle were each passionately sincere in their views about baptism. And each was skilled at appealing to the Bible in support of his views. Yet they disagreed, and the disagreement seemed incapable of being resolved. This disturbed me. How could I know—*really* know—whose view was the correct one?

I had become a bit of a theological debater in my own right as I moved into my teenage years. I had many Catholic friends around the time of our visit to Temple Square, and I would often challenge their views about going to the priest for confession, and about Mary and the Pope. Some of those friends were fairly articulate. I never convinced them of anything—nor did they force me to change the views that I was defending. In my private thoughts, however, this bothered me. Who was I to say that I had the "right" theology and theirs was simply wrong?

So when Joseph Smith described a time in his life as a young teenager when he was simply bewildered by "this war of words and tumult of opinions," his story resonated with me in the deep places. His teenage questions were mine as well: "Who of all these parties are right; or, are they all wrong together? If any one of them be right, which is it, and how shall I know it?" I was not tempted to believe Joseph's account of being visited by the divine persons and angels. But, frankly, if an angel had happened to visit me with some clear answers, I would not have refused to listen.

Two years after our visit to Salt Lake City, I sat through a series of Sunday night talks given by Walter Martin on the subject of "the cults." By this time our family had moved to New Jersey, and I had a small group of Christian friends in the large public high school I was attending. Several of them were members of the Riverdale Bible Church, and they were excited about the series of Sunday evening lectures Martin would be giving at their church.

Walter Martin was not as well known in those days as he would be after 1965, when he published his influential *Kingdom of the Cults*. But he was already a dynamic speaker who could stir up an evangelical audience with his engaging, sharp-witted critiques of Mormonism, Christian Science, Jehovah's Witnesses, and Seventh-Day Adventists. (This last group he would later remove from his list of dangerous cults.) For his Riverdale talks he took on each of these movements on four successive Sunday nights. I made a point of attending the whole series.

The sessions were widely advertised, and the small church was packed for each of the evenings. Martin was an effective rhetorician, and I was captivated by the way he made his case against non-Christian groups. He had a fine one-liner, for example, about Christian Science: just as Grape Nuts are neither grapes nor nuts, Mary Baker Eddy's system of thought is neither Christian nor science.

On the evening of his talk about Mormonism the atmosphere was electric. A dozen or so Mormons were in attendance, and they sat as a group near the front of the auditorium. We had seen them walking in, carrying their copies of the Book of Mormon—and several of the men wore their LDS "Elder" name tags. It was clear that they had come armed for debate, and Martin was eager to mix it up with them. He was in top form for his lecture.

During the discussion period, one of the Mormon men was quite articulate as he argued that Martin misunderstood the Mormon teachings regarding atonement and salvation. But Martin was not willing to yield an inch, and what began as a reasoned exchange ended in a shouting match. The young Mormon finally blurted out with deep emotion: "You can come up with all of the clever arguments you want, Dr. Martin. But I know in the depths of my heart that Jesus is my Savior, and it is only through his atoning work that I can go to heaven!" Martin dismissed him with a knowing smile as he turned to his evangelical audience: "See how they love to distort the meanings of words?" I am paraphrasing the preceding from a memory reaching back over about five decades, but I can still hear in my mind what the young Mormon said next, with an anguished tone: "You are not even *trying* to understand!"

I came away from that encounter strongly convinced that Martin's theological critique of Mormonism was correct on the basic points at issue. But I also left the church that night with a nagging sense that there was more to be said, and that the way to let it be said was captured in the young Mormon's complaint: both sides had to *try* to understand each other. I hoped that the day would come when I could do something to make that possible.

I have often thought of those two teenage encounters—reading Joseph's First Vision account and witnessing the exchange between Walter Martin and the young Mormon—as what really pushed me toward the study of philosophy. For one thing, the teenage Joseph Smith's question about how we can decide who is right in "this war of words and tumult of opinions" has always been high on my own intellectual agenda. On countless occasions, when I have listened to someone appeal to an inner feeling of certainty about the truth of some Christian doctrine, I have been inclined to ask, "But suppose a Mormon said that same kind of thing about an inner 'testimony' to the truth of the Book of Mormon?"

The Mormon young man's poignant complaint to Walter Martin— "You are not even *trying* to understand!"—also had a lasting influence on the way I have approached disagreements about the basic issues of life. I have tried hard to understand people with whom I disagree about important issues, listening carefully to them, and not resorting to cheap rhetorical tricks. Even if I have fallen short of this commitment, it has regularly guided me in my philosophical and theological endeavors.

For over a decade now I have been codirecting a Mormon-Evangelical dialogue with Professor Robert Millet of Brigham Young University. For the first several years we met "under the radar." We engaged in off-the-record discussions, with roughly ten persons representing each tradition, on issues about which evangelicals and Mormons have strongly disagreed. More recently, our project has begun to receive public attention—and we are not without our critics, especially in the evangelical world. But already much has been gained. Not only have deep friendships been formed, but on both sides we have also come to see that we have often misunderstood each other in the past, mainly because we have not been willing to set aside the angry rhetoric and engage in genuine listening to each other. Many deep differences remain, but at least we are coming to more clarity about what those real disagreements are all about. For me this has been a matter of getting around to dealing with questions that arose back in my teenage years.

23

"Oh How You've Spun Me 'Round, Darling"

Homayra Ziad

In the winter of 2000 I had the privilege of visiting the monasteries of Bucovina in Northern Moldavia, Romania. In the painted church of Sucevita, I witnessed an act of worship that deepened my own prayer life. What was it that so moved me—the simple and familiar act of prostration.

Prostration, resting on palms and knees and placing the forehead on the ground, is the quintessential Islamic act of worship. It is the culmination of every cycle of prayer, performed more than twenty times a day. Portraits of this striking physical action abound in images of Muslim worship. Prostration drives home the intense physicality of the Islamic tradition—that religion is expressed both through body and soul. Islam is an ascetic tradition in love with the body. The material body is revered, a fistful of earth fashioned by the very hands of God, carrier of soul, deserving of care. And yet the rigorous discipline of the body in such acts as the fast of Ramadan brings the soul into stark relief against the vanishing of the body; the body is further adored for its willingness to act as a vessel of transformation that, paradoxically, transcends the material.

To see my "own" form of worship performed in an unfamiliar setting unsettled me. Even more, performed before a portrait of Jesus, a prophetic figure who I was taught was never to be represented physically. And yet I understood the power of prostration more deeply in that moment than I ever had. Before this experience, prostration was "mine"—and possession had dulled its sharp edge. Now, watching this act as if for the first time, I was struck by the submersion of self that conscious prostration demands of one—anyone—who enacts it.

With the clarion call of iconoclasm ringing in my ears, I took three quick, furtive photographs of one particular icon of Christ, coffee-brown against an ochre backdrop. Back in Bucharest, where my parents would be living for the next three years, I spent several evenings in contemplation of this photograph. It was when my eyes met the still, steady gaze of Christ the icon—who bore the burden of divine love—that I began to understand Jalaladdin Rumi's commentary on the link between body and soul. Rumi's reference is to the Quranic story of the birth of Jesus, in the nineteenth chapter entitled Maryam, where God lovingly tends to the body of Mary in the pangs of childbirth. Rumi writes:

The body is like Mary.
Each of us has a Jesus, but so long as no pain appears, our Jesus is not born.
If pain never comes, our Jesus goes back to his place of origin on
the same secret path he had come, and we remain behind,
deprived and without a share of him.[1]

Later, Meister Eckhart would say, as if picking up the thread of a conversation that spanned centuries, "the spiritual being will be born in the human soul, provided one willingly takes upon oneself the burden and pain caused by Divine Love."[2]

A Sufi teacher once told me that all ritual is imitation. He compared the action of prayer to the spinning of a record in a gramophone—the record spins to recreate the sounds of an intangible experience. Determined, intent, on and on it whirls, but the sound can be no more than mere imitation. Is it the pain of never-reaching that makes us ever-reach? Caught in this whirl, what else can we do but fall to the floor, place our forehead to the ground in a gesture of surrender, palms outstretched . . . waiting? Perhaps that is what the Sindhi Sufi teacher Sachal Sarmast meant when he cried out:

---

[1]   Translation by Annemarie Schimmel, *I am Wind, You are Fire: The Life and Work of Rumi* (Shambhala Publications, 1996), 122.
[2]   *Ibid.,* Schimmel makes this connection.

Oh how you've spun me 'round, darling!
How you've spun me around!
You distill, you're the tavern
You're the serving boy.
You're the drinker, you buy the rounds
And you're the stumbling drunk, darling!
You romp around in your own lap
Just like little Krishna, darling!
Oh how you've spun me round, darling.
How you've spun me around![3]

My experience in the monasteries of Bucovina spun me 'round. It not only led me to a new and thus deeper understanding of the ritual act of prostration, but reanimated a basic tenet of my belief structure: that faith is created and refined in encounter. In the Islamic tradition, God is a plural singularity. Lover, Destroyer, The Subtle, All-Knowing: God's names—the ones we know—are relationships, how God gives birth to what is not God. In the creation story shared by the Abrahamic traditions, God breathes life into the first human being, fashioned of earth, carrying God's own breath within. If God is composed of relationship, this is the only mode in which I may truly exist.

Human encounter, then, is an essential way to experience something of that Ultimate Reality. I believe this is similar to what Martin Buber had in mind when he spoke of the other as thou, and of the ultimate Thou. The dialogical relationship, whether experienced in speech or in silence, possesses the possibility of transformation. In dialogue, I am fine-tuned: my rituals, prayers, and pathways are enriched, even recalibrated by these encounters. As I observed the Christian worshippers in Romania bend and bow in a manner entirely familiar and utterly foreign, at first, I was shaken. And then, reflective. The stillness of wonder reshaped my conception of prayer.

---

[3]   This is my own translation, which originally appeared in *Kabir in Pakistan (Pakistan Mein Kabir): 12 Qawwalis and Sufi Folk Songs*, ed. Shabnam Virmani (Bangalore: Srishti School of Art, Design and Technology, 2008).

24

Theological Goosebumps:
A Turning Point in My Interfaith Journey

Paul F. Knitter

O ne of the most transformative—that means, mind-expanding and heart-energizing—experiences that I have had in my rather long lineup of interfaith encounters came from a source that, especially as one surveys the Catholic Church nowadays, is not marked by its transformative energies: the bishops. Way back in the mid-'60s, in Rome, the Eternal City, the Roman Catholic bishops so expanded my mind and energized my heart that they set my life in a direction that I have been trying to catch up with ever since.

I Wanted to Be a Missionary

What brought me to Rome in September of 1962 to begin my theological studies was a decision I had made ten years previously when, fresh out of eighth grade at St. Joseph's Elementary School in Summit, Illinois, I decided I wanted to be a missionary priest. So, despite my parents' almost tearful admonitions that God's call might be coming a little prematurely, I left home to begin the long road to the priesthood. Part of that preparation was to study the religions of all the people, whom, because I loved them, I would try to save by bringing them to Jesus. I truly believed the prayer we prayed in the seminary chapel three times a day: "May the darkness of sin and the night of heathenism vanish before the light of the Word and the Spirit of grace!"

But the more I studied these "heathen" religions, the harder it became for me to detect the darkness of sin that was beclouding them. On the contrary, in the teachings and practices of Hinduism, Buddhism, Islam, and the indigenous religions that I was exploring, I found deep, often enticing claims about the Oneness of the divine and the finite, about the sacredness of the earth, about the call to sacrifice oneself for the sake of not just humans but of all sentient beings. Sure, there was corruption and abuse and violence. But there was plenty of that as well in my own Christian backyard.

So when I was selected to be sent to Rome to finish my last four years of theological study at the Gregorian University, I brought with me a suitcase full of theological questions: If there's one God, why are there so many religions? Does any one religion have a corner on salvation? What's the meaning of missionary work? These were not just intellectual questions for me: they touched my heart, my very identity as a future missionary, indeed, as a Christian.

The Right Time at the Right Place

Little did I realize when I arrived in Rome at the end of September 1962 that I was landing at the right spot at the right time to find answers—or at least to begin to find answers—to my questions. The pope had called an ecumenical council that would gather all the Catholic bishops of the whole world, and it was to start right around the time that our classes began at "the Greg." I had the historic privilege of standing in the Piazza San Pietro on October 11, 1962, about thirty feet from Pope John XXIII as I snapped a black and white picture of him (which I still have) balanced on his *Sedes Gestatoria* (portable throne), leading a huge row of more than two thousand bishops, with mitered heads wobbling behind him, into the Basilica of St. Peter to begin the first session of the Second Vatican Council.

What I didn't realize that day is that the council would become very much a part of my own theological education in an immediate, practical way. You see, I belonged to a missionary order called the Society of the Divine Word, and there were twenty-four Divine Word bishops from various "mission countries" attending the council. A number of the American bishops were, to put it kindly, a little rusty in their ability to read Latin. This was a bit of a disadvantage since all the homework they brought home with them every day from the council—all the *sub secreto* (confidential) documents that they had to study and vote on the next day—were written in the official language of the Catholic Church which they, as Catholic bishops, were presumed to know: Latin.

Well, as any good Catholic knows, presumptions either about the laity or about the bishops are never quite accurate. So these American bishops, knowing that all our lectures and all our textbooks and exams at the Gregorian at that time were in Latin, humbly turned to us for help. And we humbly obliged—knowing full well that this was our way of finding out what was going on at the council—and, who knows, maybe whispering a theological suggestion or two in a compliant bishop's ear. (Of course, if he couldn't speak Latin, it would go nowhere!)

It was in the course of these charitable relations with the Divine Word bishops in Rome that I had my transformative dialogical experience. I still remember where I was standing in the Collegio del Verbo Divino (the name of our house of studies)—right outside the chapel door—when Bishop Simon showed me an early draft of *Nostra Aetate—The Declaration of the Church's Attitude toward Non-Christian Religions.*

I could not believe what I was reading! Yes, I had known that the council, under the earlier bold urging of Pope John XXIII and the wise and even bolder guidance of Cardinal Augustin Bea, had crafted a new view of Judaism that would finally move the Catholic Church beyond the attitude that Jews belonged to the religion that killed Jesus and that therefore Judaism had to be replaced by Jesus' church. And I knew that bishops from other areas, especially Muslim nations, were pressing for statements that would open possibilities of better relations with other religions.

But the document I was holding in my hands—and that would still be honed in further debate on the council floor—was going beyond anything the church had ever done in its entire history. I sensed that this declaration was removing "no trespassing signs" and inviting Catholics and other Christians to look for God's presence where, previously, God had not been expected—or allowed!—to be found. Like so many Catholics, I had been educated doctrinally within the walls of "outside the church there is no salvation." One could be saved only inside the Roman Catholic Church. If there seemed to be exceptions to that ironclad rule, they were explained by theological machinations that somehow got pagans or non-Catholics clandestinely into the back door of the church through the workings of the Holy Spirit in the person's individual conscience. But in this process, never was any positive value attributed to the any other religion, or any other church, besides the Catholic religion.

The document I held in my hand changed all that! I felt theological goose bumps as I read in that early text of *Nostra Aetate* not only gracious summaries of the main teachings of Hinduism, Buddhism, Islam, and primal religions, as well as of Judaism, but also a clear recognition how all these religions enable humans to respond to "those profound mysteries of the human condition," and how they are all animated by a "profound religious sense," how they "reflect rays of the Truth that enlightens all people." Neither I—nor any other Catholic in the history of our church—had ever read anything like this in an official church teaching!

What was the most surprising statement of *Nostra Aetate*—and what turned out to be, as I look back, its most transformative announcement—was the new "obligation," or challenge, that the bishops were laying before all Christians: they were "exhorting" the people of God "prudently and lovingly to *dialogue and collaborate*" with followers of other religions and so "in witness of Christian faith and life, to acknowledge, preserve, and promote the spiritual and moral goods found among these people." So from then on, the job description of a follower of Christ would contain the following requirement: to dialogue with believers of other religions so as to learn from and "promote the spiritual and moral goods" in these other religions!

Was I still in the same church I had been baptized into?

The Answer Is Still Working

A lot has happened, within the Catholic and other Christian churches and within my own life since Vatican II. (I left the priesthood in 1975 and married in 1982.) But I can say with certainty that on that day when I read the early draft of *Nostra Aetate* standing outside the chapel of the Collegio del Verbo Divino in Rome, together with other documents of the Second Vatican Council dealing with religions, my questions about how to make sense of my Christian beliefs in the light of religious pluralism received an answer. Or more accurately, they received a firm foundation on which I could keep up the effort of looking for answers. The hope that filled my twenty-six-year-old heart when I first read *Nostra Aetate* is still there as this heart keeps going at seventy-two!

Part IV

Unpacking Our Belongings

And ye shall know the truth, and the truth shall make you free.
John 8:32

Pilgrims who venture beyond the borders of home for an extended stay must eventually unpack. Though they intended to pack lightly, they inevitably find themselves burdened with cargo they do not recall personally having loaded. For the things we carry include the cultural baggage that each generation of a community consciously or unconsciously bequeaths to the next. Interfaith encounter forces its practitioners to assume responsibility for both the actual and perceived histories of their groups. The authors of the essays in Part IV all confront troubling elements in their religious traditions.

Abdullah Antepli's essay "Never Again: The Transformative Power of My Journey to the Nazi Death Camps" chronicles his experience of seeing firsthand the horrors of the Holocaust and his subsequent work with fellow Muslim leaders to combat the legacy of anti-Semitism.

What is there to unpack as we confront the painful particulars of our religious training? Ramdas Lamb, a Hindu convert who grew up Christian, recounts in "The Lessons We Learn as Children" some of the negative messages he received about the unsaved, unclean, unrighteous other.

The lines that separate religions internally may not appear on the maps given to tourists, but as the plethora of sectarian turf wars attest, they are deeply gouged into the landscape. The essay by the Muslim scholar Ali Asani, "Encountering the Muslim 'Other' at Harvard," addresses the daunting but necessary task of mending fences within one's own tradition; surely pluralism begins at home.

Mary Boys, author of "It's Complicated," reminds us that interfaith education is serious work. Her classroom is composed of students with a rich tangle of traditions and ethnicities. Her syllabus intentionally and accidentally inspires discussions of a plethora of controversial issues: Christian anti-Semitism, African American anti-Semitism, white privilege, Jewish suspicion, Christian exceptionalism, and politically charged reconstructions of the historical Jesus (Jewish rabbi or Palestinian peasant?). As a tenacious teacher who refuses to stop listening, prodding, struggling, and learning, she creates a space where the complexities of what connects and divides us are not simplified but are authentically engaged.

In Rodney Petersen's "What I Learned in Zenica about Forgiveness," a Christian discovers an uncomfortable reality: that Bosnian Muslims, fairly or not, initially view him as kin to their predominantly Orthodox Christian Serbian oppressors, and not as the American Protestant agent of reconciliation he seeks to be. In Michael Lerner's "Learning to See God in Everyone," a Jewish American overcomes suspicions about Christians based on several negative experiences and finds himself making common cause with progressive fellow travelers across the religious spectrum. Anantanand Rambachan in "The Ambiguities of Liberation and Oppression: Assuming Responsibility for One's Tradition" reflects on the need for Hindus to grapple with the oppressive legacy of the caste system.

Lakota Christian Richard Twiss, invokes a traditional tribal greeting, "Mitakuye Oyasin" or "All My Relations"; we are ultimately all fellow travelers from the perspective of our shared connection to creation. Coming to Jesus before he came to church, Twiss sees hope for peaceful relations across differences despite the reality of brokenness.

25

Never Again: A Muslim Visits
the Nazi Death Camps

Abdullah Antepli

O ne of my most painful and transformative interfaith encounters was a recent trip I made to four of the Nazi concentration camps in Germany and Poland with a small group of American Muslim leaders. The trip came as an unexpected answer to many years of personal prayer. As a recovering anti-Semite, who is deeply pained by current Jewish-Muslim relations in the United States and elsewhere, I knew I needed to develop a deeper understanding of the Shoah and its impact on several generations of Jews. As an imam and chaplain working actively to help heal the wounds between Jews and Muslims, I had to open myself more to the pain of my Jewish brothers and sisters.

Our trip included visits to Dachau, Auschwitz, Birkenau, and Krakow, and conversations with several Holocaust survivors. I cannot fully articulate how powerful it was for me to actually walk in the footsteps of millions of brutalized and murdered people in a matter of a few days. Although I had read books and seen films about the Holocaust, to stand on the very grounds where so many innocent men, women, and children were ruthlessly murdered was overwhelming.

Among the things that struck me most forcefully as we were guided through the camps was just how "ingenious" the Nazis were in their design of these killing centers. The death camps became so efficient in the last three years of their functioning that the Nazis were able to turn people into ashes in less than three hours after they arrived. It also became clear to me that the Nazis could not have pulled off this diabolical and complex undertaking without the contributions of countless people from different sectors within European society. Traveling from Germany to Poland, from one camp to the next, I thought about all of the people who participated directly or indirectly in this demonic campaign to exterminate the Jewish people and others considered marginal and unworthy of humane treatment.

Before this trip, I also never quite understood the scale of the destruction. Twelve million people were killed, six million of whom were Jews, making up about one third of the world's Jewish population at the time. There were 3.5 million Jews living in Poland before World War II. Fewer than 200,000 Jews were left by the end of the war, and today, there are approximately 1,000 Jewish families in Poland; this, after Jews had lived in this region for over a thousand years. Images of old men walking to synagogue for Shabbat services, young boys and girls playing in the streets after school, and men and women working in stores, factories, hospitals, and government agencies crowded my mind—all of them murdered simply because they were Jewish.

Because numbers—especially such enormous numbers—can be difficult to relate to, I want to share one very personal story from my trip. For me, among the most painful images was seeing the hills of human hair in Auschwitz and Birkenau. The Nazis used to shave Jewish bodies and sell the human hair to various factories for commercial use. I will never forget those hills of human hair and the inhumanity it represented. My ten-year-old daughter has beautiful, long, thick hair. I used to find so much comfort in running my fingers through her hair at the end of a long and tiring day. Since my trip, I find it very difficult to do this anymore. Whenever I touch her hair, those horrific images rush through my mind. And I was merely a visitor to the camps: not a survivor, not the child or grandchild of survivors, not even a member of the Jewish people.

As I continue to process my trip, I pray that people throughout the world take the message of NEVER AGAIN into their hearts, and that we develop the courage and compassion to work to end genocide and other forms of mass atrocities.

Although I have only begun to articulate in my own words the power of this transformative experience, I share here a joint statement that my colleagues and I drafted upon our return to the United States.

*   *   *

The following is the official statement from the imams who visited the concentration camps.

> *"O you who believe, stand up firmly for justice as witnesses to Almighty God."*
> —Holy Quran, al-Nisa, "The Women," 4:135

On August 7–11, 2010, we the undersigned Muslim American faith and community leaders visited Dachau and Auschwitz concentration camps where we witnessed firsthand the historical injustice of the Holocaust.

We met survivors who, several decades later, vividly and bravely shared their horrific experience of discrimination, suffering, and loss. We saw the many chilling places where men, women, and children were systematically and brutally murdered by the millions because of their faith, race, disability, and political affiliation.

In Islam, the destruction of one innocent life is like the destruction of the whole of humanity and the saving of one life is like the saving of the whole of humanity (Holy Quran, al-Ma'idah, "the Tablespread," 5:32). While entire communities perished by the many millions, we know that righteous Muslims from Bosnia, Turkey, Tunisia, Morocco, and Albania saved many Jews from brutal repression, torture, and senseless destruction.

We bear witness to the absolute horror and tragedy of the Holocaust where over 12 million human souls perished, including 6 million Jews.

We condemn any attempts to deny this historical reality and declare such denials or any justification of this tragedy as against the Islamic code of ethics.

We condemn anti-Semitism in any form. No creation of Almighty God should face discrimination based on his or her faith or religious conviction.

We stand united as Muslim American faith and community leaders and recognize that we have a shared responsibility to continue to work together with leaders of all faiths and their communities to fight the dehumanization of all peoples based on their religion, race, or ethnicity. With the disturbing rise of anti-Semitism, Islamophobia, and other forms of hatred, rhetoric, and bigotry, now more than ever, people of faith must stand together for truth.

Together, we pledge to make real the commitment of "never again" and to stand united against injustice wherever it may be found in the world today.

- Imam Muzammil Siddiqi, Islamic Society of Orange County, Calif., and chairman of the Fiqh Council of North America
- Imam Mihamad Magid, All-Dulles-Area Muslim Society; President Elect, Islamic Society of North America, Washington, D.C.
- Imam Suhaib Webb, Muslim Community Association, Santa Clara, Calif.
- Ms. Laila Muhammad, daughter of the late Imam W. D. Muhammad of Chicago, Ill.
- Shaikh Yasir Qadhi, Dean of Academics for the Al Maghrib Institute, New Haven, Conn.
- Imam Syed Naqvi, Director of the Islamic Information Center in Washington, D.C.
- Imam Abdullah T. Antepli, Muslim Chaplain, Duke University
- Dr. Sayyid M. Syeed, Director, Interfaith and Community Alliances, Islamic Society of North America

26

The Lessons We Learn as Children

Ramdas Lamb

I grew up in a poor section of Los Angeles known as Watts, raised primarily by my Italian Catholic mother and grandfather. My mother worked as domestic help in private homes and also at the nearby Catholic church. Because she had very little formal schooling, she worked hard so her three children could become educated. The church allowed us to go to its elementary school for free because of her work there. Going to Catholic school was a great experience in that I was taught very early on about the concept of devotion to God, and it became one of the foundation blocks upon which I sought to build my life. It also gave me a heavy dose of guilt and fear of hell. As a result, by the time I started third grade I had decided I wanted to be a priest.

However, two events happened that radically changed the way I understood life and that on reflection were pivotal in shaping my future. The first had to do with a Jewish boy named David. His family had just moved into the neighborhood, and his parents had decided to send him to my school since the education there was seen to be superior to that in the local public school.

From almost his first day we became best friends, regularly playing together and spending time at each other's homes. We were soon inseparable. Then, one day in third grade, the nun who was our teacher pulled me aside just after lunch to tell me that she was worried about the amount of time that I was spending with David. When I asked her why, she replied, "Because he is going to hell." I was stunned. I had been under the impression that only really bad and evil people go there, and as my best friend, I could not imagine he could have ever done anything that wrong. Seeing my look of disbelief, she continued, "It's because Jews don't believe in God. All of them are going to hell." I knew then that she was wrong, since David and I talked about God a lot, and I told her so. She got quite upset, so I said nothing more.

After school that day, I went straight home, crying along the way, and told my mom what the nun had said. Her reply was simply, "Pay no attention to such comments. God loves everybody, especially children." Whenever my heart was troubled, my mother always had simple answers to my questions that would soothe me. Now, she had given me the freedom to ignore what the nun had said. Moreover, after that day I began to have doubts about much of what the nun and the church were teaching me.

Whenever questions about God and life came up, I would ask my mom instead. I once asked her why, if God loved us, he made our family poor. She replied, "Because God loves poor people. That's why he made so many of us. He only made a few of the rich ones." Words like this are how she taught me. Her simple view of the world and life was far warmer and more loving than that which I was being told in school. Both my close relationship with David and my growing distrust of what I was being taught continued, to the chagrin of my nun.

My mother did not read well, so whenever she did get a book, she would bring it home for me to read to her. Through those moments, I developed an abiding love of books and reading. One day, several months after the incident with the nun, my mom brought home a children's book that someone was discarding, and she asked me to read it to her. It was a child's biography of Mahatma Gandhi. I had never heard of him or of India, but my mother said she heard he had been a great person from a faraway land. As I began to read, many of the issues that had started to become important to me because of my relationship with David seemed to be answered. The book said that as a Hindu, Gandhi believed everyone is loved by God, irrespective of their religion, and he, too, had Jewish friends. He also said that God loves the poor and that serving them was a good way to show our love back to him. Here was a man who was not Catholic, but he sounded a lot more like Jesus, and my mother, than my teachers at school did. Once I finished the book, I told my mom I wanted to go to India. My words brought a smile to her face, since she had always wanted to travel but was never able to do so. She said she hoped I would go one day and that I would come back and tell her stories about it.

Since that time, my life has gone through many phases; from wanting to be a Catholic priest to becoming an atheist; from hating anything to do with the church and Christianity to finding much goodness and appreciation in some of the great Catholic mystics and for the selfless charity works that so many Christians have done.

As a teenager, I found Gandhiji's autobiography and devoured it. It added to my resolve to travel to India. Within a few years, I was able to get a ticket as far as Europe and hitchhiked the rest of the way. Not long after arriving in India, I took initiation as a Hindu monk and remained in that life for nearly ten years. I began working with poor villagers as well as helping promote education and a broader understanding of life. I saw my mother and the hardships she faced reflected in their lives and the eyes of so many village women.

Eventually, I returned to the United States to help care for my aging parents, pursued an academic education, and began teaching comparative religion. All along, I have maintained my connection with India and the Hindu tradition, and with the rural poor who have so much to offer in their simplicity and sincerity. My work with rural youth is done in hopes of fostering the kind of educational environment that can help those in the region of my adopted village to have the opportunities that I had to expand my understanding of the world and of the divine. In all my undertakings there, the teachings and love of my mother, the words and life of Gandhiji, and the teachings of my monastic guru serve to inspire and guide me.

When I look back at the words of my third grade teacher on that early spring day, I recognize how they were a catalyst for a series of important changes in my life. As an eight-year-old who had been indoctrinated with fear of hell by his teachers, I was forced into a difficult decision: a choice between adhering to narrow sectarian beliefs and the love of my friend. Fortunately, my mother provided the guidance I needed. So much of what happens to us in our youth, especially the more challenging and difficult situations, can sow seeds that lead to a much broader and deeper understanding of life if nurtured properly. We need to be challenged. Sometimes we need to suffer. Sometimes we need to face real difficulties and hardship, for all of these can be the fodder that helps us grow, mature, and truly learn to have compassion for those whom others look down on.

From time to time, people ask me what made me go to India and why it has become such an indelible part of my life. I tell them about a children's book that caused me to dream, and about a mother who nourished my dreams. I usually do not mention the nun, but she, too, played an important role in such a pivotal event for me. She did more to teach me in those few sentences than anything else she ever said.

27

Encountering the Muslim "Other" at Harvard

Ali S. Asani

As a scholar who studies and teaches about Islam in the academy, I have been asked many questions about Islam. In the aftermath of 9/11 many people want to know whether Islam is truly a religion that advocates tolerance of peoples of other faiths. Does it encourage Muslims to live in peace with non-Muslims, or is it a religion prone to create conflict? What I am rarely asked are questions concerning tolerance among Muslims: How do Muslims handle differences between themselves regarding doctrine, ritual practice, and other matters of faith?

Growing up in Kenya in a Nizari Ismaili Muslim family of South Asian origin, I never felt that my identity as a Muslim was suspect simply because I belonged to a minority Shia community. In Kenya, Muslims of other persuasions, the majority of whom are Sunnis, seemed (at least outwardly) to accept Ismailis as fellow Muslims despite differences in interpretation and practice.

It was only when I came the United States to pursue my undergraduate studies at Harvard that I became aware of issues concerning intra-Muslim pluralism. As a seventeen-year-old in a new country, I faced many challenges. Surprisingly, the biggest challenge was to my religious identity. During my first semester at Harvard, I enrolled in an intensive Arabic course taught by a visiting professor from Lebanon. One day during class the professor, who was a Sunni Arab, asked me whether I was Sunni or Shia. When I replied that I was an Ismaili, he exclaimed in Arabic, "*la hawla wa la quwwat illa billah*" ("There is no protection or strength except with God"), a remark usually made when a person seeks God's protection from evil. He then declared that he was shocked to find out that I was an Ismaili since he had always considered me to be a good Sunni Muslim.

That moment was the first time I experienced humiliation on the basis of my religious beliefs. Needless to say, after that day, I noticed a subtle difference in the professor's attitude toward me. In another class the instructor, alluding to the fantastic myths about Ismailis as murderers and assassins propagated by medieval Sunni polemicists and European orientalists, constantly made snide remarks that I was on a secret proselytizing mission. Eventually, I became used to such barbed comments. Fortunately, professors in many of my other Islamic studies and religion courses were not so prejudiced.

Three decades later, as a Harvard faculty member teaching a variety of courses on Islam, I sometimes overhear some Muslim students impugn my ability to teach Islam "correctly" simply because I am Ismaili. Such perceptions are not limited to students. Several years ago, a prominent and highly respected Muslim scholar of Islamic studies remarked to a colleague about me, "What does he know about real Islam? He is Ismaili." The intent of such comments is clear: unable to distinguish my academic training from my personal religious convictions, they are meant to marginalize and delegitimize my thoughts, opinions, and ideas because I am judged not to be a "proper" Muslim.

Viewed within a historical perspective, these attitudes are hardly surprising because, as a minority, the Ismailis have been marginalized and variously stereotyped as heretics and infidels by other Muslims. In my case, I experienced this marginalization when I came to Harvard.

Encountering the Muslim "Other" at Harvard has greatly influenced how I have to come to think about Islam and conceive of Muslim identity. How does one define Islam and determine who is a Muslim? Who has the authority to do so? On what basis? Why was my identity as a Muslim not questioned by other Muslims in Kenya? Why did I encounter prejudice in the United States? These have become key questions for me personally and professionally that I have explored through my scholarship and teaching.

My encounters with the Muslim "Other" have also led me to recognize the existence of a great paradox among Muslims when it comes to thinking about diversity within Islam. Some Muslims, feeling beleaguered by hostility from non-Muslims, believe that acknowledging and accepting plurality of religious beliefs and practices within the *ummah* or Muslim community is a sign of disunity and hence weakness. They, therefore, respond to questions concerning diversity of practice and interpretation among Muslims by vehemently denying that it exists. Differences among Muslims are cultural, not religious, they proclaim. They insist that there is only "one" Islam. As Tariq Ramadan aptly points out, the conception of Islam as a uniform theological monolith and the inability to recognize or engage with intra-Muslim religious diversity have resulted in the strange situation where Muslims, either as individuals or groups, will ignore or exclude one another, even insult one another and yet claim to the outside world that we are all brothers and sisters. Such enigmatic attitudes have deeply affected the way in which Muslims understand the concept of pluralism.

Given the deep historical wounds that have festered for centuries, the mutual demonization of groups, and the ongoing competition for religious and political hegemony, intra-Muslim dialogue may seem to be an impossibly difficult task. Indeed, it can be justifiably claimed that intra-Muslim dialogue does not exist in any meaningful way. Dialogue with one's nearest is emotionally fraught with many risks and fears. Grappling with points of view that are different from one's own and respectfully agreeing to disagree can often be challenging, testing one's patience and humility. But these obstacles should not deter us from aggressively pursuing this as a worthwhile goal. Does not the Quran say, "O humankind We [God] have created you male and female, and made you into communities and tribes, so that you may know one another. Surely the noblest amongst you in the sight of God is the most godfearing of you. God is All-knowing and All-Aware" (Quran 49:13).

28

It's Complicated

Mary C. Boys

Each Monday's *New York Times* includes a delightful column, "Metropolitan Diary," featuring vignettes of life in New York City. One submission in early February 2010 seemed particularly apt for the initial meeting of my course "Studies in Jewish-Christian Relations" at Union Theological Seminary.

> *Dear Diary:*
>
> Here's Abbott and Costello, as unwittingly performed by my husband and mother-in-law, who came to baby-sit last month:
>
> *Mother-in-law:* "You're going to a movie, then brunch?"
>
> *My husband:* "No, brunch then the movie—'It's Complicated.'"
>
> *She:* "Then do the movie first. What are you seeing?"
>
> *He:* "I just told you: 'It's Complicated.'"
>
> *She:* "What's so complicated? If you can't see the movie you want, I heard that new one with Meryl Streep is good. What's it called again?"[1]

---

[1] Submitted by Susan Kleinman and published on February 8, 2010. http://www.nytimes.com/2010/02/08/nyregion/08diary.html?ref=metropolitandiary.

Just how complicated this course would prove to be came home to me a month later. In order to illustrate some of the pernicious effects of Nazi propaganda overlaid on Christian anti-Jewish teaching, I showed several color slides taken from a study of the curriculum of German schools under Hitler.[2] The first slide, the cover of a 1936 book by Johann von Leers, *Wie Kam der Jude zum Geld (How the Jew Came to Money)* pictures a malevolent-looking Jew grasping the world with grotesquely outsized hands; his elongated fingers hook into the globe.

"Well, if I showed that to my congregation, that would be pretty much how they see Jews," remarked one of the students, a young black man.

I have no memory of what I said in response. I do remember the jumble of my own emotions. What do I say now? How might I make this a teachable moment? How do I make the course safe for everyone, but especially for the Jewish members of the class, visitors to Union and outnumbered by the Christians? And what about the students of color in the class: How do I show respect for their experience of racism while helping them to confront the toxic legacy of anti-Semitism?

We viewed the remaining slides. The class ended.

But not everyone left. A group of about ten, many students of color, remained. Although I recall few of the specifics of that conversation, it was lively and lengthy—and candid. At the back of the room, one of the Jewish men sat listening to the postclass exchange along with a Catholic woman from Union. The next morning, concerned he might have been offended, I emailed him. He replied that while the conversation had not been an easy one, it was an eye-opening discussion that wouldn't have been possible at his own institution.

In retrospect, many factors seem to have contributed to the tensions of that evening. The "wounds of history"—ironically, that was how I had named the topic for that class—have not healed. Before showing the slides, I had sought to make connections between racism and anti-Semitism by distributing an illustration of Nazi race science, "The Soul of Non-European Races in the Jewish People." Taken from Karl Hahn's *Volk und Rasse: Das neue Reich (People and Race:*

---

[2]   See Gregory Paul Wegner, *Anti-Semitism and Schooling under the Third Reich* (New York: Routledge Falmer, 2002), 107f.

The New Reich), it posits that Jewish people are constituted by the many negative characteristics of four "races": Near Eastern, Oriental, Ethiopian, and Negroid.[3] But distributing that chart and discussing it too briefly was insufficient. At a minimum, the preparatory reading for the course should have included more on race science in the Third Reich and its connections to racism in general.

This year's syllabus included a session devoted to the intersections of racism and anti-Semitism. In preparation for that topic, I mentioned a book that had recently been recommended to me, *Plantation and Death Camps: Religion, Ideology, and Human Dignity.* Yet the minute I mentioned the book and showed its cover—a juxtaposition of the electric fence of Auschwitz and slave cabins, and of a Jewish prisoner and a slave—a Jewish student commented that one shouldn't lose sight of the uniqueness of the Holocaust.

So in the following week's presentation, I began with two claims: (1) the concrete, historical particularity of the Shoah; and (2) its common patterns with other deadly phenomena such as that form of dehumanization we term racism. The black slaves and Jews in the Shoah were set apart as pariahs, wrenched from their families, humiliated by degradation, brutalized by their oppressors, endured the agony of nighttime transports, and shamed and outraged by their own filth. The great commonality, Beverly Mitchell claims, is that both slaves and Jews bore witness; they left personal accounts for posterity that told the "truth from the inside of what it was like to live through a heinous assault on their dignity as children of God."[4]

However significant these commonalities, the issues of race, class, and power in New York City (and beyond), continue to hover over us all. This year I included readings that spoke to the complexities of multiculturalism, to white privilege, and to the developments by which many Jews have come to understand themselves as "white." The discussion seemed quite muted, perhaps because these are difficult topics to address in such a diverse group—especially when the discussion is led by a white professor. Yet more seems to have happened in

---

[3]   The chart is reproduced in Wegner, *Anti-Semitism and Schooling under the Third Reich*, 128.

[4]   Beverly Eileen Mitchell, *Plantation and Death Camps: Religion, Ideology, and Human Dignity* (Minneapolis: Fortress, 2009), 32.

the discussion groups than I noted. For example, when I received the final papers for this year's course, one of the rabbinic students from the Jewish Theological Seminary (JTS) of America, Yael Hammerman, wrote the following:

> There was one in-class small group discussion that was particularly memorable and significant for me, and never could have happened at JTS or in other academic contexts I have been in. During our session about "Racism and Antisemitism," I sat with the two African American women in our class as we discussed the articles by Greenberg and Goldstein. . . .
>
> Greenberg's argument about how the Jewish community in America tends to see itself as Outsiders, while African Americans tend to see Jews as Insiders—because of their white skin and because they tend to be middle or upper class economically —spoke to me powerfully as well. . . . At the same time, most Jews do not see themselves as privileged, insider white-folk. . . .
>
> It was difficult to express the forcefulness of Greenberg's argument about Jewish Outsider/Insider status alongside two African American students, and to share how I do in fact often feel like part of an outsider group despite my white privilege. The article was no longer theoretical—Black ink on a White page. Instead we were a group of real White Jews and Black Christians speaking about our experiences in the world around us. I was uncomfortable naming the difference in economic status between the Jewish and African American communities but I forced myself to bring it up. Also, A. [another Jewish classmate] and I both spoke about how as Jewish women we often feel like outsiders but as white women we can blend into society and "pass" when we may not want to stand out. . . . We have no permanent visible markers of our Jewishness. The two African American women in the group spoke about how they do not have this luxury to "pass" and always carry their black identity with them front and center. They felt that it is the first thing by which they are judged by others. This conversation was particularly significant for me because I forced myself to talk about sensitive topics that made me uncomfortable, and

for which I did not necessarily have the "right" words, but I appreciated that the space was made in an academic context to take these risks.[5]

I continue to rethink the structure of the course. Typically, the early weeks of the course include a critique of supersessionism—the belief that Christianity supplants Judaism—and an encounter with Christianity's anti-Jewish teachings. These are topics fundamental to reconciliation between Jews and Christians, and the subject of rich scholarship. But in my familiarity with this material, I may have taken insufficient account of how shocking this history is to those unfamiliar with it. Some regard this as focusing only on the negative aspects of Christianity: Not only am I "hanging the dirty laundry" of the Christian tradition, but I am doing it in the presence of the religious other—the victim of that harmful teaching.

Moreover, by situating Jesus in the world of Second Temple Judaism, I am challenging certain conventional understandings. No one has said "You've taken away my Jesus," but I sense I've at least "messed" with some precious notions. And, as Kim Harris, a black PhD candidate who has served as the Teaching Fellow for the course remarked after reading a draft of this essay, "For some black students, what may be happening is that Jesus, whom we think of as sharing the types of oppression that we experience, once again becomes White Jesus as we explore his Jewishness. Is this Jesus, then, still an ally to Black oppression?"

When I insist, in the words of "A Sacred Obligation," that "revising Christian teaching about Judaism and the Jewish people is a central and indispensable obligation of theology in our time," students from churches with many members on the economic and social margins of society remind me that other issues are far more central and indispens-

---

[5]   She is referring to an essay by Cheryl Greenberg, "Pluralism and Its Discontents: The Case of Blacks and Jews," in *Insider/Outsider: American Jews and Multiculturalism*, ed. David Biale, Michael Galchinsky, and Susannah Heschel (Berkeley: University of California Press, 1998), 55–87. The Goldstein article to which she refers is the "Epilogue," in Eric Goldstein, *The Price of Whiteness: Jews, Race, and American Identity* (Princeton: Princeton University Press, 2006), 209–40.

able.[6] True. And yet, the New Testament is proclaimed and preached, so what sensibilities will inform their interpretation?

While teaching this course, I have been working on a manuscript on the death of Jesus that deals with two fundamental issues: analyzing the effects of the Christian charge that the Jews were/are responsible for the death of Jesus and proposing alternative understandings in the light of current biblical and historical scholarship. The more I have learned about the history and consequences of the "Christ-killer" charge, the more I feel the need to take responsibility for the past. I struggle with how to present this past in ways that will not paralyze with shame but rather encourage commitment to a different future. I am aware that the pedagogical challenge will necessarily involve a considerable degree of disequilibrium among the Christian students—and for Jewish students, albeit in different ways. Disequilibrium is necessary, both because we Christians *should* be disturbed by our history vis-à-vis Jews and because learning involves disruption, wrestling with information and ideas that challenge previous understandings. Yet I need to learn from my own moments of disequilibrium when I sense that the material at hand is too threatening to be taken in, or my approach is too limited by my own social location.

Stephen Brookfield observes that teaching involves "crossing borders of chaos into zones of ambiguity."[7] I suspect his observation is true of those of us who work in interreligious endeavors. Crossing religious borders is risky work. And complicated—and holy.

---

[6]   For the full statement, see http://www.ccjr.us/dialogika-resources/documents-and-statements/ecumenical-christian/568-csg-02sep1.

[7]   Stephen Brookfield, *The Skillful Teacher*, 2nd ed. (San Francisco: Jossey-Bass, 2006), 3.

29

What I Learned in Zenica about Forgiveness[1]

Rodney L. Petersen

The de-escalation of conflict can have nothing to do with forgiveness. It can also have everything to do with it.

When we were filming the material for the documentary *Prelude to Kosovo,* our group from the Boston Theological Institute (BTI) was in the city of Zenica, where we had been invited to speak with some local Muslim leaders. Given the continued instability of the region, our hosts provided a military escort for our group. When we arrived, we introduced ourselves, about twenty students and their professors, all affiliated with Christian theological institutions.

We had come to do a series of interviews for a film on human rights, with a strong sense of solidarity with the Muslims of Bosnia as with all others who suffered abuse in the conflict subsequent to the breakup of the former Yugoslavia. Perhaps thinking we were from the "objective" media, when we explained that we were from Christian institutions in the Unitd States, we were abruptly "dis-invited" to speak in the upper chambers of the Islamic Academy. Instead, we were ushered back to the front porch of the building where we began an impromptu and somewhat strained dialogue about the nature of the

---

[1]   Portions of this piece were taken from my article, "A Theology of Forgiveness," in *Forgiveness and Reconciliation: Religion, Public Policy and Conflict Transformation,* ed. Raymond Helmick and Rodney Petersen (Philadelphia: Templeton, 2002).

conflict in Bosnia from the perspective of our hosts. We quickly realized that we were insufficiently aware of the continuing depth of pain of the Bosnian Muslims known as *Bosniaks* and of the ways in which being Christians from the United States implicated us indirectly in the conflict.

In the 1990s Bosnia, a part of the former Yugoslavia, had been ravaged by seemingly endless conflict. Its Muslim population, formerly integrated into a multireligious state, had experienced continued discrimination and devastation. Although the United Nations declared the besieged Bosnian enclave of Srebrenica a "safe area" under UN protection in 1993, the United Nations Protection Force (UNRPO-FOR) failed to prevent the town's capture by the Army of Republika Srpska (VRS), representing a form of Serbian Orthodoxy, and the subsequent massacre in 1995.

The forcible transfer of more than 25,000 Bosniak (Muslim) women, children, and elderly, which accompanied the massacre, was found to be confirming evidence of genocidal intent. A paramilitary unit from Serbia, the Scorpions, formerly part of the Serbian Interior Ministry, participated in the massacre along with others from the region. The Srebrenica massacre was determined to be the largest mass murder in Europe since World War II. We were in Bosnia as a part of a workshop on what it meant to be "church" in the context of such a humanitarian disaster, traveling through Serbia, Croatia, Bosnia, and the region of south Yugoslavia known as Macedonia.

We recounted what we knew of this history in an effort to open up conversation toward our intended interviews. However, the response was only an increasing silence with at best curt and even saturnine responses to our questions. After getting almost nowhere in the conversation for some time, a young professor of Sharia (Islamic law) turned to me and said, "All we really want is for someone to say 'I'm sorry.'"

We had not been involved in the slaughter and devastation of Srebrenica, but we were from the West, from countries that had participated in the UN mandate to protect the "safe area" of Srebrenica. We were a group of Christians—Orthodox, Roman Catholic, and Protestant—who talked in lofty terms about the principles of the United Nations' Declaration of Human Rights. We often grounded these rights in our religious traditions and confessions. We send missionaries and establish nongovernmental agencies around the world to foster these ideas. Yet we did very little to defend the humanitarian rights of these Bosniak people and seemed to show little of the compassion that we say lies at the heart of our confessional traditions. We were, thereby, implicated.

I did not know what to say. Silence overcame our BTI group. It appeared as if no one knew what to do. As one of the leaders of the group, I did not know what to do either. It seemed so simple to say, "I'm sorry," yet the questions in my own mind included those about the nature of apology: When is it appropriate? When is it "cheap"? Who has a right to ask for forgiveness on whose behalf? How do we deal with restitution for a crime so large? Were we operating with compatible notions of forgiveness? What would it mean for each of us if I as a Christian, even as an evangelical Christian, asked for forgiveness from my Muslim hosts? My own understanding of forgiveness was rooted in very specific theological propositions, all centered on the figure of Jesus. To forgive or to be forgiven was a particularly Christian notion that I had not thought deeply about beyond these theological boundaries.

Then, too, I also felt a sense of shame for my own religious community. Forgiveness is a central element of Christian confessional identity through its orientation to what is interpreted as the person and work of Christ and the way that event is understood and appropriated through different theories of the atonement. The identity of my understanding of Jesus was grounded in this theology as seen in a trajectory of interpretation that ran from the Apostle Paul, through the theology of Augustine, doctrine of grace in Martin Luther and other Protestant reformers, and a history of piety grounded in Anglo-American Protestantism. Yet that ideal now seemed hollow and distant in what we had done, or failed to do, in Bosnia. In short, I (and we) were speechless.

Mustering as much courage as I was able in the immediacy of the moment, I apologized and asked for forgiveness from this young professor of Sharia. Our host graciously received my apology, and we were able to proceed with curiosity and caution into a more fruitful, if still tentative, conversation. We were in new and uncharted territory.

Although we remained on the front porch, our ecumenical group of students from Boston was beginning to learn something of what it meant to be religious citizens of the world, a world of complex yet very simple human emotions, a world in which theological terms such as "forgiveness" are of inestimable importance but with communal boundaries that are seldom what they seem. I was learning theology in a new "key."

This encounter was a moment in which I was challenged by a member of another religious tradition to think more deeply and to practice more broadly my own understanding of forgiveness. It finds parallel examples throughout personal and political life in the early twenty-first century as more attention is given to stories of forgiveness. Evidence of the transformative power of forgiveness to effect personal and social change is seen in similar encounters from southern to northern Africa, in the Middle East, and throughout the world. The stories of people of diverse faiths and cultures seeking to find the way forward in personal or common civic life, finding the courage to reconcile with their enemies toward social healing after wrongdoing is in itself remarkable.

This is all the more striking given the cultural evolution that has brought us to the place where forgiveness is no longer simply the concern of religious people or a matter of irrelevance or an unworthy moral ideal in the face of injustice. Rather, forgiveness is integral to a world on the verge of destruction. As an evangelical Christian it is increasingly clear to me that a theological understanding of forgiveness needs to find its place next to a general human desire to say, "I am sorry." This is perhaps something akin to what Elizabeth Spelman means when she defines a central human desire as being "to repair" (*homo reparans*).

In one recent collection of narratives recounting the transformative power of forgiveness, Michael Henderson (*No Enemy to Conquer: Forgiveness in an Unforgiving World*, 2009) gathers together the stories of persons such as Desmond Tutu, Benazir Bhutto, Rajmohan Gandhi, Jonathan Sacks, the Dalai Lama, and others in an anthology of hope toward a "geopolitics" of mercy. Weaving together threads of politics, inherited identity and history, wisdom and theology, Henderson gives us an account of how forgiveness has touched private and public life through processes of transitional justice. Henderson provides examples from South Africa's Truth and Reconciliation Commission as well as the Forgiveness Project and additional illustrative cases. With the high-profile emphasis on forgiveness in the public/political arena, greater attention is being given to the nature of forgiveness in university research departments and related disciplines in the arts and sciences as well as from schools of theology.

Such added attention has led to a clearer realization that forgiveness is not a concept that stands by itself. Its appropriate partner is justice and its end is reconciliation. When heartfelt and meaningful, it connects to issues of rehumanization, decisions to reengage persons no longer chosen to be perceived as enemies. For forgiveness to be meaningful, it must be related to the establishment of justice, particularly "restorative" justice. This may also involve the reexamination of history as part of an effort toward meaningful reconciliation. In this way forgiveness leads to social healing, even healing an estrangement pervasive in human existence.

Something like this happened in our own encounter in Zenica. We arrived at the academy thinking we were "friends" in solidarity with those there. However, for them we were in an ambiguous category, perhaps even closer to "enemies." We needed to apologize. Our journey toward restorative justice began when we were willing to examine our own understanding of and relationship to the conflict in Bosnia.

Forgiveness can speak to the heart-wrenching massacres of the Balkans, Bosnia, or the Middle East, Rwanda, and Sri Lanka, to take other examples, and create a new political narrative. It can take the atrocities of Gujarat or Peshawar and inaugurate deeper religious understanding. It can take the missteps of settler Australians and open new paths of cooperation with Aboriginal people. It can lead from the shackles of slavery to the highest governing office of a land. Healing the wounds of history can take priority over waging war. This is not easy or unambiguous work, but forgiveness can be a doorway to reconciliation and community as it was for our small group gathered on the front porch of the Islamic academy in Zenica.

30

Learning to See God in Everyone

Michael Lerner

My mother was a veritable cauldron of creativity and energy, which she poured out in every possible way, including toward her children, her Zionism, and her activism in the Democratic Party. I loved my mother's plays, the Jewish music that she played so beautifully in the tiny piano room in our home on Porter Place just a block from Weequahic Park in Newark, New Jersey. As president of the local Hadassah, my mother was one of the most prominent Jewish women in Newark, and she worked tirelessly to forge alliances between the leaders of the Democratic Party and the Jewish community. My dad was also active in this political scene, and even as a young child, I often felt uncomfortable with my parents' attempts to charm and win the favor of these non-Jewish politicians.

My mother, hoping that I could become the first Jewish senator from New Jersey (ah, the fantasies of the postwar American Jewish women who projected onto their children the recognition and fulfillment that a deeply sexist society had prevented them from achieving for themselves; my mother would have made a great senator), had decided to send me to what was then called a "progressive" private school, Far Brook Country Day, in Short Hills.

As it turned out, it was in many ways a wonderful school, with deep spiritual values rooted in a serious commitment to Congregationalist, Presbyterian, Unitarian, and Methodist Christianity. There was a focus on small classes, and there were hours each day for un-structured free play in the early grades when we could explore the surrounding wooded forest. The teachers at Far Brook avoided the monotonous performance orientation of public schools and developed instead our capacity to think critically.

At first, I was the only Jew at this school and the only student from Newark (the rest lived in the suburbs and came from families with a lot more money than mine), and though the teachers thought that I was quite "fascinating," I clearly didn't fit in. In addition to the religious divide, the other students were almost all from suburban neighborhoods and my family lived in the city, making after-school and weekend playdates very difficult.

So when my fifth grade teacher encouraged me to paint a Cha-nukah menorah on my window while all the others were painting Christmas symbols on their windows of the classroom, little Dickie Holden felt empowered to express the sentiment of many when he slugged me in the eye while informing me that "you killed Christ." I couldn't remember having done so, and my parents told me not to worry about it, but increasingly I began to feel much more drawn to my Hebrew school, which I attended twice weekly at Temple Bnai Abraham on Clinton Avenue in Newark. Sadly, most of the students there hated being there, felt resentful that they couldn't just be playing baseball, and didn't resonate much with the young Israeli teachers who couldn't understand why these young American Jews would not care about God or would not be preparing to make aliyah.

I couldn't understand why my parents, who lived thoroughly Jew-ish lives, had sent me to a non-Jewish school. They told me that if I was going to be the first Jewish senator from New Jersey, I'd need to learn how to be more like non-Jews in order to succeed. For me, this seemed crazy. I didn't want to be like everyone else; I wanted to be a Jew. And if Christians hated me just because I was Jewish, why would I want to be like them? I would not sing another song about Jesus, or participate in a Christmas play, or be one of the token Jews at whom anger could be projected. I was unwilling to return to Far Brook Country Day, a decision that outraged my mother (but secretly pleased my father, who was finding it harder and harder to afford the tuition at Far Brook). So off I went to Maple Avenue public school in

Newark, then to the Hawthorne Avenue Annex for ninth grade, and finally to Weequahic High School for grades 10–12.

Everything felt very safe for me at Maple Avenue School where a non-Jew was a rarity. But in an experiment in randomized integration at the ninth grade annex, I encountered another type of non-Jew—not the ones who were largely pleasant and accommodating in person, while putting me down behind my back and slyly agreeing with Dickie Holden's assessment of me as a Christ-Killer—but a handful of tough inner-city teenagers, the likes of which I had certainly not been prepared for at Far Brook. Remanded back into classrooms with younger kids by a new law that made it illegal for them to stop attending school until age seventeen, these bullies took out their frustrations by terrorizing Jewish teens like me, demanding a quarter (out of my daily allocation of 65 cents, the price of a hamburger and potato *knish* from the nearby kosher fast food store) to ensure safety for the day. My classmates and I quietly rejoiced the day the two most violent of these young men were arrested and permanently removed from our school.

My image of non-Jews was only further sullied by watching my parents increasingly trying to win the approval of the power elite of the Democratic Party of New Jersey, working through the Tammany Hall-like Democratic leadership of Essex County and Hudson County. I will never forget the dreadful telephone calls from the Essex County Democratic Party leader, who would order me to "get me the Judge" (my father having been appointed a judge at age thirty-nine) in a gruff, and obviously inebriated, voice.

But as a young adult I discovered what I had intuited in some of my encounters at Far Brook—that I actually shared many core values in common with non-Jews, particularly those involved in progressive politics. First inspired by Dr. King and the March on Washington, and by my teacher and mentor during my years at the Jewish Theological Seminary, Abraham Joshua Heschel, I became intensely involved in the antiwar movement in Berkeley, where I moved to do a PhD in philosophy. My non-Jewish friends in the "the movement" were every bit as passionate and idealistic as me and the other young Jews involved in these causes. Amazingly, four out of the twelve kids in my class at Far Brook ended up in Berkeley as part of the peace and justice efforts of the '60s!

Moreover, as a religious Jew I found many non-Jews more tolerant of and interested in Jewish sacred practices than my Jewish comrades, who had suffered from very negative Jewish educational experiences as children. Tragically, those Jews were never introduced, as I was, to the radical teachings of the ancient Hebrew prophets and to the many profound rabbinic teachings that issued from these biblical sources. They also did not have the blessing of studying with a mentor like Rabbi Abraham Joshua Heschel, whose spiritual vision merged seamlessly with his passion for social justice. To this day, Heschel's work with Dr. King, with the Reverend William Sloan Coffin, and many other religious activists remains for me a shining example of the transformative potential of interfaith cooperation.

Thus started my path into radical politics and religious activism in which I found myself partnering with Mario Savio to create the Committee for a Progressive Middle East, with Chip Marshall to create the Seattle Liberation Front, with Nan Fink to found *Tikkun* (who converted to Judaism and married me), and eventually with Cornel West and Joan Chittister to create the interfaith Network of Spiritual Progressives.

All of these experiences led me to feel more secure and even passionate in asserting the idea that God cares as much for non-Jews as for Jews and that as a religious Jew I must seek to embody the oft-repeated (and oft-ignored) commandment in the Torah to "love the stranger." Although most Jews would agree with these ideas in principle, my attempts to enact them have often put me at odds with others in my community. The most painful example of this is the Israeli government's dehumanizing treatment of the Palestinian people and the unwillingness of many Jews to name this sinful behavior and demand change. I say this knowing full well that the Israeli-Palestinian conflict is not a simple, one-sided affair and that there are Palestinians guilty of terrible misdeeds. Nonetheless, it is too easy to show respect to those whom we perceive as "good" non-Jews without struggling to recognize the humanity and image of God in those with whom we are in conflict.

So in the last fifteen years I've spent much of my time trying to build ties with Christians, Muslims, Buddhists, Hindus, Jews, UUs, and others who believe in the sacredness of all life and want to work to create a world based on wonder and awe at the grandeur of the universe, ecological sanity, caring for the well-being of everyone on the planet, love, and generosity. And for all the fear that Dickie Holden and others instilled in me as a child and teenager, I think I've been able to forgive them and continue to work hard to discover the divine presence in everyone.

31

The Ambiguities of Liberation and Oppression: Assuming Responsibility for One's Tradition

Anantanand Rambachan

In February 2006, I was invited as a Hindu guest at the Ninth Assembly of the World Council of Churches in Porto Alegre, Brazil. In the very first discussion, a session focused on interreligious relations, the presence and participation of Hindus in the assembly was vigorously challenged and denounced by a Christian bishop from South India. He chastised passionately the World Council of Churches for giving legitimacy to Hindus and their tradition by inviting us to the assembly. He described us as his oppressors and characterized the Hindu tradition as intrinsically unjust and bereft of any redeemable feature. He concluded his contribution by issuing an invitation to everyone to work for the eradication of Hinduism and not its validation. I learned later that the bishop came from the Dalit (oppressed) community, the name preferred by many who have been relegated historically to the lowest rungs of the hierarchical caste ladder and demeaned as untouchables.

The bishop's angry denunciation of Hinduism for the oppression of the caste system was not, of course, the first time I had heard such a rebuke. Yet, his words struck me with a special force. I had never before heard anyone describe me as an oppressor, and I never struggled with the fact that I am perceived to be an oppressor in the eyes of another. I was born of Hindu parents and raised in Trinidad and Tobago. My great-grandparents migrated from Northern India in the late nineteenth century as indentured workers to escape hunger and poverty in India by taking the place of freed African slaves on sugar plantations. The conditions under which they labored did not differ very much from slavery.

Paradoxically, those living conditions, and especially life in plantation barracks, contributed to the erosion of caste differences. In the shared and common living space of a barrack the observation of caste strictures was rendered quite difficult. Caste, therefore, although not entirely absent, was a minimal feature in our everyday lives. We were aware that most of the Hindu priests claimed status as *brahmins*, but other traditional features of caste such as hereditary work-specialization and regulations governing inter-dining, intermarriage, and social relations were minimal or nonexistent. Our friendships in school and in village playgrounds were spontaneous and free and not constrained by caste considerations. Hindu temples were open to all.

Since the Hindu community and tradition in which I was raised had shed the most unjust and brutal features of the caste system, I found it disconcerting to be called an "oppressor." In my mind, the word conjured a person who intentionally inflicted suffering on others, curbed their freedom, and took perverse delight in the exercise of power and domination. I did not recognize myself to be an oppressor.

I was challenged, however, by the bishop's denunciation of my tradition to recognize that he encountered it in ways that were radically different from my own experience. His context, historical, cultural, and social, was India, and he encountered Hinduism, in the practice of caste, as an oppressive tradition that negated the dignity and self-worth of his community. I had to see my tradition through his eyes and understand the source of his pain and anger. The same tradition that affirmed my self-value denied his. His experiences had convinced him that caste injustice was intrinsic to Hinduism.

It was important for me to understand and admit that, whatever might have been its historical origin and intent, the caste system developed into an unequal ordering of society on the basis of birth and ritual purity. At the apex of the social order are the *brahmins* (priests and teachers), followed by the *kshtriyas* (political leaders and warriors), the *vaishyas* (merchants and farmers), and the *shudras* (laborers and servants). The system resulted in the creation of a large group of outcastes or untouchables who were considered ritually impure and denied the privileges belonging to members of the fourfold caste order. I had to see also that caste practices sought and received legitimacy through particular interpretations of Hindu teachings. The Hindu teaching on karma, for example, was seen as implying that birth into a particular caste was the outcome of actions in past lives and that one should, therefore, be resigned fatalistically to one's circumstances.

Today, about 15 percent of the population of India, consisting of 160–180 million people, is labeled "untouchable" or members of the "Scheduled Castes" in the language of the Indian constitution. The constitution prohibits discrimination on the grounds of religion, race, caste, sex, or place of birth. Despite such constitutional provisions and commendable legal measures intended to redress historical injustices, untouchability continues to manifest in contemporary India. Sharp distinctions between self and other, the pure and the impure, are still drawn and asserted.

This was the reality out of which the bishop spoke, and I had to admit the truth of his reality. The bishop helped me see that my experience of Hinduism in Trinidad, and now in the United States, though different from those of India, does not justify silence or free me from all responsibility for oppression practiced in the name of my tradition. By claiming and professing a Hindu identity, I share accountability for what my fellow Hindus claim to be the meaning of our tradition. My accountability is not limited by geography. I must affirm or contest their interpretations and practice.

This issue of accountability for our tradition came to the fore recently when the Hindu American Foundation, a Hindu advocacy group based in the United States, released a report on caste injustice and violence in India.[1] The report documented numerous cases of violence against Dalits. It was received with hostility by many Hindu commentators, leaders, and groups. Many questioned the legitimacy and right of Hindus in the United States to comment on matters af-

---

[1]   See http://www.hafsite.org. The report is titled " Not Cast in Caste."

fecting Hindus in India. "Let's leave India out of it, since you are the Hindu American Foundation. Will you undertake such intervention for American temples?" asked on irate Hindu writer.[2] Another opened his response by contending that discussion on caste "pertains to India since it is of marginal significance for Hindus in Europe and North America."[3] "Only Indians living in India," contends the same writer," are qualified to initiate and make policy for themselves because the outcomes primarily affect them and that is the appropriate democratic procedure." Criticism of the caste system was seen as a betrayal of a necessary loyalty to Hinduism and as an exposure of its weaknesses that will be exploited by those who are hostile to the tradition.

My encounter in Brazil helped me see clearly the dangers and the contradictions of the argument advanced by these Hindu commentators. A tradition cannot make a claim for its universality and for being a global community while asserting geographical limits and boundaries to critical inquiry and questioning. Voices of dissent within a tradition do not become irrelevant when these are critical. The experiences of Hindus growing up outside of India, and of persons of other traditions, when such experiences are offered constructively and with humility, are very important for helping us see and understand ourselves more clearly and for fostering a self-critical attitude to our tradition. We are unlikely to question our inherited ways of understanding and practicing our traditions without the challenge that comes from others, internal or external. We need their voices to see ourselves more clearly.

I claim a theological vision at the heart of Hinduism that invalidates the assumptions of inequality, impurity, and indignity that are the foundations of caste belief and practice. I have to become a more vigorous champion of this way of being Hindu. The interreligious encounter in Brazil made me see even more clearly the necessity for intrareligious engagement. Contests about the meaning of our tradition occur not only across religious boundaries but, more urgently, within these boundaries.

---

[2]   See http://www.medhajournal.com/caste/haf-caste-report/1098-aditi-banerjees-critique-of haf-report.html.

[3]   See http://medhajournal.com/caste/haf-caste-report/1099-the-political-implications-of-haf-on-caste-and-hinduism-prof-gautam-sen.html.

The Hindu teachings on divine equality and nonviolence are at the center of the meaning of my religious commitment. I draw my inspiration from a long line of Hindu teachers, past and present, who challenge caste and who speak of human equality and unity. I see clearly that this commitment is incompatible with caste structures and practices that assume inequality, demean others, and condone violence. Hindus must get to the heart of this matter by questioning the legitimacy of a hierarchical social system that assigns varying worth and privileges to human beings on the basis of ridiculous notions of purity and impurity. The use of religious doctrine and ritual to provide legitimacy for such a system must also be critically considered.

I came away from Brazil chastised and challenged by my encounter with the Christian bishop. My self-critical attitude to my tradition was sharpened by his testimony and so was my commitment to its liberative vision of equality and justice. If the bishop had his way, I would not be invited to any of the dialogue programs of the World Council of Churches, and I am indeed aware that the decision to invite persons of other faiths to the assembly was not without controversy.

I am grateful that I was there and that I could hear and receive his protest. His faithfulness to this tradition and community was articulated in his words. It saved our encounter from superficiality and shallowness. I hope also that my own response to the bishop, in which I acknowledged the role of my religious community in perpetuating unjust practices, meant something to him. "For centuries of religiously sanctioned dehumanization and oppression of the Dalits," I said to the assembly, "we Hindus must own responsibility and work toward its overcoming. We must begin with a critical examination of the assumptions of our tradition that make this caste-based discrimination and violence against the Dalits possible." I spoke also of the vision and values of compassion, justice, peace, and nonviolence that are, for me, at the heart of my Hindu identity. At the very least, I hope that he would see that the internal diversity and ambiguities of my tradition were similar to his own and that we could find unity in our common stand for justice and in our rejection of oppression and violence.

32

All My Relations

Richard Twiss

Among the Lakota/Sioux, Mitakuye Oyasin is translated, "all my relatives or relations." However, what is communicated is a sense of one's connectedness to the bigger world of creation. It says I am part of the people who have gone before me, with the people living today, and with those who will come after me. It says I am related to things above, things below, and things all around. It says I am a small part of all that is and ever has been sacred; all living things—human and non-human persons.[1] These are my relatives. There are "two-leggeds," "four-leggeds," "winged ones," those who swim and crawl along the ground, and things that grow. These can be thought of as "nations": The Salmon nation, Buffalo nations, Huckleberry nation or peoples. It militates against the sacred/secular dichotomy and gnostic dualism of the West and aligns us with a holistic and integrated indigenous world-view. As indigenous people we have an epistemological framework that works well as a lens for reading scripture and making sense of our/the world. This epistemological lens helps us reconsider anthropology and anthropomorphic images of Creator and incarnation.

My father is Oglala Lakota/Sioux from the Pine Ridge Indian Reservation, and my mother is Sicangu from the Rosebud Lakota/Sioux Indian Reservation, both in South Dakota. I was born in 1954 and

---

[1] References to "persons" in this chapter follow Anne Fienup-Riodan's use in "Eye of the Dance: Spiritual Life of the Central Yu'pik Eskimos," pp. 182-185 in *Native Religions and Cultures of North America, Anthropology of the Sacred*, ed. Lawrence E. Sullivan. (The Continuum Publishing Company, 2003).

lived among my mother's people until age six, when we moved away. In 1972 I moved back to the reservation where I grew up.

In the winter of 1972, along with six hundred others, I participated in the American Indian Movement's (AIM) forced takeover and occupation of the Bureau of Indian Affairs Office Building in Washington, D.C., protesting the U.S. federal government's breaking of more than seven hundred congressionally ratified treaties that it had made with our tribes. For eight days we occupied the building and were surrounded by riot police. During this period of my life, I began to allow hatred toward white people and Christianity to grow in my heart. In 1974, however, after years of many painful experiences with drug and alcohol abuse, time in jail, and a growing despair of my own lostness, I became a follower of Jesus while living in Hawaii.

I am only *Ikce Wicasa,* a "Common Human Person." I am not a chief, tribal leader, nor do I speak for all Native people. I am only a pitiful human being who follows the path of beauty that some of us call the Jesus Way.

Many tribes refer to North America as Turtle Island. More that 700 different tribes believe that Creator put them on this land long before Columbus got lost in his search for a new trade route to the East Indies and we discovered him floating around in the Caribbean. Paul writes in Acts 17:26 that Creator predetermined set times and geographic places for people to live. We are the First Nations peoples of Turtle Island. It would appear Creator brought the Europeans to Turtle Island too. Perhaps in Jesus, we could have walked together as brothers and sisters and a great new nation "The Body of Christ" made of many nations could have grown here between our peoples. But it did not. Instead, the most horrific incidence of genocide and ethnic cleansing in the Western hemisphere occurred here among our people.

Our people were decimated by war and disease from some 20 million in the Unites States in 1400 to barely 230,000 in 1895. There are numbers of documented cases where smallpox infected blankets were sent to villages (biological terrorism) and bounties were paid for the heads and scalps of Native men, women, and children. Today we are 2.4 million in the United States and 1.2 in Canada. But, perhaps what makes the story most tragic is that so much of this was the result of the misappropriation of the biblical narrative that was co-opted as a tool of colonial imperialism. However, the story is not finished.

Over the years as I have reflected on my experience in Hawaii, I am glad I did not find faith in Jesus in a church building or institution. It spared me from having to then become Christian Reformed right away; I didn't have to become Baptist right away; I didn't have to become a Presbyterian right away; I didn't have to become an Anglican right away; I didn't have to become a Pentecostal right away; I didn't have to become a Methodist right away. I just became a follower of Jesus. Soon after beginning my journey of following Jesus, I learned I needed to become a Christian too. And from there I became a Calvinist, Wesleyan, Lutheran, Quaker, Pentecostal, Dispensational, Armenian, and Evangelical Christian. And then I learned that I had to decide on a Bible to read—the RSV, NRSV, KJV, NIV, CEV, NKJV and that some English speakers believed only English speakers could have a Bible that was "Authorized" by God. And then I was taught there was such a thing as Christian pants, shirts, dresses, shoes, and socks, Christian haircuts, Christian music, Christian instruments, Christian buildings, and Christian nations and governments.

Somehow when Jesus came into my life and overwhelmed me with his love and kindness, I wanted nothing more than to simply follow him because he truly rescued me from a life of addiction, abuse, self-destruction, and likely a premature death. Following the ways of Jesus seemed one thing, but becoming a Christian seemed quite another thing.

As the years passed I began to resist the pressure to accept interpretations of the Bible that said, "When a person becomes a Christian, they become a new creation and old things pass away and all things become white," interpretations that said following Jesus in the context of my Native cultural ways, music, dance, drumming, ceremony, and culture were out. I encountered Euro-American Christianity.

In reference to my Native culture I was informed the Bible said I needed to leave my Indian ways behind me, because I had a new identity in Christ, and it WAS NOT Indian! The Bible was used to demonize just about everything important to our cultural sense of being one with the Creator and creation. So, while Jesus found me, the church began to lose me! The church became complicit in the colonialism of indigenous people.

One of the points of colonialism is to displace people from their culture and then their land. African scholar, Ngugi Wa Thiong'o (n-Go-gay-wa-ti-ONG-go), in *Decolonizing the Mind,* sees that the way control was introduced and managed was to deconstruct the people's sense of self and replace it with that of the colonizer—the cultural bomb. The effect of the cultural bomb was to annihilate a people's belief in their names, in their languages, in their environment, in their heritage of struggle, in their unity, in their capacities and ultimately in themselves. It makes them see their past as one wasteland of nonachievement, and it makes them want to distance themselves from that wasteland . . . the control, through culture, of how people perceived themselves and their relationship to the world . . . tools of self-definition in relationship to others.

Sadly, the hegemony of the prevailing worldview assumptions of the European immigrants not only lingers today but has morphed into a distinct christianized cultural bias against Native and indigenous culture, ways, and spiritualities. Because of clashing worldview values Native North American / Indigenous people have never been embraced as co-equal participants in the life, work, and community of Jesus. In 1 Corinthians 12 Paul uses the human body as a metaphor to describe how people of diverse social and cultural backgrounds should regard and interact with one another. In verse 20 he says, "The eye cannot say to the hand I don't need you and the hand cant say to the feet I don't you." If you look at a thing and you cannot identify any perceived sense of value in it, then you get along without it. You cannot see how it will in some way benefit or add value to your life.

The Euro-North American expression of Christ and his kingdom has said to the Native North American expression of Christ and his kingdom, we don't need you. You have nothing we need. You can add nothing of benefit to us. But we in turn have everything you need.

It has created and only reinforces a benefactor/beneficiary paradigm in the church. We exist in the minds, policies, and attitudes of the North American church as the perpetual mission field: needy recipients, unreached peoples, marginalized, etc. We are not seen in the light of the scripture as co-equal participants in the life and mission of the American church.

Yet, in the light of all of this, I still follow Jesus. I find in Christ the possibility for forgiveness, reconciliation, and the path toward Shalom alongside my Euro-American friends, family, and fellow human beings. We are all *ikce wicasa,* "common human persons," on this road.

Although many questions and issues remain unresolved in my heart regarding land, restitution, justice, and healing, and much work remains to be done, I seek to embrace my own brokenness and that of others saying, *Mitakuye Oyasin,* "All My Relatives."

Part V
Stepping across the Line

There are more things in heaven and earth, Horatio,
Than are dreamt of in your philosophy.

William Shakespeare, *Hamlet* 1.5.165–67

Part V features accounts of transformative religious experiences mediated through the practices or among the precincts of a faith foreign to their respective authors. There are no simple conversion stories here, but there are new questions. What does it mean to experience an epiphany through the hospitality of your neighbor's faith? How can one be both Christian and Buddhist, as Ruben Habito explores in "A Christian Confronts a Zen Kōan." Authors in this part describe profound, often inexplicable, moments of stepping across conventional lines between religions, or lines between heaven and earth for that matter. But these are not accounts of theological thrill seekers eager for the amusement of exotic mysticisms. These writers remain committed to the paths on which they entered the spiritual life; in fact, it is their committed practice of the spiritual disciplines in their home religions that authenticates for them the integrity of their encounters across religious lines.

A Sikh, Valarie Kaur encounters a powerful sense of the Oneness prized in her tradition in the unexpected setting of a Christian church in "Double-Edged Daggers." Charles Gibbs, an Episcopalian, meets

Jesus "again for the first time" in a Sikh garden outside New Delhi in "Jesus Appeared to Babaji."

In Varun Soni's "Under the Bodhi Tree" a Hindu recounts his odyssey through Buddhism, inspired by a chance encounter with His Holiness, the Dalai Lama—under the Bodhi Tree. Daniel Berman, a young rabbinical student in chaplaincy training, reflects on what it does or does not mean—theologically, spiritually, and interpersonally—to be asked to pray to Jesus on behalf of a grieving family. In Rodger Kamenetz's "The Canine-Buddhist Dialogue," an American Jew offers a tale about interfaith engagement along two borders, between Buddhism and Hasidism and the thin transmigrational space between species. The title of Mark Heim's "Otherness and Wonder: A Christian Experiences Moksha" frames the religious border-crossing experience of its author. Heim has a glimpse of an altered reality while studying in India. Although it is a mind-expanding experience, he maintains a steady commitment to his own Christian location in this bigger universe. John Makransky's "What Mast Ram Baba Dropped into My Bowl" closes Part V by describing the gift of a question posed to him by a Hindu guru that helps him see his own Buddhist tradition in a new light.

33

A Christian Confronts a Zen Kōan

Ruben L. F. Habito

I was a Jesuit seminarian in my early twenties when I first encountered Zen.[1] Sent from my native Philippines to Japan to help in the Jesuit educational and ministerial work there, I was first assigned to the Jesuit Language School community in Kamakura, an ancient city with many Buddhist temples founded in the medieval period of Japan. Father Thomas Hand, S.J., an American Jesuit from California who was the spiritual director of the seminarians there, invited me to join him for *zazen* (seated meditation) at San-un Zendō, or "Zen Hall of the Three Clouds," located in that same city.

After the required six-week orientation period, in the fall of 1971 I was formally introduced to Zen Master Yamada Kōun in a one-on-one encounter, called *shōken*, literally "being illuminated and seen," and became his Zen student. This marked my initiation into the Zen Buddhist community that practiced according to the guidelines of the lineage established by the three Zen Masters (Rōshi) represented by the "three clouds"—Harada Dai-un (Great Cloud), Yasutani Hakuun (White Cloud), and Yamada Kōun (Cultivating Cloud).

During this encounter the Master asked me: "Why do you wish to engage in Zen practice?" My response, following the format prescribed

---

[1]   Some segments of this essay are excerpted from a longer piece titled "Being Buddhist, Being Christian, Being Both, Being Neither," in *Converging Ways? Conversion and Belonging in Buddhism and Christianity*, ed. John D'Arcy Mays (Sankt Ottilien: EOS Klosterverlag, 2007), 165–80.

in the preparatory talks, was: "I wish to discover and realize my True Self." The Master then gave me the Kōan *MU* as my "assignment" for Zen practice.

Seeing through Mu

A Kōan (*Kung-an* in Chinese), literally meaning a "public case," usually consists in a verbal exchange between a Zen Master and a monk, with a question, or a phrase to spur the practitioner on in the practice of *zazen*. The Kōan *MU* goes like this: A monk asked Zen Master Jōshū (Chao-chou in Chinese): "Does a dog have Buddha nature or not?" Jōshū answered, "*MU.*"

The Chinese character that corresponds to this curt reply "*MU*" can be read literally to mean "No!" or "No way!" Read in this manner, the Kōan would seem to be negating the received doctrine in Mahāyāna Buddhism to the effect that "all sentient beings are endowed with Buddha nature." If one accepts this doctrine, and also acknowledges that a dog belongs to the class called "sentient beings," the logical conclusion would be: "Yes, elementary, my dear Watson, a dog IS, or *must be*, surely endowed with Buddha nature."

But in this Kōan, Zen Master Jōshū seems to be either overturning this doctrine (that all sentient beings are endowed with Buddha nature) or denying that a dog is a sentient being, which of course goes against common sense or accepted convention. In any case, in responding "No!" to the question, "Does a dog have Buddha nature or not?" the Zen Master is throwing out established Buddhist doctrine, or common sense altogether, or both.

A Kōan, however, is not about having or not having Buddha nature. It is not a matter of accepting or rejecting Buddhist doctrine at all. Rather, a Kōan is meant to take the practitioner beyond the dualistic opposites of yes and no, of having and not having, of dog and human being, and being opened to a transformative experience. Just put your whole being and entrust it to *MU* as you breathe out, the practitioner is told, focusing your mind on *MU* and become totally absorbed, or better, dissolved into it, and you will "see."

Having been given these instructions, I took to my *zazen* practice, consisting usually of a half hour, once or twice daily, sitting in a cross-

legged posture, with the back erect, breathing in and out in full awareness, accompanying each outbreath with the silent sound of *MU*.

It was not more than a few weeks after being given this Kōan for
my practice when one afternoon, coming home after a day of *zazen*
at San-un Zendō and sitting on an easy chair in my room, *it* suddenly
dawned on me. That instant I *knew from within* what this doggone
MU was ALL ABOUT! This sudden realization that shook me from inside out made me laugh out loud, leap from my chair in exuberant
joy, and rush out of my room, looking for Father Hand whose room
was on the floor above mine, to tell him, "I got it! I got it!"

What did I "get?" The image I recall was that of the Buddha with
the half-smile, an image I had previously seen in pictures. In that flash
of an instant as I sat on my easy chair, I *realized* from inside, what that
half-smile was all about. With that half-smile, the Buddha, in an all-
knowing and all-compassionate way, is answering the question "Who
am I?" "What is the nature of the universe?" "What is this matter of
being born, getting sick, getting old, and dying, all about?"

I could not contain myself with the excitement and laughter and
tears that ensued, and at Father Hand's urging, I phoned Yamada
Rōshi's residence and requested an appointment for an interview. After two successive visits over the next few days, wherein the Master
tested me with the usual checking questions related to the Kōan *MU*,
he confirmed that I had indeed experienced what in Zen is known as
kenshō, literally, "seeing into one's true nature." He then handed me a
small booklet that was to be my "syllabus" for continuing Kōan work
under his guidance. This was in early December of 1971.

Fast-forwarding to 2011, I write this after leaving the Jesuits, moving to Dallas to take a teaching position at Perkins School of Theology
in 1989, and marrying and raising two sons now of college age. In the
years since I "passed" that initial Mu-Kōan, as well as the entire set of
Kōans in the Sanbo Kyodan training program under Yamada Rōshi's
guidance, I have had further experiences confirming that initial one.
I have also gone through the entire set, Kōan by Kōan, several times
over with my own Zen students who come to practice with me here
at the Maria Kannon Zen Center in Dallas. Still there is one BIG Kōan
that continues to confront me. It is one that will be with me through
my remaining days on this earth, which I can refer to as my life-Kōan.

The Crucified One

For the background of this life-Kōan I need to go back once more to my early twenties as a Jesuit in the Philippines, before being assigned to Japan. At that time I was struggling with the question of how God's "omnipotence" could be reconciled with the Christian teaching of "God's love," vis-à-vis the magnitude of suffering and injustice and evil in the world. The apparent insolubility of this question cast an unsettling doubt in me as to whether such an all-powerful and loving God existed at all, confronted by the *fact* of the existence of evil and injustice and the suffering especially of innocent children in this world. In short, my struggle with such a fundamental tenet of the Christian faith was bringing about a crisis of identity. Here I was, a seminarian preparing to become an ordained Catholic priest, that is, one who was supposed to represent God and be a messenger of God's love to all people, who was doubting whether such a loving God existed at all.

One afternoon, in the midst of this turmoil, I was pacing the corridors of the newly built Loyola House of Studies. I was living there with about eighty other Jesuits, mostly seminarians like myself, as well as our professors and spiritual directors. I was just allowing my mind to wander to and fro as I walked back and forth. Stopping briefly, my gaze fell on a wooden crucifix that was hung on a wall at one end of the corridor. As I looked at the Christ on the cross, I *saw*, in that Crucified One, the children in the neighboring village where I went to visit every weekend, suffering from malnutrition and for whom my heart ached every time I would go out and talk and play with them. I saw the parents of the children, trying to make ends meet and to give the children their best (despite a father out of work or a mother sick with tuberculosis).

This glimpse gave way to an open-ended and vast scenario. I saw every child, every parent, all the people who were ever born and lived and suffered and died on this earth, and those who continue to live and suffer, and those who will be born and will thus suffer, each in their different ways. I saw, and was, everyone, right there, as *the Crucified One*, crying out, "My God, My God, why have you forsaken me?" And at the very same moment, a voice, gently yet clearly, came from within, saying: *"You are My Beloved, in whom I am well pleased."*

Gradually I was enveloped by a deep, deep peace and inner assurance, which I could not, and still *cannot*, fully explain in words. I can only say that, upon *hearing* those words from within, I realized that in the face of all this evil and suffering and injustice, there was "something" bigger than what my puny mind can figure out logically, something more convincing, more reassuring, more overpowering, than all this evil and suffering, and that made this life all worthwhile even through all this, and to top it all, dying at the end of it. That "something" remains for me a totally inscrutable mystery, but somehow it connects to the unknown source of that voice that I heard, saying to me, and to all those who were ever born and lived and died, and who will be born and live and die: "*You are My Beloved, in whom I am well pleased.*"

What I heard was a voice of unconditional acceptance of all that was, is, and ever will be, just as it is. It is an indelible experience affirming that "all is well, all will be well," *no matter what.* It is not a message of complacency and indifference, one that makes me make light of or be numb to the pain of all the injustice and suffering in the world. Rather, it is a voice that urges me all the more to live in a way that I can be of some help in alleviating the pain and suffering of my fellow living beings, in the best way I can and with all I've got, as all this pain and suffering is mine no less.

That grace-filled moment, when I *saw* that figure on the cross, and *heard* that voice, affirming "You are my Beloved," is one that continues to reverberate in my life today. It is what enables me to identify with the larger circle of those who take that Crucified One as the centerpiece of their religious life, that is, the worldwide community of those who call themselves Christians.

Unpacking My Life-Kōan

Now back to my life-Kōan. It comes up as a question that friends, colleagues, students, or even chance acquaintances sometimes thrust at me in a casual chat.

Are you Christian, or are you Buddhist?

If I answer one or the other, it would not be true to who I am and all that I am. If I answer "neither," again that would not ring true.

In response to the question, I am sometimes tempted just to say yes (period), in a half-whimsical way. But this way of answering is an irresponsible dismissal of the question, not wanting to get into the intricate matters involved, like, "What does it mean to be Christian?" "What does it mean to be Buddhist?"

Working on my life-Kōan then means continuing to try to figure out what it *does* mean to be Christian and what it *does* mean to be Buddhist, in a way that these two do not cancel each other out. Otherwise I would be canceling my life out as well. This may be a good way to get out of all this, I am tempted to say. But that does not seem to be an option.

Let me start with a Buddhist way of putting things into words or putting words into how Buddhists see things. What I realized with that glimpse into the Buddha's smile is the fact of the "emptiness" (śūnyatā) of everything that exists. The Heart Sutra affirms: "Form (all existent things) is no other than Emptiness. Emptiness is no other than Form." To affirm all existent things as "empty" is not to deny the obvious reality of this table in front of me or of this chair I am sitting on, or to take a stance of nihilism. Rather, it is to affirm that nothing in the universe exists apart from everything else. This table, chair, the tree in the front yard, the mountains, the stars, the dog, is interconnected with everything that is and exists only insofar as everything else is what it is. In short, the question "Who am I?" is best answered by: not-I, and only "table," "chair," "tree," "stars," and so on. This is the realization that made me burst into laughter and tears at the same time and even now brings forth a half smile, sometimes more of a smirk, on my face.

On the Christian side, since the time of the early church, the followers of Jesus have sought to express what they believe about ultimate reality in a formula known as the Apostle's Creed and continued to come up with revised editions such as the Nicene Creed. This is the set of fundamental affirmations by those who saw in the Crucified One the revelation, and concrete embodiment, of God's unconditional and abiding love for all.

My life-Kōan can then be restated in this way: Am I able to recite the Heart Sutra (which I do, often) and the Apostle's Creed (which I do, often, sometimes in the Nicene "upgraded" version), without contradicting myself, without canceling myself out of existence?

An easy way out would be to turn to Ludwig Wittgenstein, who noted: *"Wovon man nicht sprechen kann, muss man schweigen"* ("Whereof one cannot speak, must one be silent") and sit back smugly with a half-smile. But something keeps nudging me to try to at least find some consistency between how I see things and how I say them, between how I live and how I articulate it. So, I am consigned to working on my life-Kōan until the day I die, with a twist on Wittgenstein.[2] *"Wovon man nicht sprechen kann, muss man schreiben"* ("Whereof one cannot speak, must one keep writing!").

---

[2] With affectionate thanks to Juan Masia, S.J., of the Japan Province of the Society of Jesus.

34

Double-Edged Daggers[1]

Valarie Kaur

Usually on Sunday mornings, my father's outside on a tractor, my mother's making *aloo pronthas*, my brother's watching cartoons, and I'm sleeping in. Sometimes, my mother crams the whole family into *Baba Ji's* room to sing *shabads* and recite scripture together. But on this Sunday morning, my grandfather has asked me to come with him to the *gurdwara*, a Sikh house of worship some miles away. At sixteen years old, I dutifully follow.

I'm still rubbing the sleep from my eyes as I slip off my shoes. Wrapped in a long head scarf, I follow my grandfather inside. One step takes us from our small farming town in California's Central Valley into an entire world transported from India.

Inside, the congregation sits on the floor. On the right, a sea of men in turbans of black, saffron, blue, and red cloth; on the left, women in silk and cotton, solid-colored, tie-dyed, and embroidered *chunnis* of all different colors draped over long braids and *jooras*. Children sit next to their mothers and fidget. A little boy runs around islands of praying people before being escorted out to the jungle gym.

---

[1]   This essay is based on an excerpt from the author's journal when she was sixteen years old.

The elderly lean against the walls, eyes closed; while the younger folks listen to the prayers, the older ones seem to reside within them.

The whole room revolves around the sacred space that holds the "living Guru": the fourteen hundred pages of Sikh verse known as *Guru Granth Sahib Ji.* The sacred book sits on a table draped in fine silvery blue cloths folded back to reveal the lines of *Gurmuki* script, whose poetry is read, sung, and contemplated. Hanging from the ceiling over the sacred book is a magnificent blue canopy embroidered with a single brilliant character in Punjabi script, the first mysterious and profound word of our holy text. *Ek Onkar:* God is One. As ever, its two linked circles drop from a top line, and the stem connecting them shoots up and umbrellas over in a long elegant stroke.

As I wait in line to bow my head before the Book, my eyes fall on the swords and daggers displayed at its base. Sikhs wielded these *kirpans* to defend the faith for hundreds of years in India, and I grew up hearing epic tales of battle and torture and martyrdom: Guru Arjan Ji tortured in a red hot caldron, Guru Gobind Ji's young sons bricked in alive, Baba Deep Singh holding his own severed head in hand as he fought in battle. These blood-soaked legends of Sikhs resisting the Moghul empire came down to us as stories of resilience and sacrifice—our ancestors died so that we might live. The *kirpans* represent an enduring commitment to fight injustice and stand tall for faith and community. But it's hard for me to eye the sharp edge. Sikh girls growing up in the Central Valley aren't taught to fight like that. I drop my dollar on the pile of donations, close my eyes, bow my head to the floor, and whisper the only words I can summon: *Ek Onkar Satnam;* One God Whose Name Is True.

I follow my grandfather and sit with him on the men's side—my modest act of defiance in a culture that too often divides women from men despite the scripture's teachings on equality. We listen to the *granthis,* singers flown from India to sing *shabads* from the scriptures accompanied by the *tabla* and harmonium; their voices—sad, meditative, and beseeching—rise, dip, and waver. As the voices soar, I close my eyes and move into deep reflection.

First I see my mother, bathed in light, hands moving swiftly over the harmonium in our little prayer room. I can hear her voice merge with the singers.

Then I picture my high school and remember the worst moment of my freshman year. After a lecture on evolution in biology class, my friends and I fell into a heated debate that led us straight into religion. As the conversation intensified, I held my half-eaten sandwich and looked up at them dumbfounded, heart thumping in my ears, and said, "So you think I'm going to hell?" They nodded and shifted uncomfortably. The bell rang.

That's when the nightmares began—dreams of Judgment Day where golden staircases to heaven disappeared before the hellfire consumed me. From then on, I talked and pleaded with friends and teachers who tried to convert me, begging them to see that my family was good and did not deserve damnation.

The greatest challenge came when my godmother brought home a strange guest: a large and powerful older woman with light skin, thick black eye-liner, and wild hair. Before I knew it, she had wrapped her arms around me, was rocking me back and forth, and in a trance-like state asked me to repeat her words: "I accept Christ as my Lord and Savior."

I stopped. I couldn't accept. "Jesus is one of many paths to God."

"You are confused. Any time you are confused, the devil is speaking to you." She began to speak in tongues to banish the demons from tormenting me any longer. And I ran away, flying through nearby fields, praying for sanctuary.

The memories jolt me; my eyes shoot open. I catch a glimmer of light on the polished *kirpans*, and for the first time, I don't want to run away. I feel the blood of warriors and soldiers course through me, and I don't want to beg or plead anymore. My grandfather once told me of Mai Bhago, a great Sikh woman warrior who led armies into battle. I want to fight like her. I want to defend my family and community against those who condemn us, starting here and now. Where can I find them? I will go to the local church and confront the priest and the whole congregation on this Sunday morning.

As the *sangat* rises for the final prayers, I hurry out of the *gurdwara* and rush through the gates of this little island of India out into the town, still in my red *salwar kameez*. A group of Mexican American kids on bicycles stops; the kids turn their heads as I pass. I run down Dakota Street, my *chunni* now draping over my shoulders, my long black hair waving, my brow furrowed, and march up to the church. I am standing on the edge of a dagger, absolutely reckless, ready to demand an answer from the priest.

I knock. The door is locked, but I hear hints of organ music inside. I knock again, filled with indignation. The door opens, revealing a white woman with fluffy grey hair and a flower-printed dress, startled to see a dark-eyed Indian girl at the doorstep. This is not the priest I was expecting. I'm tongue-tied.

"Can I come in?"

She nods and lets me in. The church is grand—and empty. I slip into the hard wooden pews and notice a grand organ bathed in the light slanting through the stained-glass windows. The woman positions herself in front of the organ, closes her eyes, and resumes her practice, the music is haunting yet steadily rising.

As the organist plays, I gaze at that symbol of judgment and damnation, the cross, in front of the church, and above it, the figure of Christ himself. The lines engraved around the figure of the Christian messiah seem to reach out and surround me. The nimbus unfurls into patterns of red, gold, green, and purple that curve and stretch and canopy over me like the embroidered *Ek Onkar* in multiple dimensions, moving and expanding with the music, surrounding the picture of the man with sad eyes and outstretched arms and this sobbing girl sitting in the pews.

I experience a moment of absolute spiritual wonderment: the organ flows into the music of the harmonium, *gurdwara* into church, Word made flesh into Word made infinite. It's a glimmer of Oneness. I'm overcome with an ecstatic love, tinged with melancholy, soaked with the blood of those who have died for it.

As the last note of the organ echoes through the grand church, she turns around and sees my tear-stained face.

"Are you okay?"

In this moment, she becomes every Christian, every church, every possible judgment. And I am an ambassador come to present my case.

"How can there be an exclusivist God?" I hear myself ask. "I don't think it's possible."

There's a pause as she considers me with a compassion I cannot express.

"I don't either," she says. "You know, I think that there are many paths to God. It just doesn't make sense otherwise. Of course, some people don't agree."

I begin to laugh and cry at once. I had marched up to this church prepared to fight the priest whom I thought would condemn me, and instead I found a Christian woman who met me in that borderland between our faiths—and embraced me. She is an ambassador too. And she had transported me up into my first spiritual experience of Oneness, the mystical vision that lies at the heart of my faith.

In her presence, the battlefield had melted into the sanctuary; the courage to fight had led me to the meaning of surrender. My ancestors must have whispered to me, "You want to experience God as One? Then to go the place where God has damned you, where God has threatened to swallow you up in hellfire. Go with your sword in your hand and your head in your palm. In that place, you will sit at the feet of Jesus and let Him do to you what He will."

And what did the messiah do? He did not send me to hell. He opened up as the gateway to the experience of Oneness I had always craved: He took me to God.

When I return to the *gurdwara,* I find my grandfather waiting for me under a great tree with roots knotted deep into the earth. I take his hand and return home.

35

Jesus Appeared to Babaji

Charles P. Gibbs

*"If the conversation isn't about salvation through Jesus Christ,
there isn't anything to talk about."*

Though I was born and raised a Christian and was ordained as a
priest in the Episcopal Church nearly a quarter-century ago, these
aren't words that I would ever say. But I've heard them many times,
and they are generally a conversation stopper in interfaith gatherings.
They betray an underlying view of this world and the next that leaves
no room for other voices. On my first trip to India in 1998, I experienced a delightful and transformational antidote to this attitude in
the person, experience, and teaching of a luminous spiritual leader:
Baba Virsa Singh.

The realities of India were overwhelming. Unimaginable poverty
was inescapable. In Mumbai, many sidewalks were lined with straw
mats that served as homes for entire families, who cooked and bathed,
ate and slept on the sidewalks. This poverty dwelt side by side with an
extravagance evident in upscale shops, and lavish, lavish wedding cel-
ebrations that took place every night in the elaborate pavilions along
the Queen's Necklace, a shimmering road that curves along a crescent
bay of the Arabian Sea.

Also, the spiritual was everywhere, and everywhere part of daily
life. The flowering of ashrams, shrines, temples, churches, gurdwaras,

and mosques, and the streams of pilgrims flowing to them bore witness to the powerful draw of the spirit that manifested both in seemingly rote ritual and in moments of numinosity.

Woven through this spiritually flavored fabric of poverty and wealth, a fabric that was to my Western senses a riot of color and sound and smell, was a visible expanse of human history. The technology and practices of the eighteenth and nineteenth centuries existed side by side with those of the twentieth. You could be in a cab racing down a winding road and come around a curve to discover a cart pulled by a camel or a water buffalo plodding in front of you.

You could see poor people in rural areas plastering dung pancakes on the sides of trees where they would dry and then be used for fuel; or you could hear a presentation on the latest developments in open-heart surgery in a five-star hotel that offered every luxury imaginable. On top of it all, in the big cities such as Mumbai and New Delhi, the air was so polluted that I often felt it would be healthier not to breathe at all.

And so it was that one late morning I found myself being picked up by a taxi at the India International Centre in New Delhi to be taken to meet a Sikh spiritual leader named Baba Virsa Singh. Babaji came from a peasant background, growing up in Sarawan Bodla, a mudbrick village in India's Punjab State. Though he had no formal education, from his youth he was recognized as having powerful spiritual gifts, including the gift of healing.

By the time I met him, Babaji was a spiritual leader revered all over India. He had founded many farm-based spiritual communities on land that had been environmentally ravaged, but was transformed (followers believed through Babaji's deep spiritual powers) into farms that bore abundant crops and offered a home, spiritual community, and human dignity to poor people of all faiths. I was to meet Babaji on one such farm, Gobind Sadan, which means House of God in Punjabi, founded in South Delhi in 1968.

Though Babaji was a Sikh, he welcomed people of all faiths, believing this was fully consistent with the founding impulse of Sikhism, which was to bridge the divisions between Hindus and Muslims, and, most important, that it was consistent with God's will. Before my visit, he had recently hosted an extraordinary ritual in which Hindu political leaders, who had been encouraging and/or turning a blind eye to the persecution of people of other faiths, took a vow before him to be accountable for the well-being of all Indians, regardless of their faith.

The hour-long drive took us through the toxic air of congested Delhi into the outskirts where traffic fell away, and shops and shacks gave way to walled farms and narrow lanes. When we finally arrived at Gobin Sadan, I stepped out into the cleanest air I'd breathed since I had arrived in India and into a palpable serenity as I walked through the gates of the ashram.

Mary Pat Fisher, a scholar of comparative religion who had left her life in Connecticut six years earlier to follow Babaji and live at Gobin Sadan, welcomed me and proved to be a delightful host and enjoyable companion. She told me some of the history of Gobin Sadan and Baba Virsa Singh and fed me lunch in their communal kitchen, which I had come to appreciate as an extraordinary Sikh practice the day before when I'd been the guest at the Bangla Sahib Gurdwara in Delhi, founded on the site where the eighth Sikh Guru had died of smallpox, and where today volunteers daily fed 25,000 people of all faiths and all economic stations, for free.

After lunch, Mary Pat walked me all over this incredibly peaceful farm. We visited three different sites where fires burn twenty-four hours a day, and twenty-four hours a day people read from the Sikh holy book, the Guru Granth Sahib. As we walked through the lush fields, she recounted stories of the miraculous effect Babaji's presence had on agriculture and how his growing system of farms on environmentally reclaimed land were providing homes and a future for many impoverished Indians of diverse religions.

At one point, we passed through the tiny cubicle where she slept and that housed all her earthly possessions, and I noticed on her bookshelf Marcus Borg's book *Meeting Jesus Again for the First Time*. When I told her how important that book had been to me, she started out of the room and asked me to follow because there was something special she wanted to show me.

We walked on dusty paths through fields lush with that season's crops, dodging cow dung that would later be collected for fuel. We reached a weathered barn and turned to walk along a stone fence.

Mary Pat stopped at a gate that led us into a beautiful enclosed garden. On the far side of the garden was a statue of Jesus, arms opened wide to embrace all who came to him.

As we stood in front of the statue, Mary Pat explained, "This is where Jesus appeared to Babaji. It was such a powerful experience that Babaji had this statue made to commemorate their meeting. Christmas is a major celebration each year at Gobin Sadan." She continued, "Babaji and Jesus still meet and talk."

To an American Christian, even one who felt he carried an open heart and an open mind, it was startling, humbling, challenging, and inspiring to see Jesus so accepted and honored in a Sikh ashram. It was even more startling and inspiring to imagine an ongoing relationship between Jesus and Babaji that would be the envy of Christians around the world. As I stood in what was clearly a holy shrine, a thought formed: Nobody owns the sacred dimension of life, and, it seems, Christians do not own Jesus.

That experience, that thought, have come back to me again and again over the years; and I have shared them again and again, often in sermons on Sunday mornings in Christian churches. When I think of that part of the history and the present of Christianity that chronicles endless divisions, power struggles, and violence done in Jesus' name, and compare those with the heartfelt respect and veneration given Jesus by Baba Virsa Singh, I feel simultaneously shamed, challenged, and inspired.

If I had never met Babaji and had only had the privilege of visiting that garden at Gobind Sadan, his impact on my life and work would have been immeasurable. Fortunately, I did have the privilege of meeting him in person.

Near the end of my visit to Gobind Sadan, I was taken for an audience with Babaji. He sat on a white couch, dressed in white from the top of his turban to the hem of his robe, with a long white beard and an expansive smile. I felt instantly that I was in the presence of a holy, humble, light-filled person who could see into the depth of my being at a glance.

Through a translator, he spoke for a timeless time, explaining his understanding of God, our source, as pure love, and of God's call to us to offer love, light, and service to the world. As he finished, he told me again that God's essence is love—boundless, overflowing love.

All God asks of God's children, he told me, is that they come to God for love. The reservoir of God's love is so vast that if all God's children came to God at the same moment and in an instant received all the love they could ever want or need from God, it would be as if a tiny bird took a sip out of the ocean. As I prepared to leave at the end of our timeless time together, Babaji admonished me to make sure I laughed enough. Then he gave me his blessing.

I often recall my visit to Gobin Sadan with gratitude and wonder. I remember that no one owns God and that Christians don't own Jesus. I believe that if our hearts and minds are open, we can meet together in God's unfathomable love. In that love we can work together to make our world a better place for all, until it is our time to journey from this world to the next. Babaji made that journey near the end of 2007. He left his body on Christmas Eve, a fitting time to be born into the next world and to be reunited with an old friend, whose arms were no doubt opened wide to embrace a good and faithful servant of the light.

36

Under the Bodhi Tree

Varun Soni

I was born in India but moved to the United States when I was two months old. My parents were among the first wave of Indian physicians to immigrate to the United States after the 1965 Immigration and Naturalization Act, and my generation was the first to be raised ethnically Hindu in the United States. Such an experience was challenging in terms of articulating a personal Hindu American identity, but it provided rich opportunities to engage with other religious traditions in the attempts of reconciling my own.

Growing up in southern California, I attended a Catholic elementary school, and most of my friends were Jewish. Our local South Asian community was small but diverse—our family friends were from India, Sri Lanka, Pakistan, and Nepal, and identified as Hindu, Muslim, Sikh, and Christian. However, my own family was more spiritual than religious, and growing up, I had a better understanding of the theological dimensions of the Abrahamic religions than I did of Hinduism.

It was not until I attended college at Tufts University that I had the opportunity to take courses in South Asian religion, history, and languages. In particular, my undergraduate religion major focused on the religions of India, and these courses were instructive in helping me formulate my own identity as an Indian American. So even though I was born in India, the first time I methodically explored my own religious and cultural identity was in the context of a Western research university as an undergraduate student.

During my junior year at Tufts, I enrolled in the Antioch College Buddhist Studies program, a semester long study-abroad opportunity in Bodh Gaya, India. Through Antioch, I spent three months living in the Burmese monastery in Bodh Gaya, where I studied Buddhist philosophy, history, and culture, and learned the meditative practices of different Buddhist traditions such as Vipassana, Zen, and Dzogchen. I also spent a month traveling in the Himalayas of Nepal doing field research on the "hidden valleys" of the Tibetan Buddhist patriarch Padmasambhava (Guru Rinpoche).

While in Bodh Gaya, I had a profound and transformative experience that exemplified the primary attributes of the "mystical" moment famously described by William James. This experience of heightened awareness and elevated consciousness lasted through the night and into the next day, which was Mahatma Gandhi's birthday. To commemorate the occasion, I went to the Mahabodhi Stupa, where a bodhi tree shades the place where the Buddha was enlightened, a sacred site often described as the center of the Buddhist universe.

I spent the early morning meditating under the bodhi tree, and when I opened my eyes, I saw a small group of Tibetan monks gathering, a daily occurrence at the Mahabodhi Stupa. What made this scene so magical was that His Holiness, the fourteenth Dalai Lama of Tibet, led the monks to the bodhi tree. Like a dream, he walked up to where I was sitting and greeted me with his infectious laughter and warmth. I immediately recognized that what I had briefly experienced, awakening my inner mind, was something that he constantly cultivated. That morning, the Dalai Lama led a small group of us in meditation at the center of the Buddhist universe. As a twenty-year-old university student, it was the most transformative and enlightening experience I had ever had.

My fortuitous encounter with His Holiness set me off on a different path, and after I graduated from college, I embarked on a sixteen-month spiritual odyssey around the globe. During that time, I immersed myself in the Buddhist world—I visited Buddhist shrines in Japan, I went on a Buddhist pilgrimage to Tibet, I traveled with Buddhist monks in Thailand, I meditated with Buddhist teachers in Sri

Lanka, and I explored Buddhist archaeological sites in Indonesia and Cambodia. I also continued to study Buddhist philosophy at Tufts University, Harvard Divinity School, and UC Santa Barbara, and my undergraduate thesis in religion focused on the Buddhist philosopher Nagarjuna and his conception of emptiness.

Throughout my spiritual and scholarly journey, His Holiness's presence in my life has been an extraordinary blessing, and I'm fortunate to have been able to hear him speak over fifty times in different countries and contexts. One remarkable occasion was the Kalachakra Initiation in Salugara, India, in 1996, where hundreds of thousands of Himalayan Buddhists from Tibet, Ladakh, Nepal, Sikkim, Arunachal Pradesh, and Bhutan gathered for two weeks to listen to his teachings. Recently, I had the profound honor of hosting His Holiness for his first visit to the University of Southern California (USC), where he spoke about secular ethics at two separate events. Introducing the Dalai Lama to thousands of USC students for the first time brought me full circle to my own college experience of meeting him for the first time.

Even though I self-identify as Hindu, I consider His Holiness, a Buddhist, to be my root guru and primary spiritual teacher, a viewpoint that is consistent with Hinduism's philosophical maxim of "many paths, one truth." Indeed, I believe that my experiences and encounters with His Holiness, the fourteenth Dalai of Tibet, have made me a much better Hindu.

37

How We Pray

Daniel A. Berman

As a rabbinical student training in clinical pastoral care at a major Boston hospital, I was consistently moved and challenged by the presence and strength of patients' faith. One of the goals in providing pastoral care is to help patients and their families "activate their subconscious": that is, begin to express their fears and concerns, and ask the pointed, at times unforgiving, questions buried but pulsating beneath the experience of pain or loss: Why am I here? What has happened? Who will take care of me? What now? Where is God anyway? My role was not to provide answers, but to join patients and their families in the process of asking questions so they didn't have to live with them alone.

In one case, with one family, my role was much simpler: sit, listen, and be still. And after they had expressed everything there was to say at that moment, help them find a language to pray.

It was early in my tenure as a chaplaincy student. I had spent the morning visiting patients in the medical trauma and intensive care unit and was walking back to the office to share my interactions with my supervisor. I walked by the visiting room and glanced at a family sitting close together. I passed by somewhat hurriedly and smiled, barely making eye contact. As I took another few steps, my mind processed the image. I stopped, took a deep breath, reminding myself why I was there, and turned around.

The room was small. Three grown children—siblings—sat in silence. It was clear they had been crying. I came in, introduced myself and sat down. I didn't know what to say, of course. What can one say? "Tell me what's happening," I uttered, in a barely audible voice. The youngest sister began to speak: "Our mother is dying." They had just come from saying goodbye to their mother, and her doctor was taking her off life support. The children had prayed with a priest at their mother's bedside, and were resigned now to waiting until the doctor came back to tell them that she had died.

I asked them to tell me about their mother, and they did, but it was clear they were exhausted. I took another breath, and we sat quietly for a minute. "Would you like to say a prayer?" I asked.

"Yes." They turned to me and closed their eyes. I, likewise, closed my eyes and turned to them.

It was apparent that we were each waiting for the other to begin. I had only just begun to pray spontaneously within a Jewish framework; I had almost no idea how to begin with a Catholic family. So I slowed us down. "Is there something you would like to pray for?" I asked. Silence. And then a response: "that Jesus take our mother's hand and hold it tight in his hand and lead her as she leaves us."

I had a lot of time over the course of the summer to reflect on my time with this family. As a Jewish chaplain in a multifaith setting, I anticipated moments like this. But it was my first time encountering such sharp differences in faith and prayer in a moment of real crisis, a family seeking guidance as their mother was in the final moments of her life.

What precisely was I supposed to do? My role was to provide pastoral care for patients and families in crisis. But was it also somehow my role as a chaplain of a different religious tradition to help them form words of prayer to Jesus? I wasn't sure I could do that. If I helped them, I feared, did their prayer somehow become mine as well? And yet: wasn't my work to join them in their questions and help them find the language they needed? And isn't prayer a serious and authentic language at critical times in our lives?

While these questions were present with me in that moment, the reality was that a family was sitting before me, they were devastated by the loss of their mother, and they wanted to pray to Jesus. "How do we begin?" they asked. "You are praying to Jesus," I said. "Start there." I sat with them, and held their hands as they slowly began their prayer.

I was deeply moved by this visit. This family was suffering. They invited me into their lives. And, in turn, I tried to offer comfort as the doctor removed life support from their mother. I did not pray to Jesus, but in sitting with them, I did face a tension I hadn't faced before. I spent some time that afternoon coming back to a place of familiarity, looking out the window over Boston, and chanting my own prayer for the family in Hebrew, ha'noten *l'yaef koakh*—God grant strength to those who are weary.

My encounter with this family was a touchstone in my training in pastoral work in a hospital with patients of different faiths. I don't know how I might respond in similar circumstances in the future, but the experience helped clarify for me what is at stake in these critical moments: shared humanity, compassion, and spiritual integrity. I had spent a year in rabbinical school studying different Jewish approaches to death and dying—including law, ethics, and theology—and I knew important questions of faith would be part of the experience of serving in a medical trauma and intensive care unit, but still I was unprepared for this first encounter with a family facing imminent loss. Since that morning, my work as a rabbi has presented many challenges, sometimes including the need to make quick and difficult decisions. These moments are simply imperfect. So I come back to prayer, hoping that my words and actions, even when partial or flawed, be received with hesed—grace or loving kindness—and help in some way to uplift those whom I am serving.

38

The Canine-Buddhist Dialogue

Rodger Kamenetz

Some people may know that I have written on and participated in the dialogue between Buddhists and Jews. But they may be less aware of my work in another significant dialogue: between Buddhists and dogs. Here's the story.

Years ago, a learned Tibetan Buddhist teacher from Montreal, Geshe Khenrab, came to my house to give a teaching. (Geshe was his title, indicating a learned monk.) I was living in Baton Rouge then, and my house had become a way station for wandering Buddhist teachers. Geshe Khenrab's driver was Garry. They were coming up from New Orleans to Baton Rouge. I told Garry it might take an hour and half. He arrived in a half hour. I'm not sure how he did that.

Geshe-la, as I called him affectionately, was wonderful. He was a contemporary of the Dalai Lama's. We talked for hours about his life in old Tibet. He had been living in exile for quite a while, but as a young boy in the Amdo region he'd loved being a monk. I asked him what sort of animals they had there.

He said, "Oh rabbits, deer, *yeti*, mountain lions."

I said, "Wait a minute, hold on, what did you say?"

He repeated, "Rabbits, deer, *yeti*, mountain . . . ."

I had to break in, "Stop! *Yeti*? The abominable snowman? Did you see one?"

"Yes."

"What did he look like?"

"Like a man but very big and hairy."

With this Geshe-la leaned forward across my kitchen table with the gravity of a sherpa burdened with watch care for a Westerner on a Himalayan adventure, "If they find you alone, they like to tear off your face." He then gave a deep laugh.

That was when I realized that Geshe Khenrab came from a realm where there were realities other than the kinds I knew about.

Meanwhile, Garry rearranged our living room, covering our bookshelves and television with a Tibetan *thankga*, a traditional silk painting of Buddhist deities. He took our nicest stuffed chair for the teacher to sit in and moved a table near him with a bouquet of flowers that someone had donated. That evening, the room filled up with bayou Buddhists, Baton Rouge seekers, and Arcadian adepts who came to hear Geshe Khenrab's teachings.

My dog liked the teaching a great deal. Taxi was a pretty good-sized mature mutt with beautiful sad brown eyes and a broad forehead like a Labrador, but he was hairy all over like a Muppet, like a *yeti*. He was also extremely intelligent. He walked into the room and immediately put his big head on Geshe Khenrab's knee. Geshe-la gently moved him aside, but Taxi came back and put his head on his knee again, so Geshe Khenrab simply let it rest there. It didn't seem to bother anyone.

The next day Geshe Khenrab was leaving. I saw him in a nook of the house talking to my dog. I came closer, he was saying something in Tibetan, and Taxi was taking it in very carefully. I said, "Geshe Khenrab, what are you doing with my dog?"

The swami said, "When a dog keeps coming into the temple, it means he aspires to learn *dharma*. So I am saying prayers that when he is reborn, he will be reborn as a human so he can learn *dharma*."

You know how people say that all traditions convey the same truths but use different idioms to describe them? For instance, according to the Tibetan teaching of the Dalai Lama, every person is your mother. Since there has been an infinite series of rebirths in the past, at some point, every person you encounter was your mother in a previous life, and you have been a mother to every person you encounter.

On the other hand, Judaism is a householder family religion. So to get to the same idea—that everyone is related to everyone else—we say that the first human beings were called Adam and Eve and that everyone is descended from them. So in terms of lineage, nobody really has any bragging rights. This idea gets expressed in a different way in the Jewish mystical tradition of Hasidism: namely that a retinue of angels, a host of holy servants not unlike the swami's chauffeur Garry, precede the approach of every person, announcing, "Make way for an image of the Blessed Holy One." Each of us is a fractal, a reflection of the face of God. That's another way to get to the destination of the dignity and worth of every person.

Still, for all that, I do not think that the sages of my Jewish faith ever counted on canines being part of the parade.

So Geshe Khenrab left in his nice used convertible car that he purchased for the trip. Then Taxi ran away.

He usually ran away whenever I left town because, according to my wife, he missed me. We did, I now understood better than before, have a special relationship that transcended the sentiments of "man's best friend." After all, Taxi had been my mother once, and I'd been his mother. But this time, I was still home. Why did he leave? The answer occurred to me later. *Because he was trying to follow Geshe-la, his new master, to Houston.*

Time went by. I heard that the car broke down in Texas, that they got a new car, that Geshe Khenrab arrived in San Francisco and stayed with a friend of mine. Meanwhile, Taxi came home after two weeks of mysterious pilgrimage. And a little later, he was clearly in pain. An x-ray showed the bone was rubbing against the socket of his rear leg. After the surgery, I spent the summer in servitude "walking" my dog by holding its rear legs up in a towel. It was another of karma's revolutions. Who was now master of whom?

Finally, Taxi was getting better and could walk on his own. I didn't have to be my dog's towel boy, the captain of his angelic retinue. Then I got the bad news. Geshe Khenrab unexpectedly died just after returning to Montreal from his fund-raising mission.

Suddenly, startlingly, Taxi lost his energy. He just lay down all the time in his favorite spot on a rug near the front door where he could still pretend to guard the house. When I took him outside, I had to pick him up and carry him because he could no longer walk. Something was very wrong with Taxi's transmission.

Then the day came when I heard barking outside. Taxi was at the bottom of the front porch steps, standing for the first time in weeks.

I went down, picked him up, and carried him inside. As I lowered him down onto his beloved rug, his brown eyes met mine. And then he was just gone.

Taxi was gone, the disciple following his *dharmic* master into the circle of transmigration. After Gesha-la left our home, Taxi had followed him to parts west, on the first leg of the odyssey. And now Taxi had followed his teacher on the second leg of the journey. Taxi had finally caught up with Gesha-la on the other side of nowhere. But somewhere, if you check around in a monastery, two little boys are hearing about the *dharma*, and they are inseparable.

A shaggy dog story? If you can explain it better, that's fine with me. But I'm sticking to my story. Because I believe there are things that remain undreamt of in our philosophies and that unless we make room for them we will be marooned in a very flat world.

39

Otherness and Wonder:
A Christian Experiences Moksha

S. Mark Heim

We are experts on our own lives, if such there are. But often it is hard for us to see the answer to even obvious questions about ourselves. When have I been transformed through relation with someone from a different religious tradition? One would at least have to distinguish between the times when this was true and I knew it and the times it was no less true and I didn't. The second category may be by far the largest. It includes all that is involved in growing up the son of a Baptist minister whose closest clergy colleague over thirty years was our neighbor the rabbi. I almost lived at church, but the house of worship where I was next most likely to be found was the synagogue. I knew Judaism through the restricted but rosy lens of the coming of age of my classmates, seders, festival meals, and the admiring regard of my father for his friend. I knew it through the even more restricted lens of the rabbi's three daughters whose notable achievements and virtues were much praised by my parents to their three sons with an almost familial pride that breathed a vague incest taboo.

I went to an elite New England college at the tail end of the sixties, a time and place where the religious tide was definitively going out and the future was assuredly secular. I remember a large lecture class in American literature where we had been reading Puritan poetry. Our teacher had been throwing himself into it, but he suddenly paused to look at us all ironically. "Does anyone here actually believe any of this stuff?" I can't say for sure that mine was the only hand; it was the only one I could see. My own four-year trend line ran counter to the counterculture. It moved steadily toward faith, nurtured more by my disillusion with a series of the alternatives to it then prominent among teachers and students than by a living Christian community in or near the college.

As I look back I realize that in those days the most profound supports for my own religious life came from other traditions than my own. This was true personally: the tiny but evident number of observant Jews, the single Muslim, a handful of Buddhists—anyone willing to stand out in the secular milieu was a welcome testimony to me and felt in some way like a comrade. They somehow counted more than the couple of Christian faculty members, as if their example were less tainted with my self-interest. History was choosing sides, and we had chosen the losing one. We were going down together. This sense of solidarity was also true intellectually. The attacks on Christianity came mostly as an attack on religion generically, and that made us allies. So all my (minimal) encounters with great thinkers and texts of other traditions did not register them as antagonists but as precious evidence that intimations of transcendence and the integration of faith and reason were matters worthy to occupy the wise.

On the great moral challenges of the antiwar and civil rights movements, the churches and religion generally seemed like weak and hesitant echoes to the vibrant passion of campus consensus. But in that great fire sale of the sixties as I struggled to make my own decisions on these matters, I could not deny that it was religious convictions that finally counted. Nor could I fail to observe that there was a steadied endurance to the engagement of many religious people I knew that contrasted dramatically with antiwar passions that evaporated with a low draft number.

All this fits under the heading of being transformed and not knowing it. That changed when I started crossing some literal borders. My wife and I spent a year after our marriage on the road in western and eastern Europe living in various Christian communities. It was an experience that primed us later to spend a sabbatical leave in India. I had taken up religious pluralism as an intellectual interest and even written a book about it. In what seems now embarrassingly backwards, having treated religions in terms of ideas, I wanted to see what lay behind the ideas. And India seemed as far as I could go.

During that year there were many moments that deeply affected me. Some were vivid then, and I barely remember them now. Some were modest at the time but have grown in resonance by later connection. One stood out then and now.

Over several months on Sunday afternoons at Dharmaram College a small group of Muslims, Hindus, and Christians met to listen to presentations and discuss them in small groups. The college campus where we gathered was an oasis of calm in the crowded bustle of Bangalore in South India. In those weeks after our arrival, it still felt to me as though I left our seminary compound and ventured across the city to the college like a swimmer taking a deep breath and then submerging in a brilliant chaotic ocean of colors and smells and faces until I surfaced at the Dharmaram gate.

I had read quite a bit about Advaita Vedanta, even taken a seminar one summer focused on Sankara, its great figure. But it is almost as though the more it made sense to me philosophically, the less I could really find any access to it religiously. One member of our little group was a Hindu acharya from an ashram outside the city. I do not remember his name because none of us ever called him anything but swami-ji. He was a person of preternatural calm (my trip through the traffic might have somewhat heightened this impression) and easy delight.

This particular afternoon, he had been the speaker and had led us in a kind of meditative search for the "I" of our own consciousness, a search whose futility would point us to the need for a larger I. As he spoke, I realized that he was describing with disarming simplicity an experience I remembered from my own childhood: the experience of attempting to catch the "I" in my mind who was the observer of my own thoughts. Once he had led me to that discovered connection, he took me on a breathtaking tour of my mind. Over the course of a few moments, what had appeared an edifice of speculative philosophy began to look like a map of my own soul.

Afterwards a group of us walked in the gardens and talked with him on the meaning of moksha, "release" or liberation for Hindus, which had been the theme of this talk. In his presentation he had stressed a favorite metaphor for this state of fulfillment: waking up. When we are in it, a dream can be extremely vivid, he told us. We feel its objects, we move in its world. Yet in the instant of awakening we realize completely that the dream was but a veil for our actual place and being. Just so will our present world appear when we achieve moksha. One of the Muslim students frankly shared his puzzlement. If this world is like a dream, he asked, then what are we to you, or you to us? Are we illusions, figments of each other's imagination? The acharya adjusted his robes with a smile. "We are dreams, talking to dreams." He was silent for a moment, while we savored the peculiar beauty of this image. "But of course," he went on, "you will ask me 'Who is having this dream?' And I will tell you that it is Brahman who is having this dream, and it is Brahman who each of us is when we wake up."

Our conversation meandered further into the well-worn dialectics of the great Hindu philosophers and their distinction between the faces of Brahman clothed with the appearances of our world—Brahman with qualities—and Brahman without qualities, on which such appearances have no purchase. To read of these things in a textbook is one thing. The reader can at least clearly sense there the deeply subtle intelligence of this particular part of Hindu tradition. But it is another thing to see and hear these elements expressed winningly in the concrete constitution of a life or a community. None of us in this band came away with much in the way of new information. Many came away with a new understanding of what that information might mean.

I am not of a particularly mystical persuasion. But as we walked on in the heavy early evening air and he answered our questions with this steady amused concreteness, I glimpsed, unsteadily but pervasively, what it might be like to be in the world he suggested. And then, in an unnoticed further instant, I was in that world. The best I can say is that I perceptually inhabited it, as with the reversal in perception of an image that can be seen in two ways. You cannot will yourself to see differently. When you see one, the other is an illusion. But this was not a particular image. It was everything.

No doubt, this moment was the result of more than the swami's talk. In some way, it was fueled by all the experiences of those weeks—of walking every day by the vast slum where tiny, humble shrines ringed each stunted tree, stopping in the coolness of temples with their riotous deities, stepping around living cattle and dead bodies on the sidewalk.

Whatever the reasons, I remained in this state for some time . . . for the time that it took for the rest of our conversation, for the tea and good-byes, for my walk and auto-rickshaw back across the city. It was not a trance. I was, some of the time, aware of this altered view of the world as one might be aware of a changed quality of eyesight. I would suddenly "come to" and observe it in that third person way with the startled certainty that this would surely dispel it entirely. But it would not. And then I would simply inhabit it again, while the driver made change and the crowds passed. Dreams talking to dreams.

I try not to import into my memory what was not part of the actual moment. I probably fail. What I know is that there was no particular impetus to act in any specific way, no changed moral outlook, but a very strong sense of being on another side of a great divide, a realm of peace. On the new side of this divide striving and its preconditions seemed totally impossible.

I was in no hurry for all this to end. I stood in the street outside the seminary for some period, short or long. I remember seeing the familiar lawn and buildings through the front gate in this state. And then I went through the gate myself and it was gone.

I remember feeling deeply grateful for this experience and expressing that gratitude directly to God in mental phrases of prayer. But I was not sad to see it end. I did not have any desire to recover it. Nor did I see any particular relevance of all this for the questions of religious diversity. It was not, at least then, a vision with a moral. I went home and ate supper.

But that experience has never been far from my mind when I read about other traditions or meet with those who follow them. This is not because I am at all certain that this experience corresponds precisely to what my swami friend believed and experienced in his own right. It is only because I am quite convinced that behind each tradition in principle there lies something of this same order of otherness and wonder.

40

What Mast Ram Baba
Dropped into My Bowl

John Makransky

"Mast Ram Baba" is what they call him, she said, a gleam in
her eyes. "He is a holy renunciate, with long gray hair and
unkempt beard, who wears only a loincloth even in the coldest part
of winter. He lives in a cave on the bank of the Ganges River. His ap-
pellation, 'Mast Ram Baba,' means 'God-intoxicated ascetic.'"

I was a young PhD student and committed Buddhist from the
United States, who had traveled to the Hardwar-Rishikesh area of
North India to learn from Hinduism and, if possible, from a realized
Hindu. I had spent most of the prior two years living in the town of
Sarnath, a sacred place of pilgrimage for Buddhists—the site where
Gotama Buddha gave his first teaching of the Four Noble Truths.
There I conducted research on Buddhist concepts of enlightenment
in consultation with Tibetan lama scholars and Indian Sanskritists.
I was especially drawn to a problem posed by the type of enlightenment the Buddha is said to have attained. Many of the Buddha's disciples, it is taught, attained a kind of enlightenment that freed them
from worldly passions of greed and hatred that had chained them to
the round of *samsara*, the cycle of birth and death. But the Buddha's
attainment of enlightenment not only freed himself from worldly
bondage, but unleashed a force of compassion and wisdom in him so
powerful that he could help countless *others* become free—teaching

in such profound, creative ways that his influence would inspire and uplift the world for thousands of years. Because the path of practice I was learning from my Tibetan teachers was modeled on the Buddha's paradigm, I had a strong desire to understand how freedom *from* the world could become such a powerful force of enlightened activity *in and for* the world.

Near Sarnath was the holy city of Varnasi, and I loved to go there in the evenings to stroll the ghats of the Ganges River, where I could imbibe the deep devotion of Hindu worshippers on the shore through all my senses—melodic hymns to the divine presence of Shiva and Vishnu echoing over the waters, clouds of incense, thousands of flickering butter lamps. My Buddhist practices were sensitizing me to the resonant power of the sounds and rituals of Hindu life. My personal practice, even as it deepened my commitment to Buddhist awakening, was mysteriously evoking in me an increasing wish to have a fuller encounter with the heart of Hinduism in India.

I mentioned this desire a bit sheepishly to one of my Tibetan Buddhist teachers, the scholar monk Khenpo Migmar Tsering. Some Buddhist scholars I'd known tended to distance themselves from Hindus who have been traditionally viewed as philosophical opponents. But to my surprise, Khenpo Migmar declared a similar interest in Hindu India. He spoke of meetings he'd had through the years with Hindu sadhus, holy men, in the region of Hardwar-Rishikesh, a region sacred to Hindus where the fresh, turquoise water of the Ganges River first emerges from the Himalayas. Khenpo Migmar said he'd found his encounters with Hindu holy men beneficial for his own growth as a Buddhist lama because they deepened his appreciation of the yogic depth of Hindu sages and helped clarify his Buddhist understanding of analogous meditation practices. Eagerly I traveled to the same region.

I went to an ashram in Rishikesh associated with revered Hindu teachers, where I met a female scholar and meditator from a European university who had visited the ashram over many years. She was the one who told me about Mast Ram Baba. As soon as she described him, I knew I had to meet him.

The next afternoon I walked the path along the Ganges River she had told me about, missing the turnoff to Mast Ram Baba's secluded area, retracing my steps repeatedly before finding the hidden part of the riverbank where he stayed. A community of ascetic devotees lived near this revered figure, in various caves and makeshift tents nearby. They affectionately called him "Baba-ji." I could speak a little Hindi, and when I met an old man who said he was a disciple of Baba-ji's, I asked if I could meet him. The old man nodded approval, and with a reverent look gestured toward an ancient-looking person with long white beard and unkempt hair resting on a stone slab near the river bank, his eyes shut.

Trying not to disturb, I sat in the sand at Mast Ram Baba's feet, to meditate quietly for a little while. After a few moments, to my surprise, it felt as though the power of the man's calm presence drew my mind from its usual meandering into a feeling of immense groundedness—a tranquil depth of awareness I had not previously experienced. Eventually Baba-ji stirred, sat up on his slab, and settled smoothly into sitting position. I don't know how long we sat there like that together, but my mind felt like it was beginning gently to merge with his, in a most expansive quietly compassionate way. I felt grateful to be with this man in such intimate simplicity. Out of the deep quiet of the moment, with a hoarse voice, I asked Baba-ji in Hindi, "Aap ka dharm kya hai?" "What is your spiritual teaching?" He replied softly, "Mera dharm sanaatan dharm hai." "Mine is the eternal teaching." A shiver ran through my body. I suddenly wished to ask many questions, but my Hindi was not practiced enough to converse so extensively, and Baba-ji spoke no English. He suggested I return the next morning at seven when someone he referred to as "Naani" would translate for us.

Early that evening some of Baba-ji's devout Indian disciples invited me to share a tasty, simple supper of rice, yogurt, and vegetables. A bright-eyed Sikh woman among them who spoke excellent English was curious about me, a young bearded American who had suddenly appeared in their midst. We chatted amiably and, when she asked why I had come to India, I mentioned my Buddhist studies research. She asked if I was a practicing Buddhist, and I said yes. Her face lit up with enthusiasm. "The Buddha is the one," she proclaimed, "who introduced strict vegetarianism to India as a mark of nonviolence." Her community was entirely vegetarian, and she was proud to make this link to the Buddha. But to her surprise, I informed her that the Buddha's monks and nuns were occasionally permitted to eat meat. I explained that although the Buddha taught universal compassion and nonviolence, if a little meat were dropped into the bowl of a monk or nun during their daily alms round they were to accept it as their meal for the day. The Buddha told his monastic disciples not to refuse the generosity of lay supporters, no matter how impure some of their offerings might seem. She stared at me in disbelief. But to my mind, the Buddha's instruction to accept alms without discrimination expressed his impartial compassion—he was providing a way for laypeople to generate the positive karma of giving to holy persons no matter what they had to give.

The next morning I eagerly made my way to Baba-ji's cave where a refined, early middle-aged woman with a British accent met me. She wore only a long, white cloth. This was Baba-ji's English disciple, Naani, fluent in Hindi. I later learned she had lived in this ascetic community for many years and had become a profound yogic practitioner and expert in Hindu Sanskrit texts. She graciously offered to be my translator with her guru.

Baba-ji's cave was a tiny grotto of stone and sand, big enough for just the three of us to fit. Sitting comfortably on a thin rug upon the rocky floor, he smiled and beckoned me to come in and sit with him and Naani. But before anyone had time to speak, suddenly my shoulder was bonked by the large head of a cow, who was trying desperately to squeeze its huge body into the cave with us! I was astounded, but apparently this was an everyday event for Baba-ji and Naani, who laughed with glee. Baba-ji cooed the cow's name, "Bhagavati" ("Goddess"), as he caressed the underside of her neck, letting her rub her massive muzzle along his cheek. Naani laughed. "She just loves Baba-ji," she said, and I noticed with alarm that the enormous cow had somehow inserted a third of her body into the tiny cave with us. After several minutes of this loving bovine communion, Naani gently shooed Bhagavati out of the cave so we could have a few minutes in private before numerous human devotees nearby came to offer their respects.

Baba-ji had somehow heard I was Buddhist and, with Naani's translation, took joy in asking about my studies and practices. I told him a little about my Buddhist practice, noting that my Tibetan Buddhist teachers were followers of the ancient Indian Buddhist philosophers Nagarjuna and Asanga, with whom he was acquainted. I later learned that Baba-ji was not only the "God-intoxicated" devotee of popular legend but a deeply learned master of Advaita-Vedanta, the nondual wisdom of the Upanishads. "Why have you come to me?" he asked. I mentioned my attraction, even as a Buddhist, to Hindu thought and practice in India, and the strong desire that stirred in me to learn from Baba-ji as my Hindu teacher.

But, I awkwardly confided, there was one thing about Hinduism that made it difficult for me as a Buddhist to learn from it openheartedly. "What is that?" he inquired. At the beginning of the Bhagavad Gita (the Song of the Lord, a foundational Hindu text), Krishna, who is the incarnation of God, instructs Arjuna, the central character, that he must fulfill his duty as a warrior by participating in a great war. I explained to Baba-ji that, as a Buddhist, I adhered to a position of strict nonviolence and could not accept that piece of Krishna's advice to Arjuna. In essence, the opening scene of the Bhagavad Gita had shut the door for me on serious study of the text as a whole, and with it, of Hindu philosophy, even though I found the rest of the text unspeakably profound.

Baba-ji looked at me intently for a moment. Naani translated as he said in Hindi, "I recently heard that when a disciple of the Buddha finds that someone has dropped a piece of meat into his bowl, he is to accept it. Is that true?" The woman I chatted with the prior evening must have told Baba-ji about our conversation. "Yes," I replied, "that is true." His eyes fixed mine in a firm gaze as he asked, "What if a war were dropped into your bowl?"

I was stunned. In that instant, my whole conceptual framework simply collapsed. I had no frame of reference from which to comprehend or respond to such a deep inquiry. Baba-ji's question had suddenly deconstructed my moral universe. And, in doing so, it exposed how I had attached myself to an ethical code, more than I'd been conscious, from a desire to inhabit a safely praiseworthy position than from a truly serious engagement with the problems and needs of the world.

My own prejudice had shut the door for me on serious study of the Bhagavad Gita and Hinduism. In an instant that door had been thrown open, and I felt an intense wish to learn how Hindu thought and practice had empowered and informed the wisdom of the man before me. I requested to learn all I could from Baba-ji and his senior students in the following months. He assigned as my tutor one of his close disciples—a brilliant yogi and scholar from Varanasi whom they reverently called "Acharya" as a title of scholarly wisdom. I spent the rest of the spring and summer studying the Bhagavad Gita and other sacred Hindu texts in Sanskrit with Acharya, visiting with Baba-ji, Naani, and other disciples, learning the lilting chants of ancient Sanskrit, and trying to help Acharya improve his spoken English. Baba-ji assigned me one of his spare caves (!) in which to study, meditate, and reflect on what I was learning.

In the opening scene of the Bhagavad Gita, the warrior Arjuna is caught in the most excruciating situation: he must choose whether to fulfill his sacred duty as a warrior and do battle with vast legions led by revered members of his extended family or to put aside the social responsibilities entailed by his position to avoid participating in that war. Either decision would have devastating consequences for thousands of people and for the future of his society. Desperate, he requests advice from his charioteer, Krishna, who is the incarnation of God (Vishnu). Krishna compassionately explains to Arjuna how human beings can learn, through disciplines of sacred knowledge, faith, and self-giving action, to participate in the world as an expression of the divine and as an offering to the divine potential in all persons, without being overwhelmed by the forces of greed, hatred, and ignorance that drive the societies in which they live. Over those months of study and participation (as a Buddhist) in the most beautiful Hindu rituals and inspiring texts of philosophy and praxis, I realized that the Bhagavad Gita was addressing, in its own profound way, the driving question behind my interest in the nature of a Buddha's enlightenment. How can a Buddha's attainment of nirvana, which frees him from the worldly passions that normally drive everyone's participation in the world, be the basis for his compassionate activity *in and for* the world? My study of Hinduism was opening my eyes to parallel Buddhist questions about bondage and liberation, motivation and action, in a remarkably fresh and profound way.

Blessed by my encounter with religious "others" such as Mast Ram Baba, Naani, and Acharya, when I returned to the United States and began college teaching I found myself, as Buddhist practitioner and scholar, drawn repeatedly toward the holiness of religious others similarly steeped in the spiritual depths of their traditions. Repeatedly I found the confines of my narrow understandings beneficially interrupted and expanded, a process that continues in my work at Boston College, a Jesuit Catholic university in whose program of comparative theology I teach, and in my work as a meditation teacher for the Foundation for Active Compassion, a contemplative organization of interfaith service learning.

Mast Ram Baba, I came to realize, had dropped into my "bowl" much of the direction that the rest of my life would take.

Part VI
Finding Fellow Travelers

Let there be no purpose in friendship save the deepening of the spirit.

Khalil Gibran

The varied interfaith experiences sketched in the essays of Part VI are united by the serendipity of unexpected relationships forged across religious boundaries. With different starting points, bound for alternate promised lands, these sojourners are united by their distinct pilgrimages. These are tales of odd couples and chance encounters, and of poor wayfaring strangers who forge rich friendships on the road.

Zalman Schachter-Shalomi in "What I Found in the Chapel" tells the story of a young rabbi venturing for the first time into a Gentile wilderness. He encounters there a friendly giant—no less a figure than Howard Thurman—who serves as his protector until the pilgrim gets his bearings, and then leads him into fields of mystical experience that set this Jewish seeker off on a lifelong journey of interreligious engagement firmly rooted in his Neo-Hasidic tradition. In "If Muhammad Had Not Spoken," Samir Selmanovic shares the story of how a Muslim elder in his Serbian community—Muhammad—offers him graceful support after the author converts to Christianity against the wishes of his (secular) Muslim family.

Otto Bismarck is credited with the quip that "God looks after drunks, fools, and the United States of America." In "Sewing in Silence," Laurie Patton reminds us that Providence also watches over twenty-something interfaith adventurers who manage to strand themselves on remote roads in foreign lands. Sometimes you run out of gas on the road to Nirvana. In this story, the silent companionship of two Hindu sisters of mercy knits a blanket of sacred hospitality around a traveler who is a long way from home.

In Judith Simmer-Brown's "The Solitude of Contemplative Life: A Buddhist-Benedictine Friendship," a practicing Buddhist finds a soul mate outside of her tradition and community, and reminds us of the truth that many pilgrims find: The truest friends, those who best honor and protect our religious identities, need not share our official religious affiliations.

Or Rose, author of "Holy Chutzpah: Lessons from William Sloane Coffin," finds a *rebbe*, who happens to be a lion of American Christian social activism, eager to pass on the wisdom of his years to this young rabbi. In Rebecca Ann Parker's "Out Beyond: Forging Resistance and Hope through Multireligious Friendship," a Muslim and Christian who guide a Unitarian Universalist seminary find common cause in good works and in honoring the boundaries around their respective identities.

Part VI ends fittingly with Bradley Hirschfield's "Finding Faith on the Road: Where Deep Commitment and Genuine Openness Meet." On the streets of Syracuse an odd couple, cabdriver and passenger, exchange gifts. The Christian driver receives pastoral care from the rabbi; the rabbi receives the opportunity to perform a *mitzvah* of sacred listening and counsel. As they part, their brief but mutually enriching interfaith encounter is solemnized by that most ecumenical of sacraments, a physical embrace.

41

What I Found in the Chapel

Zalman Schachter-Shalomi

In 1955, after years of intensive seminary study and service in various Orthodox Jewish congregations in New England, I began to feel the need for a broader education and a wider range of experience.[1] Up to this point, my entire religious education had taken place within the Jewish world, and it was beginning to feel somewhat narrow. I also had a sense that I could be doing more with my life, and so, with the permission of my *rebbe,* I enrolled in Boston University to study pastoral psychology and the psychology of religion. But of greater importance for my later life was my meeting with the Reverend Howard Thurman, who was then Dean of Marsh Chapel at the University.

At the time, I was living in New Bedford, Massachusetts, which was then a two-hour drive from Boston. And since it was winter, I had to be on my way under a dark sky, too early to say the morning prayers. So I would leave at five o'clock in the morning in order to arrive there at seven, leaving me an hour to pray and have a bit of breakfast before my first class at eight.

Once I was there, the problem was to find a suitable place for a Jew to pray. The Hillel student organization building was still closed

---

[1] This essay is excerpted from a newly edited version of Zalman M. Schachter-Shalomi with Donald Gropman, *First Steps to a New Jewish Spirit: Reb Zalman's Guide to Recapturing the Intimacy and Ecstasy in Your Relationship with God* (Woodstock, Vt.: Jewish Lights Publishing, 2003), xv–xviii. Used with permission.

at that hour; the only building open that early was the chapel, but this presented a dilemma. The main chapel upstairs was full of statues of Jesus and the Evangelists. As an Orthodox Jew, I simply wasn't comfortable praying there. Downstairs was a smaller, more intimate chapel for meditation, but there I was likewise inhibited by a big brass cross on the altar. Having no other option, I chose a public room called the Daniel Marsh Memorabilia Room in the same building. There I found myself a corner facing east, toward Jerusalem, and began to pray.

One morning, after I had been doing this for a while, and just after completing my prayers, a middle-aged black man came into the room and said in a casual way: "I've seen you here several times. Wouldn't you like to say your prayers in the small chapel?"

I shrugged my shoulders, not knowing what to say. The man was so unpretentious that I thought he might have been the janitor. And his offer was so forthcoming that I did not want to hurt his feelings, but how could I explain that I couldn't pray in the chapel because of the cross on the altar?

After a moment of looking at me earnestly, he said: "Why don't you stop by the chapel tomorrow morning and take a look? Maybe you'd be comfortable saying your prayers there."

The next morning I was curious and went to look into the little chapel. There I found two candles burning in brass candleholders, and no sign of the big brass cross! The large, ornate Bible was open to the Book of Psalms, Psalm 139: "Whither shall I flee from Thy presence." From then on, I understood that I was at liberty to move the cross and say my morning prayers in the chapel. Afterward, I would always put the cross back and turn the pages to Psalm 100, the "thank you" psalm.

Trusting the Holy Spirit

Sometime after this, I read an announcement about a new course in spiritual disciplines and resources, which would include "labs" for spiritual exercises to be taught by the Dean of the Chapel. The course intrigued me, but I was apprehensive about taking it. The Dean of the Chapel was also a minister, and I worried that he might feel obliged to try and convert me. So, after giving it some thought, I made an appointment to speak with him about my concerns.

When I walked into the office, the friendly black man from the chapel was sitting behind the desk, none other than Dean Thurman himself. He smiled and offered me a chair and mug of coffee. I felt a little ashamed of my initial assumption; I should have understood from our first encounter that this was a man to be trusted, but still I was hesitant.

"Dean Thurman," I said, "I would like to take your course, but I don't know if my 'anchor chains' are long enough."

He put his coffee mug down on his desk and began to examine his hands. Slowly, he turned them over and over. I noticed that the back-sides were very dark, while his palms were very light. He looked at them slowly as if considering the light and dark sides of an argument. This lasted only a few minutes, I'm certain, but it felt like hours to me. He did this with such a calm certainty that he seemed to possess great power. Moreover, he had this prominent bump on his forehead (above and between his eyes) and I could swear that it was about to open and reveal the "third eye." Finally, he spoke: "Don't you trust the *ru'ah hakodesh*?"

I was stunned. He had used the Hebrew for the Holy Spirit, something I had not expected from a Gentile. And in so doing, he brought that question home to me in a powerful way. I began to tremble and rushed out of his office without answering him.

For the next three weeks, I was tormented by that question: Did I indeed trust the *ru'ah hakodesh*, trust it enough to have faith in my identity as a Jew? Or was I holding back, fearful of testing my belief in an encounter with another religion, unnerved by the prospect of trusting my soul to a non-Jew? If I was fearful, did it mean that I didn't truly believe? Finally, I realized that his question could have only one answer. "Don't you trust the *ru'ah hakodesh*?" Dean Thurman had asked. I had to answer, "Yes, I do," and so I signed up for his course.

It was marvelous and tremendously impactful, especially his use of "labs." In the labs, we experimented with various spiritual exercises, which frequently took the form of guided meditations. In one exercise, we were instructed to translate an experience from one sense to another. We would read a psalm several times, then listen to a piece by Bach to "hear the meaning of the psalm in the sounds of the music." Another exercise was to "see music as an abstract design moving through space." In these ways, our senses were released from their usual, narrow constraints and freed to tune into the Cosmos, to touch God.

People seldom have those primary experiences in religion referred to by William James, Aldous Huxley, and others. But without this firsthand knowledge, the study of religion is impoverished. Such primary experiences allow the student to understand what is being taught. The use of experiential labs is now part of my own method; in fact, I have found that they turn out to be extremely important in the spiritual growth of many individuals.

In my exchanges with Dean Thurman and the other members of the class, I learned an important lesson that is still at the center of my thinking: Judaism and all the other Western religions are suffering from having become *over-verbalized* and *under-experienced*. Someone else's description of ecstasy or spiritual *at-one-ness*, given second- or third-hand, is simply not enough; we need—and want to have—these experiences for ourselves. And I want to make it possible for other people to have them. That is part of what a living, breathing religion is about, and that I learned from Dean Thurman.

42

If Muhammad Had Not Spoken

Samir Selmanovic

Life interrupts us. When we can't fit our life experience into our religion, something has to give, and life can't give. Like a sturdy surgical tool, life cuts back across our religion to save us from it. Just when we figure everything out, when our belief systems, traditions, and practices are beginning to play along nicely like a well-trained and tuned symphony orchestra, we stumble across something—an experience, a fact, a person. And nothing defies our religion so much as finding the sacred in one of "those people." You meet a Muslim man who resembles the character of Jesus more than anyone you've ever met in your church. You find yourself working with a Wiccan woman who is repairing the world better than anyone in your synagogue. You meet an evangelical Christian college student who puts everything on the line to protect the rights of atheists on campus. An atheist wise man or woman comes alongside you and helps you persevere on your path of faith in God. In such encounters, to use the words from Yehuda Amichai's poem "The Place Where We Are Right," the moles and plows of love soften the stomped soil of a hard ground where we are right.

That's what happened to me.

When I became a Christian, my devastated secular Muslim parents recruited one of Europe's best psychiatrists and fifty relatives to take their best shot at helping me get over my infatuation with God. Even my former girlfriends were summoned to try to evoke sweet memories and prevail over my heart. My mom was on anxiety medication, and after a couple of months, her face looked strained by an unending stream of tears. For the first time in my life, I saw my father cry. Everything evaporated; their respect for Christian institutions, the good deeds of my church, and the virtues of the Christian path were all deconstructed by a little army of people zealously researching the private lives of the members of my church. I was informed about which married Christian man had a woman on the side, who stole tools from the workplace, and who did not pay back a loan to a neighbor. After two months of this agony, my body and my spirit were weakening, and seeing my family suffer so much jolted me like nothing else ever did. I was tired, hanging on solely to the cross of Jesus, the clearest expression of God's compassion for me.

My parents did not sense my weakness at the time. Like me, they were on the brink of exhaustion, so they resorted to desperate measures and asked a religious person for help. They invited Imam Muhammad, respected in the local Muslim community as a "holy man," to attempt to throw my Christian beliefs into disarray and stir me toward Islam, which in my parents' reckoning was the lesser of two evils.

When Muhammad walked into our home, somehow I felt safe in his presence. Besides being learned in matters of scripture, he was the most environmentally progressive and socially conscious person I had ever met—a vegan who walked to our home from a far part of the city, avoiding transportation on principle, to protect the environment. A small gray-haired man with a large smile, Muhammad was emanating peace and playfulness, something my family needed so much at the time.

After being introduced, he kindly asked my parents to leave the room so that he and I could be alone. In spite of his kind manners, I still expected an attack, something I had heard dozens of times before such as, "The Torah and the New Testament are an incomplete mishmash of texts redacted by humans, whereas the Quran was recited by God and is therefore perfect, correct in all ways, superseding, and completing all previous revelations! Come to the winner!" Instead, after some initial small talk, he let time pass in silence, and I enjoyed this rare moment of rest. When I was ready, I raised my eyes and looked at him, dreading the inevitable argument. He stood up quietly, walked over to me, sat down, and lightly touched my shoulder for a moment.

Then he said calmly, "I am glad you are a believer." And nothing more.

After sitting in peace for a little longer, we stood up, and he opened his arms to invite an embrace. I opened mine. He smelled like wooden furniture and soap—old but fresh. Hugging him, I thanked God for giving me this break in life.

Neither my parents nor I knew what to do with what had just happened. After he left, my parents nicknamed him "Crazy Muhammad." My parents fell into a deeper despair, and word of Muhammad's foolishness spread in the family.

The grace and truth I had first met at the cross were embodied in this man, who was willing to be taken for a fool in order to help make me whole.

Would I be a Christian today without Muhammad's blessing?

If Muhammad had not spoken, God would have made stones talk to me, I believe. Largely because of this experience, however, I eventually got over my fantasy of Christian supremacy and signed up for the kingdom of a sovereign God who is Spirit and who cannot be controlled and, like the wind, blows wherever it pleases.

43

Sewing in Silence

Laurie L. Patton

It was November 1983. I had arrived in India only three months earlier, with a "find yourself" fellowship from my university to travel to the sacred water sources of India. I had trekked to the Himalayan shrines of Kedarnath and Badrinath in the last days of the autumn pilgrimage season. And I had even thumbed my nose, as only a twenty-three-year-old can, at the threat of snow avalanches in Gangotri and Gaumukh, the melting glacier that gives life to the Mandakini, one of the tributaries of the Ganges. With these treks under my belt, I arrived in the Hindu city of Varanasi with a sense that I knew what to expect.

But there were differences. In Varanasi, the Ganges had turned from the small mountain rivulet of the Mandakini to the silent, all-encompassing flow of the plains. In some places, the river spanned more than a mile wide. The severe grandeur of the Himalayas was replaced by the hum of urban life—but not an urban life that was familiar. Varanasi was a city filled with traffic, to be sure, but traffic interlaced with Hindu funeral rites, oxcarts carrying television sets and boom boxes, and the bells of *arati*, the evening offering of fire conducted by the Ganges and in many Hindu temples all over the city.

One of the most densely populated as well as one of the most intensely Hindu places on earth, Varanasi posed a special kind of challenge for a young foreigner. It is said that Varanasi is the litmus test for those who want to keep visiting India forever, and those who never come back again. In the midst of deep cultural difference, the wish to become *deshi*, or "of the region," dominated in the young American student community in Varanasi. The young American women wore saris, the right number of bangles (between eight and twelve), and the right metal for toe rings (silver). And all of us haggled with the rickshaw drivers to make sure we paid only *deshi* prices—not a rupee more.

Hindi was the lingua franca for most of us when we were out and about in the city. I had taken up private tutorials with the best Hindi teacher on the planet. (He has his own Facebook page now, called "I learned Hindi with Virendra-ji.") But I was silent when I was out and about with my student compatriots. While they happily chattered with children and shopkeepers in the streets, I was so ashamed of making an error, of being seen as more foreign than I already was, that I stopped speaking altogether. I was the quiet one in the lovely silk saris, the right number of bangles, and the silver toe rings. And oddly enough, this silence frequently worked in my favor.

The only trouble was that I was doing fieldwork and needed to talk every once in a while. After the breathtaking rivers of the mountains, I had become fascinated with the ponds and wells next to the Ganges—called *kupa*s and *kunda*s in Sanskrit. I frequently wandered with a translator in the back alleys of Varanasi in search of these smaller sacred sites that few visitors knew about. And I met many women at these ponds and wells, some of them incorporating these sites into their daily worship. Many were honoring a local deity in a temple near the pond and bathing as part of their morning activities. Still other women came a little more infrequently. Some visited Lolarka Kund, an ancient and deep well dedicated to the sun, for an annual festival where they released gourds and squashes into the water in hopes of gaining offspring. In most of these visits, I let my translator do the talking, and so even there I could be a woman of few words.

But at twenty-three, identity is everything. And my silence and shyness in speaking Hindi remained excruciating. The discomfort in my own silence was probably one of the reasons that I took up with a young Western man (let's call him Dan), who was fluent in Hindi and had an Enfield motorcycle. I loved listening to Dan speak Hindi effortlessly and with a lovely sense of humor in almost every situation—whether it was with a teacher, a milk vendor, a sweeper, some-one at a petrol station. We began to spend a great deal of time on that Enfield, where I could observe the world, happily settled under the roar of the engine. I could be even quieter as the female companion of the strange young Westerner who spoke Hindi so well. And thus I entered into a situation where the more Hindi I learned, the quieter I became. It was completely unlike me. Silence was never comfortable.

In late November, Dan and I decided to take a trip to Bodh Gaya, the place where the Buddha attained enlightenment under a pipal tree. It is now called the Bodhi tree (the tree of enlightenment), and its descendant grows in splendor inside the temple complex devoted to the memory of this event. I wanted to see the tree and to get out from the compression and density of everyday life in Varanasi. But I also learned from a friend that getting to Bodh Gaya from Varanasi involved a trip along a road that was famous for its *dacoits*, or robbers. Somehow, it didn't matter. Just like I had thumbed my nose at the snow avalanches, I thumbed my nose at this potential risk, thinking that it wouldn't really happen to us.

As I packed that evening, I decided that our time away should involve hours of quiet work as well as visiting the Buddhist temples that were the main attraction of the town. So I put in my backpack a book about the steppe-wells of Gujurat and the embroidery I had brought along from home. The embroidery was crewel work, and its pattern was a picture of birds on a branch in the Chinese style that is so common in American needlework of the nineteenth century. Somehow being in a Buddhist pilgrimage town and doing embroidery seemed to go together.

Dan and I set off for the five-hour journey, accustomed by now to the stares that greeted us along the main roads. Two foreigners on an Enfield, the woman in the back in a sari riding side saddle, would raise far more questions than either of us could answer, in Hindi or in English, when we stopped for chai at the tiny roadway stalls. The hours went by uneventfully, until about 5 p.m., about an hour be-fore sundown and an hour before we would get to Bodh Gaya. On the final stretch of road, Dan realized that he had miscalculated how much petrol we would need to get there. He stopped the motorcycle and checked the gauge. And then he put his foot on the pedal to start again. The motor spluttered but did not turn over. We had ground to a halt right next to a field of sugar cane. And we had ground to a halt near dark, on one of the most dangerous roads in North India.

After much discussion, we decided that the safest thing was for Dan to hitch a ride with someone to the nearest petrol station, and come back with the gas in a red canister he kept on the back of the motorcycle for just these kinds of situations. I would wait with the motorcycle by the side of the road. We waved down a large delivery truck belching smoke, and the crew was happy to oblige. I felt a clutch in my throat as I waved at him, happily smoking newly rolled *bidi*s in the back of the truck with the delivery crew, on the way to the petrol station.

In the minutes after Dan's departure, I looked around at my surroundings. I thought the best thing to do would be to make myself as inconspicuous as possible. I pulled my sari around my head and sat on the ground. In those first moments, I veered between fear and elation. When I wasn't anxious, I was enjoying the roadside anonymity, looking around every once in a while to see the life of the road around me. Oxcarts came close by, and I examined the cracks in their wheels. Rickshaws came by, and I parsed out the letters in the advertisements on the back of their cabs.

After about five minutes, I heard a rustle in the cane fields behind me. From the leaves came two women, clearly farm women who had been working the fields nearby. They were wearing red saris, frayed at the edges with wear and tear, but some of the gold threads of the trim still glinting through the dusty edges. They stood near the roadside clearing, framed by the leaves of the sugarcane. One was an older woman, about fifty, and the other I guessed to be about twenty-five. They seemed to be taking stock of the situation, looking at each other and then at me with calm, clear eyes. There was no giggling or staring, as there usually was in such encounters in Varanasi. It was instantly clear that they had not come as curiosity seekers looking for entertainment. And surely I must have seemed strange to them, even stranger than I was to Varanasi city dwellers who were used to foreigners in their midst. These two women weren't even interested in the Enfield, which was the usual topic of conversation after the other topics had petered out.

Then the older woman spoke to the younger one. I could tell from a few words that they were speaking Bhojpuri, a local dialect that shared words with Hindi but was distinct from it. And then, without any further words, they came and sat on either side of me—the younger one to my left and the older one to my right. We sat like that for about a half an hour, staring out at the road. Their presence was simple and straightforward. At first I was puzzled by their unusually disinterested demeanor. And then I realized that they had simply come to sit with me. Nothing else.

After a while I decided I would get the embroidery out of my backpack while the light was still good. I dragged out the plastic bag which held the threads and needle and cloth. I held it out to them. They nodded. Then I began to sew, and beckoned them to come closer. I did a French knot stitch in pink thread, to make up the tuft of the bird's head on the pattern. I held it out to the older woman and did another French knot to see if she understood. I then gave it to her and nodded, to see if she wanted to try. Her hands were cracked and rough, and held the needle sideways. The thread kept slipping off the needle as she tried to wind it around, and she began to laugh. I helped her hold the needle steady as she tried one more time. This time it held, and she was able to make the French knot. By this time, her younger companion was watching intently. I held out the embroidery to the younger woman, and she took it. She quickly wound the thread around made a perfect French knot. We all began to laugh.

I cannot remember how much time we spent there doing embroidery by the side of the road. I do remember the exhaust from the traffic settling on our skin and clothes. I also remember that I found a spare piece of cloth and gave it to them, with a needle and spare blue thread. With the second cloth, they became less shy about trying stitches. They showed me a stitch that was an alternation of long and short; their hands moved with a deftness that I could only barely imitate when I tried it myself.

By the time I was learning the second new stitch, we heard the sound of men shouting. It was the men from the delivery truck, with Dan, waving the red petrol canister, now full, happily in the air. As Dan and his companions came closer, the women nodded to me, covered their heads with their saris, and turned and went back into the cane fields. The cloth with their blue stitches in it lay on the ground near the Enfield.

The entire encounter lasted about an hour and a half. I believe in that ninety minutes there were five or six words spoken. Our silence was in part a result of the fact that we shared no common language. But we could easily have done what many people do in those situations—chattered away in our different languages, gesticulating and pointing and speaking loudly. But we didn't. The women came and simply sat with me. And miraculously, I felt no need to make conversation. I did feel the need to do embroidery. And embroidery was a language that was immediately understood.

I have tried not to romanticize the memory of those two women, whose names I never knew. I have reminded myself frequently that they probably led lives of struggle and resentment as well as joy, like all of us do. But the fact remains that those two women perceived my vulnerability and came to sit nearby. And that day, they transformed my built-up anxiety about silence, my own inability to speak in a new culture after twenty-three years of highly articulate chatter. As I got back on the Enfield and we continued toward Bodh Gaya, I came to understand silence differently. I believe that hour in the Bihari twilight was the first moment I genuinely knew that the compassion of presence, a teaching in all religious traditions, has no need for words.

44

The Solitude of Contemplative Life:
A Buddhist-Benedictine Friendship

Judith Simmer-Brown

The deepest level of communication is not communication, but
communion. It is wordless. It is beyond words, and it is beyond speech,
and it is beyond concept. Not that we discover a new unity.
We discover an older unity. My dear brothers [and sisters], we are
already one. But we imagine that we are not. And what we have to
recover is our original unity. What we have to be is what we are.

Thomas Merton[1]

When Brother Gregory and I were first paired as dialogue partners, it was a sunny and humid July day on the verdant grounds of the Abbey of Gethsemani. We sat gratefully under the canopy of a huge tree, and our rapport instantly ignited. Brother Gregory, easily twenty years my junior, had been a Benedictine monk since shortly after college. Clad in his black robe with a cowl and shod in sandals, he combined an eager freshness and the shy reticence of a monk. As a midlife wife and mother, professor, and Tibetan Buddhist practitioner, I was dressed in the casual skirt and blouse of a weekday shopping trip, the Buddhist *mala* around my wrist perhaps the only clue to my decades

---

[1] Thomas Merton, *The Asian Journal*, ed. Naomi Burton, Patrick Hart, OCSO, and James Laughlin (New York: New Directions, 1973), 308.

of contemplative life. It was 1996 and we were both attending the historic Buddhist-Christian monastic dialogue conference at Gethsemani, presided over by His Holiness the Dalai Lama and senior ecumenical advisers from the Vatican. Brother Gregory had traveled from the Abbey of St. Procopius in Lisle, Illinois, where he serves as infirmarian.

We each spoke of our journeys, the individual journeys of contemplative prayer and meditation. We also spoke of our journeys in community, and the challenges of our specific communities. Quickly we discovered the resonance and kinship that has continued in the fifteen years since that first conversation.

Brother Gregory has been deeply inspired by the journey of Thomas Merton, known as Father Louis at Gethsemani. Brother Gregory has followed with faithfulness his Benedictine vows and vocation, and like Merton, he has been fascinated by the practice traditions of Buddhism. He had learned the Tibetan Buddhist meditations of *shamatha* (calm abiding) and *vipashyana* (insight), and found that they deeply nurtured his life of prayer. He asked me questions about the practices from the very beginning of our conversations.

I found Brother Gregory's interest in Merton and Buddhism compelling from the first, for I am the student of Chogyam Trungpa, Rinpoche, a Tibetan lama who became fast friends with Merton on his Asian journey. In fact, the morning of Merton's death, his address at a Benedictine conference enthusiastically spoke of his plans to work with Trungpa Rinpoche in Scotland and America. As the daughter of a Methodist minister who unsuccessfully sought methods of Christian meditation before becoming a Buddhist, I had become fascinated with contemplative prayer during my years in the Naropa University dialogues between Buddhists and Christians in the 1980s. My teacher's love for Merton brought me close to him, and I had held Merton in my heart for years. Brother Gregory and I had much to share.

I discovered that Brother Gregory was an avid reader of Buddhist books and publications, often alerting me to sources I had not yet seen. His view of the greatest contemporary challenges of contemplative life was my own as well, and we found ourselves in conversation at every opportunity. I knew of the decline in monastic membership in Christian communities, and we shared a passion for Monastic Interfaith Dialogue as a mutual support for the cultivation of the heart.

We have met at conferences and colloquia, we have shared dinners with my family, and we have exchanged phone calls and emails over these many years. We have supported each other in crises of spirit and community, even when our respective communities could not understand our commitment to dialogue. We each know the anguish of the other.

Probably the most remarkable exchange we ever had was conducted entirely through email. In fact, it is unlikely we could have discussed this in person, given the delicacy of the subject. Brother Gregory was working on an essay on celibacy for Monastic Interreligious Dialogue and asked me to give him feedback. When I got his email, I was sitting in an airport lounge between flights. Reading the essay, I was so struck at the resonance I felt when Brother Gregory described the "existential solitude" of monastic life. "Solitude, then, is the dimension of the Christian mystery to which the monastic life bears witness in a special way. Hence, we can say that our 'monastic life demands first of all a profound understanding and acceptance of solitude.'"

This description struck me in that airport as akin to my own experience of being a married contemplative in an environment that exposes the fallacies of romantic love. As Rinpoche taught me, most of us seek romantic relationships because we are afraid of being alone, and we feel those relationships are successful to the extent that our loneliness is assuaged. But the contemplative recognizes that aloneness is the fundamental state of all beings and that no human can fully fulfill the inner needs of another, nor should they. Instead, when we resonate to another, we discover a special connection in our shared aloneness. Relationship, Rinpoche taught, is an opportunity to give to another and to share with them the poignant, personal qualities of being alone together. The only way to assuage loneliness is opening to the absolute.

Upon reading Brother Gregory's article, I immediately responded with a reflection on aloneness and the beautiful space of openness and warmth that we discover when we are alone together. Our rapid email exchanges that afternoon represented one of the most intimate exchanges we have ever had. I expressed the irony that marriage in a contemplative life could share the same commitments, kindness, love, and profundity that celibacy might for another.

One of the hallmarks of my dialogue relationship with Brother Gregory is that we recognize in each other the solitude of contemplative life, even when we are surrounded by the demands of being in a family, a community, a set of responsibilities that present us with challenges we would never have chosen. We know that differences of scripture, history, and community mean nothing between genuine contemplatives. We have found in our relationship some of the intimacy and resonance that our mentors, Thomas Merton and Trungpa Rinpoche, found in each other in 1968. Such a discovery is precious beyond words.

45

Holy Chutzpah: Lessons from
William Sloane Coffin

Or N. Rose

The first time I heard William Sloane Coffin speak was at a memorial service for Abraham Joshua Heschel at Congregation B'nai Jeshurun in Manhattan in the late 1990s. As I listened to Coffin preach, I thought to myself, "Now that is the kind of rabbi I want to be someday." Of course, Coffin was not a rabbi but a renowned Presbyterian minister. His eloquence, humor, and chutzpah all greatly impressed me. His strong physical presence was matched by his bold spiritual vision. He spoke lovingly and self-critically about Christianity, emphasizing the need for people across faith lines to work together on social justice and environmental issues.

Over the next several years I learned much more about Coffin's singular contributions to American civic life: his work as a chaplain at Yale University, as a "freedom rider" for African American civil rights, and as an anti–Vietnam War activist. The more I learned about Coffin, the better I understood why he and Heschel were such close friends. Like their colleague, Martin Luther King Jr., these men believed that as religious leaders grounded in the teachings of the ancient Hebrew prophets, they were obligated to engage in issues of social

concern; they possessed what Heschel once described as "moral grandeur and spiritual audacity."[1]

I had the privilege of meeting Bill in the winter of 2005. Having
heard that he was nearing eighty and in poor health, I was determined
to speak with him as soon as possible. I decided that the best chance
for me to have a real conversation with Coffin was to interview him.
As a contributing editor for *Tikkun*, I knew the magazine's founder
and editor, Michael Lerner, would appreciate such a piece given their
shared commitment to progressive religion and politics (and their personal connections to Heschel).

After reading as much as I could by and about Coffin, I made a
pilgrimage to Strafford, Vermont, where he and his wife, Randy, were
living. When I arrived at their home, I was surprised to see just how
weakened Bill had become from a stroke and other ailments. He sat
in a tattered Barcalounger, his legs covered by a heavy woolen blanket; he looked visibly smaller than the last time I had seen him, and
his speech was slurred. What remained unchanged, however, was his
fiery spirit.

It was clear from the opening moments of our conversation that
while he rarely left his living room any more, Bill continued to travel
great distances intellectually and spiritually. On one side of his chair was
an impressive stack of books on religion and politics and on the other
was a small folding table with a telephone and various notes on it.

For the next two hours, Bill spoke to me with great insight, passion, and humor about the great moral and spiritual issues of the day,
from abortion to the environment to interfaith cooperation. Famous
for his quick wit and mellifluous speech, it was striking to see him
slowly choose his words and work hard to articulate them as clearly as
possible. Although Bill made a few self-deprecating remarks about his

---

[1]   This expression comes from a telegram Heschel sent to President John F. Kennedy in 1963 regarding the need for strong religious and civic leadership in the
struggle for African American civil rights. A copy of this letter can be found in
a collection of Heschel's writings with the same title, edited by his daughter, Dr.
Susannah Heschel. See *Moral Grandeur and Spiritual Audacity: Essays* (New York:
Farrar, Straus and Giroux: New York, 1997).

ability to communicate, his methodical pace actually had a calming effect on me, allowing me to focus on the substance of the conversation without being overwhelmed by the fact that I was interviewing William Sloane Coffin!

Among the many things we discussed that afternoon, Bill was most concerned, not surprisingly, about the need for the emergence of a new generation of religious leaders willing and able to carry forth the work of social justice and environmental responsibility that was so important to him and his peers. As our conversation wound down, he paused and said, "This may sound like a crabby remark, but the world has too many 'old turks' and 'young fogies.'" He wanted more of us "turks" to take risks and speak out for justice. But he was also careful to add that one must always be mindful of the thin line between righteous indignation and self-righteousness. Work for social change, he warned, could breed in one a dangerous arrogance disguised as holy impatience. Related to this, he said, "Never hate evil more than you love the good." Because the result is that "you will become a damn good hater! And the world has enough of that kind of activist."

After completing the interview, Bill insisted that I have a drink with him. But he was also concerned that I make it home before the Sabbath. "What would 'Father Abraham' [Heschel] think if I caused you to violate the holy Sabbath!" he exclaimed.

Over the next few months I spoke to Bill several times by phone. At first, we worked together on editing the interview, but soon we just schmoozed—not idle chatter, but more open-ended discussion— about his old age, my new marriage, and the complications of religious leadership and human frailty. Bill was not shy about sharing his own shortcomings with me (particularly when I put him on too high a pedestal) and encouraged me to be honest about my own.

As we spoke, I always held a pen in hand, ready to record a quotation from the likes of Reinhold Niebuhr or Albert Camus. Most precious to me were Bill's own aphorisms, as he had the rare ability to formulate poetic insights in the course of casual conversation. One quotation that I thought about repeatedly in the weeks after Bill's death in the spring of 2006 and that continues to stand out in my mind is as follows: "The only way to have a good death is to lead a good life. Lead a good one, full of curiosity, generosity, and compassion, and there's no need at the close of the day to rage against the dying of the light. We can go gentle into that good night."

I have been blessed with wonderful mentors since my childhood. My parents instilled in my siblings and me the value of cultivating relationships with teachers and elders who were willing to share with us something of their wisdom and with whom we could engage in honest and searching conversation. These people were not to be regarded as saints, but as advanced fellow travelers, individuals of like mind or spirit who had walked farther than we had along the winding road of life. William Sloan Coffin was such a mentor to me. Although I had the opportunity to spend only a short time with him, he was a generous, insightful, and funny teacher, whose presence and passion will remain with me for years to come—*yehi zikhro barukh*, may his memory be for a blessing.

46

Out Beyond: Forging Resistance and Hope through Multireligious Friendship

Rebecca Ann Parker
in conversation with Ibrahim Farajajé

Out beyond ideas of wrong-doing and right-doing,
there is a field.
I'll meet you there.

Rumi (translated by Coleman Barks)

In Morocco, as my colleague and friend Professor Ibrahim Farajajé tells me, Muslims are the traditional keepers of Jewish graves. Jews commend into the hands of Muslims the care of their burial places and the guarding of their saints' tombs where Muslims as well as Jews perform acts of devotion and remembrance. Tending cemeteries, he goes on, is not the only cross-religious service that takes place in Morocco where he lived for a time. At the end of Ramadan, Jews prepare and bring food for Eid-al-Fitr, the great feast that breaks the month-long fast; similarly, when Pesach is over and Jews can again eat leavened bread, the first loaves are baked by Muslims and brought as gifts to the homes of their Jewish neighbors.

The image of people of one faith performing sacred duties for people of another faith captures my imagination because this is what Professor Farajajé and I do as provost and president, respectively, of

Starr King School for the Ministry. Professor Farajajé is a Muslim, and I am a Christian, and together we lead a Unitarian Universalist/ multireligious theological school whose mission is the preparation of people for ministry and for progressive religious leadership for society.

To serve the faith of another as an expression of one's own faith is something "out beyond" the usual ways of approaching interfaith relationships. Such service is more than openness, more than tolerance, more than sympathy, more that curiosity about an exotic other, and it is certainly more than dialogue for the sake of comparing and contrasting religious doctrines. Such service is devoted commitment to the well-being and the flourishing of another's religious tradition on the other's terms. It is the kind of love that does not "alter when it alteration finds," but loves the freedom, dignity, particularity, and sacred worth of the other. The other is neither subsumed into a notion that "all spirituality is the same" nor required to convert, nor asked to accept placement in a supersessionist order. The other is welcomed as irreducibly other, yet connected in creative interchange and relationship.

The collegial friendship Professor Farajajé and I have forged over years of working together grounds our school in a lived experienced of cross-religious, cross-gender, and cross-racial leadership. Our friendship began in a context of stress. Professor Farajajé had just accepted the invitation to join our faculty at Starr King after ten years as a professor at Howard University. When he began making phone calls to potential houses and apartments for rent in Berkeley that would suit his family's needs, he kept running into barriers. One landlord, on learning that he was a new professor at Starr King School at the Graduate Theological Union, quickly steered him away from the neighborhood he was inquiring about. "You wouldn't want to live here! This used to be a nice neighborhood, but now the Koreans and the Blacks are moving in." The assumption that if he was a professor he must be white spoke volumes. As a liberal white person, I was naive about racism in Berkeley. My eyes were opened as Ibrahim shared his experience with me: repeatedly, as soon as Ibrahim's mixed racial identity was revealed to a potential landlord, places were suddenly rented, or no longer available, and his status as professor was doubted.

Finally, after considerable searching, Ibrahim found the perfect house. He would be meeting the landlord at the property the next morning. "I don't want them to take one look at me and tell me it's been rented," he said. "And I am afraid that when they see me they won't believe I am really a professor. Will you come with me?" I agreed and arrived at the house attired in my most conservative navy blue suit. I had had my share of sexist reactions as one of a tiny handful of women seminary presidents in a profession almost completely dominated by men. "Do you think if the landlord won't believe you are a professor at Starr King, that he will believe I am the president?" Fortunately, the landlord knew Starr King School—he had grown up in a Unitarian Universalist congregation and had no trouble believing that Starr King would have hired each of us for leadership positions. He happily rented Professor Farajajé the house.

Our friendship unfolded from there. Friendship can open doors for people to enter spaces beyond the categories that separate us. As our friendship evolved, candid conversation, solidarity in the face of prejudice, and shared spiritual practice have become foundational to our ways of working.

*   *   *

It is late August 2002 in Berkeley. We are living in the aftermath of September 11, 2001. The halls of our school are filled with hustle and bustle as staff and faculty attend to last-minute preparations for the arrival of new students for orientation. In the midst of the flurry, in our small round chapel with its redwood walls and tall windows shaded by climbing vines, three of us with diverse religious orientations—Muslim, Unitarian Universalist, and Christian—are praying together. Professor Farajajé, Professor Lawrence, and I have gathered to observe our tradition for the start of the school year. One by one, we read each student's name—new and returning—and pray for the student through a meditation whose words are:

> *There is a Love,*
> *holding us.*
> *There is a Love,*
> *holding all we love.*
> *There is a Love,*
> *holding all.*
> *We rest in this love.*

We have not discussed what any one of us might mean by "Love." We do not offer any specific intersession for any given student— some of whom we will meet for the first time in the coming week. Our prayer arises from a shared awareness that while we might speak or think about God differently, we know that our work as theological educators takes place within the context of a benevolent power greater than ourselves, a power that upholds all of us in relationship, infuses grace and compassion into our daily work, embraces diversity, and calls us to do right by our students and by one another. "The School belongs to God," we say from time to time. We believe that we and our students, engaging one another in the sacred tasks of teaching and learning, are sheltered by the canopy of this greater love.

* * *

September 2004, fall arrives again in Berkeley. The new students have been oriented, classes have begun, and I have just phoned the police. In my shaking hands, I am holding a piece of hate mail that has arrived without postage in Professor Farajajé's mailbox at the seminary. A pastiche of insidious words and violent images threaten harm to him and his child. The letter marks an escalation in opposition to our school's affirmation of Muslim presence in our faculty and student body. It also targets our educational commitments to counter oppressions of all kinds—racism, sexism, heterosexism, classism, able-bodied-ism, and ecological exploitation. Ibrahim waits anxiously with me for the police, who arrive quickly. The police counsel us to increase security for our faculty member and students and advise us that the best way to stop further escalation will be to hold a public rally in which we state our opposition to hate and assert our values of tolerance and inclusion.

We call the rally. Friends and supporters of the school fill the street; speeches are made; songs are sung. The gathering is colorful and bold, but I nervously watch the perimeter and scan the crowd, keeping eye contact with the security team. Colleagues and students from the University of California at Berkeley, down the street, have joined with us. This same week, Muslim women on the Cal campus have been accosted at night by a group of jeering young men, taunting them to remove their head coverings.

For the remainder of the fall, Professor Farajajé teaches with a
guard in his classroom. The tension doesn't relax for months; toxic-
ity seeps into the life of the school. We adjust the patterns of our
friendship and collegial work in order to carry this burden. Prayer
becomes imperative—a sustaining source of endurance. We form a
practice of holding our staff meetings away from the school, at "Lois
the Pie Queen," where black community leaders have been coming
for decades. Religious diversity feels welcome here, even faithful, here,
where Black Muslim activists and African American Gospel singers
are equally at home. Over salmon croquettes, fried chicken, and waf-
fles, we review budgets, plan agendas, brainstorm curriculum ideas,
and seek to move the school forward. As a Christian, my tradition
is to say grace at the beginning of the meal; as a Muslim, Professor
Farajajé's practice is to give thanks after eating. In his typically gracious way, Ibrahim joins my tradition, offering a grace from his roots
in the black church, "Strength for today and bright hope for tomorrow. Amen. Amin. Ashe." This prayer will accompany all our shared
meals for years to come.

* * *

Today, at Starr King School for the Ministry, people of diverse
faiths are living and learning together as people whose religious practices serve the well-being of the other's faith. We are experiencing
one another's spiritual traditions, joining in preparation and performance of one another's rituals, and we are developing the arts
of religious leadership and ministry by learning from one another.
Our students, faculty, and staff are Unitarian Universalists, Muslims, Christians, Jews, Pagans, Wiccans, Buddhists, Religious Hu-
manists, Hindus, people of American Indian spiritual practice, and
people who identified as "unaffiliated but interested in religion."
Our curriculum is shaped around three emphases: countering oppressions, creating just and sustainable communities, and cultivating
multireligious life and learning. A Jew teaches pastoral care; a Buddhist teaches religion and the arts; a Muslim teaches storytelling and
preaching; a Unitarian Universalist teaches approaches to religious
education; a Christian teaches ethics; a Hindu mentors students in
discerning their vocational path.

Friendship and spiritual practice have enabled those of us who lead the school to endure through tumult and strife. At moments of shared meals and nourishing conversation, we have a taste of paradise. My own preached words come back to me, "This way of living is not utopian. It does not spring from the imagination of a better world, but from a profound embrace of this world. It does not begin with knowledge. It begins with love, and love transforms what we know."

47

Finding Faith on the Road:
Where Deep Commitment and
Genuine Openness Meet

Bradley Hirschfield

I flew into Syracuse, New York, on a windy evening in October of 2000. After we landed, I hailed a cab. This not being New York City, where I am from, there was no cab line, no wait, and no time to look at the car I was jumping into.

As soon as I was in the cab, however, I noticed that pretty much every surface of the car's interior was covered with a Jesus Loves You sticker, that there was a crucifix mounted on the dashboard, and there were even little green pocket bibles hanging on strings at the point where the windshield meets the frame of the car. This wasn't just a cab, it was a rolling cathedral!

Part of me thought I should just jump out of the car, but we were already pulling away from the curb, and I didn't want to cause any trouble or cost the driver his fare.

As he pulled out of the airport, the cabdriver, a middle-aged man with a scraggly beard, long greasy blond hair, and wearing a red checkered shirt, cut off at the sleeves, was checking me out in the rearview mirror. He was actually using his rearview mirror to see if what he thought he saw on the back of my head (a kippah/yarmulke/skullcap) was really there.

Having decided that it was really back there, which it was, he finally asked in the raspy voice of a heavy smoker, "So, what do you do?"

I hesitated. Every fiber of my being said, lie. In fact, I actually recall thinking of the other careers I had explored, and telling him about one of those. You see, I travel one hundred nights a year for the work I do teaching, speaking, and consulting, and although I love and miss my wife and kids, most of the time I relish the adventure of connecting with all the different types of people I meet on the road. At that moment, however, I did not want to connect with the cabbie.

All I wanted to do was sit quietly, get to my hotel, brush my teeth, put on a tie, and go give my lecture.

"I'm a rabbi," I said. I couldn't lie. Not because I'm so pious, but somehow, at that moment, it did not feel like the right thing to do.

"A rabbi!" he replied. "There are so many things I want to ask a rabbi."

"I bet there are," I responded, looking once more at my surroundings.

"So," he said, "can I ask?"

"We are going sixty-five miles an hour down the highway, where am I going?" I said. "Ask away!"

He studied me. "You believe in the Bible, right?"

"Yes," I said, figuring this was not the time to bring up Old Testament, New Testament—those distinctions didn't seem relevant.

"What do you think of Jesus?" he asked.

"Oh, an easy question," I deadpanned. " If you are asking me if I believe that Jesus is God's only son and the only way we can find salvation, no, that's not what I believe about Jesus. If you're asking if I believe that Jesus is one of humanity's great teachers from whom we all can learn, then yes, I believe in that Jesus."

A long silence followed my response to his question, followed only by a very loud "huh" from the front seat of the cab. I didn't know whether he was impressed or offended. Perhaps he felt I was mocking Christianity.

"But if you think Jesus is so great, shouldn't he be your path to salvation? Why if you believe the first thing, don't you believe the second, and why if you don't believe the second thing, do you believe the first?"

"I can believe that Jesus is a great teacher without believing that he is God's son and the only path to salvation. One truth doesn't negate the other. I can love Jesus in my way. And you can love Jesus in yours.

There is room for both of our understandings of Jesus. I don't believe that you have to be wrong for me to be right."

"Whoooah," he said. "A rabbi who loves Jesus!" He was watching me so intently in his rearview mirror that he drifted off the road. Chunks of gravel flew up from under the wheels as we veered onto the shoulder and then back onto the highway. Was the price of my honesty going to be death by car wreck? I actually thought about all those times I had commented on God having a wicked sense of humor, and that this might be one of those times.

Eventually both the cabbie's breathing and his driving returned to normal. We were back on the road and staying in one lane, mostly. With that, my own breathing returned to normal, apparently enough for my driver to notice and continue our conversation.

"Rabbi!" he exclaimed. "That whole you don't have to be wrong for me to be right thing, I've never heard anything like that before! Now there are so many more things I gotta ask you."

I didn't explain that I had never said it quite that way before—I didn't see how that would help. I was struck, however, by the fact that in many ways, much of my life and work had been leading up to that formulation for most of my life. It was, it turns out, a momentous occasion for both us.

Even as I clutched the armrest and prepared myself for whatever was coming next, I empathized with the cabbie. I suspected that he lived a life in which his way was the only way, and it was incomprehensible and not just a little bit maddening that everyone didn't share his particular point of view.

I had been there. In the early 1980s, when I was a teenager, I had been a religious fanatic. I had left my family's upscale North Shore suburban Chicago neighborhood to join a group of settlers in the West Bank city of Hebron. I felt absolutely sure of myself, absolutely sure of the meaning and purpose of my life, absolutely sure that my way was the only way to live.

I led tours for Jews through Hebron, with a Bible in one hand and a gun in the other, pointing out every building with a niche for a mezuzah, the handwritten scroll that marks the door of a Jewish home. I showed them that regardless of contemporary maps, this land was ours. The Bible was our deed, because, according to the Book of Genesis, Hebron was the place where Abraham, the first Jew, had bought land for the tomb of Sarah, his wife. It is the place where Genesis says Abraham, Sarah, and their children are buried.

Then something happened that shook me to the core. A group of Jewish settlers was attacked. In running down one of the assailants, three of the settlers fired into a school and killed two Palestinian students.

I was stunned by their deaths. When I sought the advice of one of the settlement movements leaders, he said, "Yes, this is a problem, but it is not a 'fundamental problem.'" That was when I knew something horrible had happened. Staying in Hebron was destroying the very things that had brought us there: the desire to take back power and walk the land our ancestors had. These are good things. But even the best things have limits. A lesson that I learned in Hebron was that the best things can become the most seductive and deadly—great dreams become absolutist dogmas and people suffer on all sides.

The deaths of those students cracked me open. I realized that perhaps I didn't have all the answers, and the beliefs that had been driving my life were deeply flawed, or at least the entire program of their implementation was. I found myself suddenly outside the fold of the settlers' movement, and I felt desolate and not just a little bit lonely.

I tried to stay in Israel after the incident, but it wasn't working for me. The feelings of disillusionment and alienation persisted. So I came home. America, even with all of its materialism (much of which I happen to like) and consumerism, its culture of Coca-Cola and McDonald's, felt more spiritually healthy to me than the Holy Land. Because with all of its problems, this is basically a pluralist, inclusive culture, or at least more of its members aspire to that ideal than do the members of any other society I've experienced. I enrolled in the University of Chicago to study religion while remaining a traditionally observant Jew; I wanted a wider perspective on the forces and beliefs that had run my life. I wanted to explore the forest and not just hug one particular tree.

The University of Chicago provided that for me. I was influenced by Jonathan Z. Smith, who gave all religions a hard time but respected them as well. He moved with ease from Cargo Cults to ancient Israel to medieval Islam to the letters of Paul. I was also influenced by Jon

Levenson, a warm, engaging man with a wicked, and sometimes cutting, sense of humor. I decided to continue on with my studies, and I enrolled in the doctoral program at the Jewish Theological Seminary in Manhattan. I wanted to go into academia. I had no interest in becoming a rabbi.

I felt that rabbis just persuaded other people to imitate the rabbi, that they scored points by getting you to join their institution, and measured success by how many people they signed up. Although that was different from what was going on in Hebron, it seemed so to me only in degree, not in consciousness. I now know that many rabbis aren't like that, but I still feel that too often success for religious leaders of any faith is about getting their students to look, act, and think more as they do. I aspire to use what I know to help people look more like the person they want to be; to find, to use an overused term, "their best self." I try to offer my teachings as a way to do that, not as an instrument of affiliation.

When I gave the cabbie my take on Jesus that night in Syracuse, I was speaking to him through the prism of my Hebron experience and how it had changed me. I was trying to help him see that my way was not the only way, and that although each of us was deeply committed to a particular tradition, we could remain open to the wisdom found in other traditions. I wanted him to appreciate that I could love and learn from his tradition, and that we did not need to agree in order to share that love.

I assumed the cabbie's strong reaction had to do with the fact that, as he said, he had found a rabbi who loved Jesus. But it was more than that.

"Rabbi," the cabbie said. "Can I ask you another question—it's about my wife."

Although I didn't say it, what I thought was, can I just have another Jesus question, please. But what I said in response was simply, "Sure."

The cabbie said that for years and years he had been a drug addict and an alcoholic. He had been in and out of detox programs. He had suffered relapses and broken countless promises to himself and others. He had been unable to hold a job and was often in trouble with the law. He had lived his life that way for as long as he could remember.

And then he had been introduced to his church and his pastor, had found Christ, and had become clean and sober. Jesus had saved him.

I've talked to many addicts over the years, and I know what a difference Jesus can make in their lives. In Jesus they find a source of unconditional love—an affirmation of human dignity and infinite worth, no matter what transgressions they have committed—an image of someone who suffered more than they have, no matter how much they have suffered. And in Jesus they find someone who literally came back from the dead, who was reborn.

Jesus had showed the cabbie how he could start over, and evangelical Christianity had been his salvation. But, he told me, he had a problem: his wife of twenty years wanted nothing to do with his religion, church, or pastor. "She doesn't go to church with me, and she doesn't want to go to church with me," he said. "She doesn't believe what I believe. But she never gave up on me, through all the dark times. She stuck with me. And now . . . ." His voice broke and he couldn't get out the words. "Plus," he finally added, "My pastor says that if she doesn't get the Message, then maybe I should get a new wife."

I could feel how torn he was. His most important teacher had told him that he had a choice to make. He felt pulled in different directions by the two things that mattered most in his life: his wife and his faith. Nobody had told him that his wife could be completely with him on his journey even if they were never going to be in complete agreement. My teacher in Hebron, for whom any difference was an excuse for disconnection, expressed the same mind-set. Either the cause was perfect and for everybody, or it was flawed and therefore for nobody.

"Look," I said to him, "I can't tell you what to do, but I can tell you this—you are a very lucky man. You are doubly blessed; first you were saved by your wife and then you were saved by your faith. I can't imagine why you would give up on either one of them. You can make room for both of them and for each other."

"Whoaaaaaa!" he shouted, and again we were swerving sharply to the right and heading off the road. I couldn't believe it—I thought I was handling things so well, and for the second time in one day, I was about to die in the back of this guy's cab! But, it turned out that while he was very excited about my response to his question, and was moving very fast, we were turning into the driveway of my hotel.

"Can I still pray for her?" he asked.

"For her to see the light? To believe what you believe? I guess so," I replied. "You probably wouldn't be you if you didn't pray for her. But if your praying starts to make you appreciate her less or any less able to sustain your relationship, then you are praying too much. Your wife doesn't have to be wrong for you to be right, and when it comes to Jesus, you don't have to be wrong for me to be right either."

Having arrived at the hotel, I thought that we were done. I was wrong. As he screeched to a halt, he jumped out of the car and was coming around to open my door. He was moving with such speed and determination, that I thought this time I really had offended him. He threw open my door and was literally reaching in for me!

As I got out of the cab, I realized he wasn't upset at all, but he was shaking. He literally fell into my arms and put his head on my shoulder. It was only moments before I felt my collar wet with his tears.

So there we were, two middle-aged men standing in the parking lot of a Syracuse hotel, hugging each other. We must have made quite a picture. After what seemed like a very long time but was probably only a couple of minutes, the cabbie pulled himself together, stood facing me as he sniffled a bit and wiped his eyes. He straightened himself, brushed his hair of his face, tucking it behind his ears, and stared at me hard in the eyes.

"Rabbi," he said, "You'd make a good pastor!"

I felt honored—it was his highest form of praise. I gave him one last hug and we were each on our way.

I have no idea what became of the driver, but I carry the lessons of our ride with me each and every day, and now you can too.

Part VII

Repairing Our Shared World

Is not this the fast I have chosen,
To loose the bands of wickedness,
To undo the heavy burdens,
And to let the oppressed go free?

Isaiah 58:6

The essays in Part VII are from interreligious activists, persons whose deep attachment to their particular traditions calls them, like the biblical patriarch and Quranic prophet Abraham/Ibrahim, to devote themselves to the cause of justice and righteousness. The final frontier of interfaith engagement is that terra incognito visualized and unrealized in all our varied sacred texts and holy rites. Critics claim it is religion itself that is a barrier to the harmony of living beings and have amassed enough evidence to make their case. In our closing, we summon a handful of faithful persons, who stand in for a greater cloud of witnesses, to offer their testimonies to how their religious commitments compel them to join with others of a different or no religion in common service.

Eboo Patel, author of "The Heroes I Was Looking For," writes about women both within and beyond his own Muslim community who model religious commitment with a passion for justice. This combination grounds Patel's own identity and defines his activism as a founder and the executive director of the Interfaith Youth Core.

In "A Community, Not Simply a Coalition," Jonah Pesner with Hurmon Hamilton, rabbi and reverend, respectively, write about the joys and challenges of their joint social justice efforts through the Greater Boston Interfaith Organization. Phyllis Berman and Arthur Waskow describe the power of personal relationships in the work of interfaith cooperation in "Dwelling Together in the Tent of Abraham, Hagar, and Sarah." In her essay "Practicing in the 'Temples of Human Experience,'" Zen Buddhist priest Ji Hyang Padma describes the courage she finds through her work of repatriating refugees across the war-torn border between Cambodia and Thailand through the Dhammayietra (Pilgrimage of Truth) movement. This newfound courage empowers her to bring her voice more fully to the interfaith conversation in the United States.

In "The Value of a Peso," by Miguel De La Torre, we learn about someone who taught its evangelical Christian author about authentic social action, a Catholic woman impatient with paradigms, unlettered in theologies, and unattached to any high-minded institutions dedicated to social change.

A generation before the interfaith movement in which many of the writers in this volume intentionally or unwittingly participate, there were a host of duly celebrated religious pioneer activists whose names keep appearing in and between the lines of this book, such as Thomas Merton, Dorothy Day, Howard Thurman, the Dalai Lama, Martin Luther King Jr., Mother Teresa, William Sloane Coffin, and Abraham Joshua Heschel. This book seeks to honor their legacy. Our reverence, however, is incomplete until with De La Torre we light a candle in honor of his and so many more unnamed, unsung heroes whose humble charity and piety inspire our continued journeys.

We close *My Neighbor's Faith* with Jim Wallis, founder of the Sojourners community in Washington, D.C., whose decades of social activism make him a fitting heir to the figures just mentioned. Against the backdrop of rising Islamophobia, Wallis challenges American Christians with "A Test of Character," to do no more or less than their master commands them, to love their neighbors as themselves.

48

The Heroes I Was Looking For

Eboo Patel

I spent my high school years in suburban Chicago dreaming of the
future comforts of fat paychecks. When I went to college at the
University of Illinois in Champaign, I saw the other America—homeless Vietnam vets drinking mouthwash for the alcohol, minority students shunted to the back of overfull classrooms, battered women
unable to find space at too-small shelters. I knew that America saw
these shadows but chose not to call them. I did not want that disease.

So I flailed about wildly. I went to demonstrations and raged
against the machine, but I did not see it improving anybody's life.
I spent one summer living in communes and another traveling with
the Grateful Dead, but decided escape wasn't my trip. I pierced my
tongue and dressed in drag on campus, but realized that it wasn't a
fashion revolution I was after. "Try being constructive," a professor
advised me. So I started volunteering at shelters and schools, but I
knew a broken world needed more than flimsy tape.

Few shared my frantic outlook. Most people were happy changing
their clothes to fit the climate. Some folks left for places where the
climate suited their clothes. A handful cursed the climate, shrugged,
and went on their way. I wanted to change the climate. My loneliness was freezing. Somebody said to me, "Go visit St. Jude's Catholic
Worker house on the other end of town."

"What's a Catholic Worker house?" I asked.

243

"Part shelter for poor folks, part anarchist movement for Catholic radicals, part community for anyone who enters. Really, it's about a whole new way of living. You've got to go there to know."

From the moment I entered St. Jude's, it was clear to me that this was different than any other place I'd been. I couldn't figure out whether it was a shelter or a home. There was nobody doing intake. There was no executive director's office. White, black, and brown kids played together in the living room. I smelled food and heard English and Spanish voices coming from the kitchen. The first thing some-body said to me was, "Are you staying for dinner?"

"Yes," I said.

The salad and stew were simple and filling, and the conversation came easily. After dinner, I asked someone, "Who is staff here? And who are the residents?"

"That's not the best way to think about this place," the person told me. "We're a community. The question we ask is 'What's your story?' There is a family here who immigrated from a small village in Mexico. The father found out about this place from his Catholic par-ish. They've been here for four months, enough time for the father to find a job and scrape together the security deposit on an apartment. There are others here with graduate degrees who believe that sharing their lives with the needy is their Christian calling. If you want to know the philosophy behind all of this, read Dorothy Day."

I did. And it made more sense to me than anything my Marxist professors lectured on, or my prelaw friends dreamed about, or my rock-and-roll records drove at. Recalling the thoughts of her college days, Dorothy Day wrote: "I did not see anyone taking off his coat and giving it to the poor. I didn't see anyone having a banquet and calling in the lame, the halt, and the blind. And those who were doing it, like the Salvation Army, did not appeal to me. I wanted life and I wanted the abundant life. I wanted it for others too."

Dorothy Day's vision of a culture of kindness was joined by a radi-cal social outlook: "Why was so much done in remedying social evils instead of avoiding them in the first place? . . . Where were the saints to try to change the social order, not just to minister to the slaves but to do away with slavery?"

Most importantly for me at the scowly, skeptical age of nineteen,

Dorothy Day had lived her commitments in solidarity with the poor, not just ministering to them; she had lived in resistance to the system, with the jail time to prove it.

I spent a lot of time in Catholic Worker houses during my college years and early twenties. I cut carrots for the soup kitchen at Mary House in New York City, demonstrated at the Pentagon with Catholic Workers in Washington, D.C., even lived for a few weeks at the St. Francis House on the north side of Chicago. I marveled at Dorothy Day because she reimagined the world and lived her life in a way that created it anew. She called America's shadows to her dinner table, served them with love, and sat with them as a friend. It was the best antidote that I had seen for America's sickness.

And mine. Dorothy Day once said, "I'm working toward a world in which it would be easier for people to behave decently." I wanted to behave decently. The Catholic Worker was a chance to do justice for the marginalized and to achieve redemption for myself. Redemption meant being saved from the sickness of selfishness. Being cured meant joining humanity. And there was something transcendent in that.

It was at the Catholic Worker house that I discovered a desire to touch the pure love of elsewhere. This was the love that Dorothy Day wrote about, the love that sourced and sustained her commitment. My faith journey was sparked not by a desire to enter heaven or from a fear of hell. It was neither about escape nor seclusion. I had no interest in the sin-and-salvation kerosene of the religious right or the soupy spirituality of the New Age.

The faith I wanted would help me love and grieve and celebrate with all humanity. It would shape my eyes to see dignity and divinity in the dirty and ragged. I felt in my bones that humanity was meant for something more than we were achieving.

J. M. Coetzee says: "All creatures bring into this world the memory of justice." I knew that we had a purpose beyond providing for our own comfort. Abraham Joshua Heschel writes: "God is hiding in the world. Our task is to let the divine emerge from our deeds." I wanted to live the truth of June Jordan's vision: "I am a stranger / learning to worship the strangers / around me."

The religious life of the Catholic Worker inspired me. I loved the prayers for strength to do the work of justice. I found the Christian hymns and sermons elevating. I read the books of Worker heroes like Peter Maurin and Thomas Merton. But I always found myself standing at a slight angle to the central symbols of the Christian faith: the cross, the blood, the resurrection. And I never felt any desire to convert.

A short conversation with the leader of a Catholic Worker house in Atlanta was an important turning point in my faith journey. I asked if I could spend a summer working at his community. "Are you a Christian?" he asked.

"No," I said.

"Then it will be very difficult for you to take full part in the life of this community. Find a place where you fit, body and soul."

I understood his comment as an invitation, not an insult. It was time to find a faith home. I began reading across religious traditions. I read Ram Dass on Gandhi and Thich Nhat Hanh on the life of the Buddha. I found my head nodding to nearly every article of Bahai social teaching and felt as if I had discovered a gold mine when I came across the thought of the contemporary Jewish mystic Zalman Schachter. But my attraction to these traditions was intellectual. Similar to my experience with Christianity, I felt that my soul did not fit in any of them.

The one tradition that I did not explore was Islam, the religion I had been raised in. Islam was the tradition my parents carried with them when they left India. America was the situation that provided them with possibilities both stated and shrouded, opportunities that facilitated upward mobility but scattered centering values. My father was a successful advertising executive. My mother earned her CPA and began building a career. The ritual dimensions of Islam never fit comfortably into our American-style lives. We rarely attended Friday prayer and only occasionally gathered at home as a family to bow our heads to God. Still, we were Muslims. We did not eat pork. We said *Bismillah* ("In the name of God") when beginning new projects. We prayed *tasbi* during difficult times.[1] And we helped people, especially Muslim immigrants, do everything from getting driver's licenses to earning advanced degrees.

Neglecting Islam was not so much a comment on the content of the religion as it was an adolescent habit of discriminating against the

---

[1]   Tasbi is the Muslim rosary.

familiar. But, as James Baldwin writes, "Later, in the midnight hour, the missing identity aches."

I began a Buddhist (at least, what I thought was Buddhist) meditation practice when I was twenty-two. It consisted of sitting still and thinking about nothing. But the Ismaili Muslim mantra my mother whispered in my ear when I was a child—Ya Ali, Ya Muhammad—kept rising into my consciousness.[2] In an attempt to stick to the program, I tried to push it out. Finally, it occurred to me that this was the program—I was a Muslim. My spiritual home had lived in my soul since my birth and before.

Later that year, I went to India to visit my grandmother. I woke up one morning to find, sitting on my grandmother's sofa, a person I had never met before. She was barefoot and wearing a torn white nightgown several sizes too large for her. "Who is she?" I asked my grandmother.

"Call her Anisa. I don't know her real name," she told me. "Her father and uncle beat her, so she has come here. We will keep her safe."

My grandmother has been sheltering abused women for forty years by hiding them in her home. Those who are interested in education, she sends to school. For those who want to live with family in other parts of India, she pays for their travels. Others just stayed and helped my grandmother around the house until they got married and started their own families. My grandmother has pictures of some of them, faded black-and-white shots, with pencil scribbles on the back telling the story.

After hearing the stories of about a dozen of these women, I wanted to know one more—my grandmother's. "Why do you do this?" I asked.

"Because I'm a Muslim. This is what Muslims do," she said.

My grandmother was a Muslim Dorothy Day. Her home had been a Muslim Catholic Worker house. The heroes I was looking for were within my religion, in my very family.

I immersed myself in Islam. I sought examples of giants who had fought tyranny with love, and found them in Farid Esack and Badshah

---

[2] "Ya Ali, Ya Muhammad" is a common Shia Muslim mantra. Ismaili is a Shia Muslim community.

Khan. I desired beauty and found it in the poetry of Rumi and Ibn Arabi. I discovered the stories that revealed the grand purpose of humankind that Allah made humanity *abd* and *khalifa*—Allah's "servant" and "representative," on earth. I felt the truth of Islam in my soul—that Allah created Adam through the spirit in Allah's breath, that Allah chose Muhammad to be Prophet, and that Allah wanted me to submit to the will of Allah. I felt embraced by the compassion of Allah, forgiven by the mercy of Allah, and guided by the light of Allah.

I found full nourishment in Islam for ideas I initially encountered in other traditions. I am a Muslim whose first faith hero was Dorothy Day.

49

A Community, Not Simply a Coalition

Jonah Pesner with Hurmon Hamilton

In 2006, Massachusetts made history when it passed legislation requiring every citizen of the Commonwealth to have access to quality, affordable health care. I was honored to co-chair the grassroots campaign that fueled the legislative process with the Reverend Hurmon Hamilton, the pastor of the storied Roxbury Presbyterian Church. At the time I was a rabbi at Temple Israel in Boston, and we were leaders of the Greater Boston Interfaith Organization (GBIO). The victory in Massachusetts demonstrated what is possible when the faith community comes together across lines of race, class, and faith, and holds political and corporate leaders accountable to a higher moral purpose than more typical, narrow interests.

At the same time, Massachusetts also made history when the supreme judicial court required that our Commonwealth provide marriage equality to couples of the same gender, and the legislature codified that principle into law. Rev. Hamilton and I found ourselves fighting together for health reform and pitted against each over the question of marriage rights for gay and lesbians. Because we were deeply committed to our relationship, we were determined to do more than agree to disagree about our divergent perspectives.

Similarly, the members of our church and synagogue yearned for more than polite dialogue. In fact, it was the practice of GBIO to challenge us to be more than simply a coalition that came together for common interests and then dissolved. Instead, grounded in the practice of congregation-based community organizing, GBIO challenged us to be a *community* not simply a coalition.

What is the difference between a community and a coalition? Coalitions are utilitarian. Members collaborate on a common purpose, and once that purpose is achieved, the coalition dissolves. In a community, the relationships are as important as the shared purpose. They transcend specific issues; the whole is greater than the sum of the parts. Humans yearn for community, not coalitions. In community, we find inspiration, comfort, and joy. Sometimes, in community there is tension. The test of a community is its ability to deal with such tensions productively and strengthen the relationships despite or even because of it.

Such was the case when GBIO confronted the question of gay and lesbian marriage. I remember standing on the Boston Common at a rally for marriage equality, and there was my friend and partner of more than a decade, Rev. Hamilton, speaking in direct opposition to my position; we knew right away we owed each other more than politely parting ways.

Trained with a model of leadership developed by the national Industrial Areas Foundation (based on Saul Alinsky's work in 1930s Chicago), we had helped many people from different walks of life participate in one-on-one conversations, encouraging them to share their personal narratives and their core beliefs. Such story sharing, we believe, becomes the glue that binds us together as a community with a sacred purpose.

It was time for us to return to the table and have such a conversation. I spoke about my brother and his own struggle as a Jewish, gay man in American society. Rev. Hamilton talked passionately about a member of his family, telling a similarly compelling story of human sexuality and identity. We spoke honestly and allowed ourselves to be vulnerable in the safe space we created together. After we spoke at length, we widened the conversation as we heard from other pastors, priests, and rabbis on the issue.

In this context, I also shared stories about the women and men whom I knew that struggled with issues of health care, parenting, and caring for dying loved ones, because of inequality faced by lesbian, gay, bisexual, and transgendered people in our country. I was amazed by how moved and touched my colleagues were by these stories. I was also amazed by the stories they had to tell about their understanding of the stakes of marriage in their own communities. I heard from others leaders who were deeply committed to a traditional view of marriage, whose congregations were being devastated by patterns of out-of-wedlock births, who feared polygamy could become a reality if same gender marriage was made legal. Ultimately, these same leaders sat with lesbian and gay families, heard from their children, and were able to understand the questions with more nuance and depth.

And we studied scripture. In particular, we reread and meditated on the verse in Genesis that tells us "God created the human person in God's own image." As we had grounded our fight for health care access in the belief that all humans were a reflection of the divine, we committed to discuss marriage equality in the same spirit.

None of us was trying to change the other's mind. That would have been a fruitless effort of exchanging positions. Instead, we were seeking deeper understanding of one another and, in turn, a strengthening of our relationships. In fact, I believe the way we religious leaders practiced community created a turning point in the debate. What had been a poisonous atmosphere of vitriolic attacks and caricature-like articulations of opposing views became a respectful conversation. Opposing leaders assumed good faith. They stopped debating the issue in the press. At the end of the day, both sides spoke out in defense of the true concerns of the other.

And so we became a community created in God's image, not just a coalition.

50

Dwelling Together in the Tent of Abraham, Hagar, and Sarah

Phyllis Berman and Arthur Waskow

During the past decade—even before 9/11/01, but with more intensity afterward—we have taken part in several gatherings of interreligious leaders and scholars hoping to stem the explosions of violence throughout the world that have been undertaken in the name of G!D, YHWH, Jesus, Allah, and all the other intimate names known to the faithful.

Many of these gatherings were sponsored by important global religious organizations, governmental agencies, and human rights groups, and hosted in beautiful locations in Europe, the Middle East, and North America. Through these meetings we have been blessed to meet some remarkable people from an array of religious traditions—Christians, Jews, Muslims, Hindus, Buddhists, Animists, Wiccans, Jains, Sikhs, and Shintoists. Although we certainly have learned a great deal from these gatherings, we have also returned from several of them deeply disappointed.

When we come together, whether with friends or strangers, what we most want to happen is to feel our hearts opening to one another, recognizing the humanness, and the presence of the infinite, in one another. When this happens, our time feels rich; when this doesn't happen, our time feels at least partly wasted.

Why was it, then, that at so many of these fine gatherings of intelligent, peace-loving folks, we came away with so little sense of personal connection? It was because the planning committees focused far too much of their attention on what Jewish mystics would call only two of the Four Worlds: the world of *Asiyah* (the physical world of action) and the world of *Briyah* (the intellectual world of ideas) rather than including as well the worlds of *Yetzirah* (the emotional world of feelings) and *Atzilut* (the soul world of Oneness).

So at each conference dozens of us sat in rows, listening to four or five leaders (almost always men) speak in panels from a podium. The papers they gave were all about interfaith dialogue—but they/ we never really dialogued! They talked at us, rarely with one another, and very rarely with the rest of us. So our heads got stuffed with information and ideas, including some good proposals for joint action. But our bodies stiffened, our hearts remained closed, and our souls slumbered.

And so, when it was our turn to organize our own interfaith initiative at the Shalom Center—"The Tent of Abraham, Hagar, and Sarah"—we tried to learn from our past experiences and create a more holistic experience. Although we certainly made mistakes throughout the project, we do feel that we were able to help create some important contexts for genuine relationship building.

We designed our first meeting as an intimate weekend retreat for just over a dozen Christian, Jewish, and Muslim religious leaders and scholars on the banks of the Hudson River. September 11 was in the recent past and still very much in the air. We were puzzled to see half a dozen military helicopters circling around a set of buildings right across the river, until we realized that this was West Point, and the U.S. Army was protecting one of its most sacred sites from a potential terrorist attack. We could not help but replay the horrifying images of faith-gone-wrong on that fateful September morning and the smoldering rubble of the towers. We could not help but keep in mind and heart that what we wanted from our coming together was not only a plan of interfaith action and an increased intellectual understanding of one another, but also a real sense of knowing and caring about one another as fellow human beings created in G!D's (whatever her name) image.

We began all of our sessions by inviting each participant to share briefly with the group something of his or her spiritual journey. We wanted to know what brought them to this peacemaking point in their lives. Each of us had fifteen minutes to share our moments of trembling and turning in our lives.

From that powerful beginning, it was possible for us to create real intimacy as a group, even to pray together (not just observe one another in prayer) in ways that were both authentic to and respectful of one another's religious practices. We invited Muslims to lead prayer services on Friday, Jews to lead on Saturday, and Christians on Sunday. We arranged for every meal to begin and end with prayer from one or another of the three traditions. In each case, we asked the prayer leaders to shape the services in ways that were true to their own spiritual paths and at the same time allowed the rest of us to participate in the experience.

We also worked diligently to formulate ways that we could help build peaceful relationships among our communities and in the broader world. Together, for example, we drafted a religiously rooted statement calling urgently for an end to the U.S. military intervention in Iraq, arranged to reach out to signers and donors in our respective communities, and ultimately published it as a full-page Abrahamic ad in the *New York Times*.

The name we chose for our project—"The Tent of Abraham, Hagar, and Sarah"—stemmed from an ancient rabbinic tradition that the Abrahamic family kept its tent open in all four directions, so as to be able to see travelers at a distance and to be able to welcome them quickly, to assuage their hunger and their thirst. Our hunger and our thirst were for spiritual sustenance and communal peace.

One of the great gifts of this project is our friendship with Imam Al-Hajj Talib Abdur Rashid. Imam Talib, the leader of an African American mosque in Harlem, was from the outset of the project one of the most engaged Tent dwellers. His politics were vigorously progressive; his religious commitments were seriously conservative. So conservative, in fact, that when we formed a circle for contemplation or celebration, he was unwilling to hold a woman's hand. We responded by shuffling who stood next to whom. But it turned out that his deeply conservative understanding of gender relations in Islam went beyond the touching of hand with hand, and this sparked an unexpected crisis at the Tent's first gathering.

Talib led a Muslim prayer service through which he taught us some of the chants in Arabic, showed us how to kneel and prostrate and when to rise—and kept the Muslim women among us at a distance. The service ended with one of those women in tears. Many of the Jewish and Christian men and women of the Tent were used to full and equal participation—including leadership—in their own communal prayer services. It was clear that we could not move forward together meaningfully without addressing this issue. So gently, respectfully, we explored other possibilities. The result was that in our later gatherings, we asked women to lead the three major prayer services, doing so in ways that we all felt were honorable and inclusive.

Our explorations were never one-directional—religiously or politically. In fact, one of our most memorable learnings came from Talib. This time it was not from his graceful and thoughtful response to the group on ritual matters, but in leading us to a deeper awareness of the complexities of Muslim life in post-9/11 America, and our work as religious leaders in this new and confusing reality. One morning, his cell phone buzzed with what, he explained, was an urgent call. Two members of his Harlem congregation had been detained for interviews by the FBI. The FBI thought these men might have been involved in some sort of terrorist plot. Talib skillfully explained to his congregants on the scene how to care for the members who had been detained, and then turned to us.

"There's no way I can know for certain what has happened," he said. "But I truly doubt that these two men have done anything wrong. And I do know that my brother Imams all across the country have reported again and again that everywhere some members of our mosques are being harassed, detained, and threatened."

For a few of us, the notion that the FBI might be acting outside the law, or on its edges, was information learned through political action long ago. But for most of us, it was a new possibility to face. For some of us, indeed, if the *New York Times* reported someone's arrest on suspicion of terrorist activity, it had been easy for us to slip quickly from suspicion to certainty. Yet our Talib was uncertain. How could we—who did not even know these people, but who knew and respected and had grown to love Talib—be more certain about their guilt or innocence than he?

A few days later, when we saw him quoted in the *Times* about his deep uncertainty about the detention of his congregants, he was no mere configuration of inky letters on a gray field of newsprint. He was no abstraction—he was our friend. We could not simply set aside for intellectual reflection the complexities created by reading a reporter's version of the statements of a religious leader. Talib's dilemmas were no longer his alone: they forced us to think again about our own faith and faithlessness, our own trustfulness and trustworthiness, our own community and loneliness, our own loyalty and skepticism. At that moment, it became clear that our "interfaith dialogue" was not of the mind alone, but of the heart and soul, and even of the body.

Talib is tall—really tall. Arthur came to know how tall, how big, how strong, in a scary moment just outside the White House gates. Each of them—not knowing the other was going to attend—came to participate in the clergyperson part of a large demonstration against the Iraq War. But the press was far less interested in them than in Cindy Sheehan, who like the ancient prophet Nathan facing down King David, had haunted George Bush's ranch in Texas to challenge the president after her son died in a war she, and countless others, believed was sinful. When a number of the clergy came forward to hand letters to the White House guard for delivery to the president, Cindy Sheehan—not a clergyperson, but also no shrinking violet—was at the front of the pack.

Clamoring media from all around the planet wedged themselves around her, trampling us lesser-known priests and rabbis, ministers, and imams in the crush. Buffeted, stumbling, Arthur looked up to see a broad black face he knew towering over the others. Talib spread out his arms, and Arthur fell into them. Arthur regained his footing, caught his breath, and then chose the moment he was ready to be arrested in this act of nonviolent protest.

The next time we saw Talib was a few years later. The two of us had been invited to a gathering organized by African American imams in New York to honor rabbis who had spoken out for the right of Muslims to build a mosque and community center in Lower Manhattan. As we walked to our table, we looked around for Talib. He had not yet arrived, but one of our hosts assured us that he was on his way.

Once at our table, we began a conversation with several of our dinner partners about how to greet one another. A few of the Muslim men made it clear that physical contact of any kind between men and women (other than family members) was not allowed. All right, when in Mecca do as the Meccans do! And we remembered learning years before, in our Abrahamic gatherings, that Talib (like some of our Orthodox Jewish friends) would not touch hands with women. So we prepared ourselves: when he did arrive, Phyllis could express her joy at seeing him, but no touching.

A few minutes later Talib entered the large hall and strode toward us. We stood to say hello, *Salaam aleikum*, tears of joy and reconnection in our eyes. And then, Talib rushed forward, scooped up Phyllis in his arms and didn't put her down until he and she were finished hugging. No one at our table said a word. Talib was not making a statement; he was simply embracing a sister in a heartfelt moment of reunion.

Love—the ancient teaching of the Torah and Koran—is still today the most powerful force for overcoming fear, prejudice, and violence. Because it is such a powerful force, it must be channeled with great care and consideration. For us, Talib has repeatedly served as a model of responsible and responsive love in times of pain, uncertainty, danger, and discomfort. To him, and to all who take up the deep internal journey of true loving "dialogue" to welcome all thirsty travelers into the opened tent of Abraham, Hagar, and Sarah, our thanks, our admiration, and our love!

51

Practicing in the
"Temples of Human Experience"

Ji Hyang Padma

The beginning of my interfaith work, my first religious "border-crossing," came in 1993. I had just been ordained as a nun in a Zen temple in Korea, and returned to the Boston area, offering pastoral support and meditation classes to HIV-AIDS patients through the Boston Living Center. In the course of this work, I met Jeannette Normandin, a Catholic nun who was also working the front lines of this health crisis. She was dividing her time between Boston Living Center and Ruah House, which she had recently founded as a housing option for women with AIDS. She invited me to attend the Boston Clergy and Religious Leaders' Group, a gathering formed to promote fellowship among downtown congregations. It had originally been an ecumenical Christian group, and was still warming to the presence of people of other faiths. It took me some time to break in, to make connections, and to find my place at the table. This ice-breaking period tested my own commitment to the work, as I am a shy person by nature and this required me to stretch myself in new and uncomfortable ways.

In this period of growth and challenge, I took inspiration from my mentor, Maha Ghosananda, the Gandhi of Cambodia, who frequently visited, in the midst of his work to promote peace, the Zen Center where I lived. Maha Ghosananda served as a member of the international Peace Council, a diverse group of religious leaders, well respected in their home countries, who came together regularly to support each other's peacemaking efforts wherever this support was most urgently needed. Maha Ghosananda led an annual walk for peace in Cambodia that grew to become a social movement, the Dhammayietra. The first walk began at the Thai-Cambodia border and included escorting refugees back to their home country to tearful reunions with their family members.

On one of his trips through Boston, Maha Ghosananda spoke to me about his upcoming Dhammayietra to bring about peace during Cambodia's first democratic elections. He said to me, "Please come." The preelection murders and campaigns of intimidation had brought people to anticipate tanks in the streets, as had occurred just a year before. At the risk of his life, Maha Ghosananda was practicing in the "temples of human experience," and I recognized this opportunity to walk with him as my own initiation into a path of border-crossing. During the seven-day walk, people associated with both the ruling Cambodian People's Party and of FUNICPEC, the opposition party, came out of their homes to their show support of the walk. While banners for each party hung from the doorways of neighboring homes, men and women from both parties knelt and prayed as we passed. The energy of four hundred people walking together silently, with a shared practice of mindfulness and loving-kindness gave these communities an opportunity to pause and reflect on whether there might be another way to experience their shared life. Interspersed throughout the lines were banners with the words of a prayer this sharply divided community shared in common:

> *Great compassion makes a peaceful heart.*
> *A peaceful heart makes a peaceful person.*
> *A peaceful person makes a peaceful family.*
> *A peaceful family makes a peaceful community.*
> *A peaceful community makes a peaceful nation.*
> *A peaceful nation makes a peaceful world.*
> *May all beings be at peace.*

This prayer describes the effects of mindfulness practice suffused with *metta* (loving-kindness). When we embody this practice, it spreads, and more and more people begin to rest in their natural state of kindness. These widening circles of care create the peaceful communities in which we aspire to live. To achieve world peace, we must begin with our own hearts.

We completed the walk on the seventh day in Phnom Penh, three thousand people joined us. Ahead of us, there was a sea of saffron: the Theravadan monks' robes shining among ancient stone buildings. Behind us, there was a sea of white: the Theravadan nuns' robes, as bright as their clear, compassionate eyes. When a reporter asked Maha Ghosananda after the Dhammayietra walk, "What difference do you think you have made?" he replied, simply, "I feel more peaceful." Our way of being in the world brings about the change we would like to see happen, step by step. Every word, every action, makes a difference.

Through the Dhammayietra, I discovered the path of meditation practice and the path of social engagement to be one continuous practice. The work of creating peaceful communities through interfaith dialogue is nurtured by my commitment to mindfulness meditation. My meditation practice deepens through the active engagement of compassion in service and action. Maha Ghosananda's meditation practice of *metta* (loving-kindness) gave him the capacity to extend compassionate awareness to whoever was around him; that continues to be the way I seek to hold space within the context of interfaith dialogue. My faith in meditation practice deepened through seeing the tangible effect it had on Cambodian society. I returned to Boston with renewed courage and confidence in engaging in interfaith dialogue.

52

The Value of a Peso

Miguel A. De La Torre

I was sitting on the dirt floor with about a dozen of my seminary students. Bugs crawled along the walls of the shack constructed of discarded wood, cardboard, and plasterboard. Empty plastic bags and trash littered the flimsy structure, hugging the hut as if they were adornments. The "owner" of the house, an indigenous woman who had been aged prematurely by the ravages of poverty, patiently engaged us in conversation.

Routinely, I bring my students to Cuernavaca, Mexico, on missionary trips. Usually, the purpose of missionary trips in these parts is to evangelize "nonbelievers," to convince them to accept the doctrines of the missionary, worshiping and believing like North Americans. My missionary trips are somewhat different. We go to be evangelized by the poor, to learn from the disenfranchised and dispossessed who God is. We go to "get saved."

Our host welcomes us into her home and offers us hospitality. She prepares a snack of jam on stale saltine crackers, giving what she can barely afford to give. As in past encounters, I encourage my primarily Protestant Euro-American students to ask this poor, illiterate, Catholic indigenous woman about her faith. With me translating, my students begin asking, "Who is God? Who is Jesus? Who is the Virgin Mary? What is the Church?" Like a teacher instructing the young, she begins to provide us with her understanding of faith, doctrine, and church teachings.

As I translate her responses, I am struck by how illogical, uninformed, superstitious, and syncretistic is her faith. This mixture of local indigenous teachings, medieval Roman Catholicism, and a sprinkling of self-help New Ageism is more than my trained theological mind can handle. I fight the urge to correct her, to reveal the incongruities in her beliefs. I find myself slipping back into the traditional missionary role of becoming her savior and righting her theological wrongs. Although I continue to faithfully translate her words, I begin to contemplate how I can challenge her with the "truth."

Just then, her nine-year-old son returns home. A dirty, undernourished boy shyly enters the hut barefoot and meekly interrupts his mother. He hands over about fifteen pesos which he collected— during school hours—selling Chiclets at a downtown street corner. The mother places all but one peso in her pocket. This one coin she places on a box in the middle of the room that serves as a makeshift table. After a while, I ask her what she plans to buy with the peso she set aside.

"Oh, that," she responds, "that's for the poor."

In that moment I learned more about God than I had from all of the theology books I had ever read. When those who have so little *do* their faith by providing for those who have even less, those of us privileged by class should be profoundly humbled. It is the privileged who see the oppressed and do nothing that are the ones that do not know God. I may have had the educational training to tease apart the inconsistencies in this woman's beliefs, but she knew far more about God than I did. This is not a romanticization of the poor, for surely there is nothing romantic about poverty. Rather, it is a theological truth that I learned directly from this poor woman's actions.

When we all get to heaven, we will discover how wrong we all were. No group has a monopoly on truth. So in a sense, orthodoxy— correct belief—is not that important (I say as a working theologian!). What should take precedence is orthopraxis—correct action. Calling oneself a Catholic, Protestant, Jew, Hindu, Buddhist, Muslim, *curandera/o*, or *santero/a* is less important than living one's faith, and each of our traditions instructs us to care for the poor and marginalized members of our societies. This reminds me of the New Testament passage found in the book of James: "You say you believe in one God—big deal; even the demons believe and tremble with fear. You idiots, don't you know that faith without praxis is dead!?" (2:19–20, my translation).

53

A Test of Character

Jim Wallis

In the fall of 2010, we saw a disturbing rise in religious intolerance in the United States. From the much-politicized opposition to a proposed Muslim community center near Ground Zero in New York City to a fundamentalist pastor's threat to burn Qurans, a wave of Islamophobia appeared to be sweeping the country.[1]

How should Christians respond? There are some key questions that get to the heart of the issue, and our answers say a lot about ourselves, our own faith, and the collective character of our country.

The first question is this: Does our judgment of our neighbors come from their religious labels or the content of their character? I do not advocate a religious pluralism that blurs the significant differences between religions, but I do believe that my religious tradition calls me to be a peacemaker and to love my neighbors, especially when I do not agree with them. When Muslim leaders step up to lead an initiative to reduce tensions and promote understanding, do we judge them by the actions of terrorists (whom those leaders have condemned) or by their integrity and character? This does not mean we have to agree with them on everything, but rather that we're called to love and respect them.

The second question asks: Do we believe in freedom for my religion or freedom of religion? The "establishment" and "free exer-

---

[1]   This reflection originally appeared in a slightly different form in the December 2010 issue of *Sojourners* magazine. Reprinted with permission.

cise" clauses of the First Amendment were revolutionary statements. They represent ideals to which we aspire but have not always lived up to. Anti-Catholic sentiment, anti-Semitism, and other forms of religious bigotry have reared their ugly heads over and over in our history. But ultimately, many minority groups have flourished here because of our strong history of religious liberty. Whether we allow religious freedom for Americans of Islamic faith—near Ground Zero or anywhere else—will give evidence of our own character, the integrity of our faith, and our real commitment to the ideals that have distinguished our nation.

Finally, we must ask a third question: In the face of global terrorism, who wins when the U.S. restricts religious freedom? Religious sensitivities, especially around Ground Zero, are understandable. September 11 was a crime against humanity, and, tragically, it was the first significant encounter many Americans had with radical Islam or Islam of any sort. But this is why the mission of the Manhattan community center is so important, as it plans to run programs that reduce tensions and build understanding. In order for our country to continue healing, more of us need to build trust with those who are different—especially with the many Muslims who love this country. There are thousands of interfaith conversations, service projects, and relationships that have been built since 9/11. These should be publicized and encouraged.

One good example is that of Heartsong Church in Cordova, Tennessee, which—in a rare departure from the cable networks' steady drumbeat of conflict—was featured on CNN. In 2008, Heartsong's pastor, Steve Stone, learned that the Memphis Islamic Center had bought land adjacent to his church. Rather than protest the plans, he put up a large sign that said: "Heartsong Church Welcomes Memphis Islamic Center to the Neighborhood." The Muslim leaders were floored. They had dared to hope only that their arrival would be ignored. It had not occurred to them that they might be welcomed.

When the Islamic Center's new building was under construction, its members used Heartsong Church for Ramadan prayer services. Heartsong's community barbecues now serve halal meat. Pastor Stone said the two congregations are planning joint efforts to feed the homeless and tutor local children.

Stone also told me that he got a call from a group of Muslims in a small town in Kashmir. They said they had been watching CNN when the segment on Heartsong Church aired. Afterward, one of the community's leaders said to those who were gathered, "God just spoke to us through this man." Another said, "How can we kill these people?" A third man went straight to the local Christian church and proceeded to clean it, inside and out.

Stone says he is just trying to love his neighbors, as he says Jesus instructs him to do. For their part, the residents of that small town in Kashmir told him: "We are now trying to be good neighbors, too. Tell your congregation we do not hate them, we love them, and for the rest of our lives we are going to take care of that little church."

This conflict is really about the role that faith will play in America. It is about whether or not we will accept Muslim Americans as true Americans or as second-class citizens. It is about whether we will blame millions of American Muslims and one billion Muslims worldwide for the actions of a small number of Muslims who try to use their brand of faith to murder innocent people. It is a test of our character, and we dare not fail it.

Contributors

Ibrahim Abdul-Matin is a second generation American Muslim, radio personality, and a policy adviser in New York Mayor Michael Bloomberg's Office of Long-Term Planning and Sustainability. He is the author of *Green Deen: What Islam Teaches about Protecting the Planet*, in which he challenges Muslims and non-Muslims to be stewards of the earth.

Kecia Ali is associate professor of religion at Boston University. Her publications include *Marriage and Slavery in Early Islam, Sexual Ethics and Islam*, and *Imam Shafi'i: Scholar and Saint*. Her current research focuses on modern biographies of Muhammad. She serves as co-chair of the Study of Islam section of the American Academy of Religion and sits on its committee on the Status of Women in the Profession.

Abdullah Antepli is the Muslim chaplain at Duke University. He completed his basic imam training and education in his native Turkey. From 1996 to 2003 he worked on a variety of faith-based humanitarian and relief projects in Myanmar (Burma) and Malaysia with the Association of Social and Economic Solidarity with Pacific Countries. He is the founder and an executive board member of the Muslim Chaplains Association and a member of the National Association of College and University Chaplains. From 2003 to 2005 he served as the first Muslim chaplain at Wesleyan University. He then moved to Hartford Seminary in Connecticut, where he was the associate director of the Islamic Chaplaincy Program and Interfaith Relations, as well as an adjunct faculty member.

Ali Asani is professor of Indo-Muslim and Islamic religion and cultures at Harvard University. He graduated from Harvard with a BA in the comparative study of religion and a PhD in Indo-Muslim culture. He teaches a variety of courses concerning Islam at Harvard, including Islam and the arts, Muslim societies in South Asia, Islamic mysticism, and Ismaili history and thought,. Professor Asani has been particularly active post-September 11 in improving the understanding of Islam and its role in Muslim societies. In 2002, he was awarded the Harvard Foundation medal for his outstanding contributions toward promoting a better understanding of Islam.

Judith Berling was raised Presbyterian or UCC. In the 1970s, she experienced East Asian temples and rituals firsthand when she spent two and a half years in Taiwan and Japan researching and writing her dissertation on Chinese religion for Columbia University. She taught in religious studies at Indiana University for thirteen years and then served as dean. Now she teaches Chinese and comparative religions at the Graduate Theological Union in Berkeley, California. She is an active member of St. Mark's Episcopal Church in Berkeley.

Daniel A. Berman is the assistant rabbi at Congregation Mishkan Tefila in Chestnut Hill, Massachusetts. Prior to entering rabbinical school at Hebrew College where he was an interfaith fellow, Rabbi Berman practiced as a trial attorney in Boston for several years and held a position as adjunct professor at Northeastern University School of Law. Rabbi Berman received chaplaincy training at Massachusetts General Hospital. He is married to Sarah Meyers, and together they have two children, Elie and Mica.

Phyllis Berman was guide and facilitator for many of the sessions of the Tent of Abraham, Hagar, and Sarah. She is the founder (1979) and director of the Riverside Language Program, an intensive school in New York City for adult immigrants and refugees from all around the world. From 1993 to 2005 she was the director of the summer program of the Elat Chayyim retreat center. She and Rabbi Arthur Waskow are co-authors of *A Time for Every Purpose under Heaven: The Jewish Life-Spiral as a Spiritual Journey* (Farrar, Straus and Giroux, 2002) and of *Freedom Journeys: The Tale of Exodus and Wilderness across Millennia* (Jewish Lights, 2011).

Mary C. Boys is the Skinner and McAlpin Professor of Practical Theology at Union Theological Seminary in New York City, author or editor of five books on Jewish-Christian relations, including *Has God Only One Blessing?: Judaism as a Source of Christian Self-Understanding* and *Christians and Jews in Dialogue: Learning in the Presence of the Other,* co-authored with Sara S. Lee. Dr. Boys is a member of the Sisters of the Holy Names of Jesus and Mary.

Rita Nakashima Brock, PhD, is ordained in the Christian Church (Disciples of Christ) and is an award-winning author. Her recent book, *Saving Paradise: How Christianity Traded Love of This World for Crucifixion and Empire,* co-authored with Rebecca Parker, was a *Publisher's Weekly* best book of 2008. From 1997 to 2001, she directed the Radcliffe Fellowship Program, Harvard University, and was a fellow at the Harvard Divinity School Center for Values in Public Life (2001–2002). She founded Faith Voices for the Common Good in 2004, directs it, and led the planning team for the Truth Commission on Conscience in War (http://www.conscienceinwar.org), which generated the Soul Repair Project for healing moral injury in veterans.

Joan Chittister is a Benedictine sister and author of some thirty books. She is the Executive Director of Benetvision: A Resource and Research Center for Contemporary Spirituality and is a past president of the Leadership Conference of Women Religious. Chittister is also a regular columnist for the *National Catholic Reporter* and an active member of the International Peace Council. She has been recognized by universities and national organizations for her work for justice, peace, and equality for women in church and society. A theologian, social psychologist, and communication theorist, she takes seriously her teaching ministry.

Miguel A. De La Torre, PhD, presently serves as professor of social ethics and Latino/a studies at Iliff School of Theology in Denver, Colorado. He has authored numerous articles and more than twenty-five books, including the award-winning *Reading the Bible from the Margins* (Orbis, 2002), *Santería: The Beliefs and Rituals of a Growing Religion in America* (Wm. B. Eerdmans, 2004), and *Doing Christian Ethics from the Margins* (Orbis, 2004). He is a director of the American Academy of Religion and past director of the Society of Christian

Ethics. He was elected the 2011 vice president of the Society of Christian Ethics and is in line to serve as the society's president in 2012. Additionally, he is the editor of *Journal of Race, Ethnicity, and Religion* (http://www.raceandreligion.com).

Charles P. Gibbs is the founding executive director of the United Religions Initiative (http://www.uri.org), a global interfaith network active in seventy-eight countries that strives for peace, justice, and healing through interfaith cooperation. An internationally respected speaker and author, Charles is an Episcopal priest. He brings to his ministry a strong commitment to spiritual transformation, work for peace, justice, and healing, and an abiding belief in the sacredness of all life on this planet.

Roger S. Gottlieb is professor of philosophy at Worcester Polytechnic Institute. He is the author or editor of sixteen books, including *Engaging Voices: Tales of Morality and Meaning in an Age of Global Warming* (Baylor University Press, 2011), *A Greener Faith: Religious Environmentalism and Our Planet's Future* (Oxford University Press, 2006), *A Spirituality of Resistance: Finding a Peaceful Heart and Protecting the Earth* (Rowman and Littlefield, 2003), and *Joining Hands: Politics and Religion Together for Social Change* (Westview, 2002). He is also a contributing editor for *Tikkun* magazine and columnist for Patheos.com.

Arthur Green is the Irving Brudnick Professor of Jewish Philosophy and Religion at Hebrew College. In 2003 he founded the Hebrew College Rabbinical School, where he currently serves as rector. He is former Philip Lown Professor of Jewish Thought at Brandeis University, as well as former president of the Reconstructionist Rabbinical College. He is both a theologian and a historian of Jewish mysticism and sees his work as forming a bridge between those two distinct fields of endeavor. He has a long history of involvement in interfaith activity. Among his many publications is *Radical Judaism: Rethinking God and Tradition*.

Irving Greenberg, an influential rabbi and theologian, has written extensively on post-Shoah theology, on the relationship of Judaism and Christianity, and on the ethics of power and religious/cultural issues of pluralism after the Holocaust. He served as chairman of the United

States Holocaust Memorial Council from 2000 to 2002. From 1997 to 2007 Greenberg served as the president of Jewish Life Network/ Steinhardt Foundation. From 1974 to 1997, he served as founding president of the National Jewish Center for Learning and Leadership (CLAL). His writings include *The Jewish Way: Living the Holidays* (1988), *A Philosophy of Judaism,* based on analysis of the Sabbath and holidays, *Living in the Image of God: Jewish Teachings to Perfect the World* (1998), and *For the Sake of Heaven and Earth: The New Encounter between Judaism and Christianity* (2004).

Ruben L. F. Habito, born in the Philippines, was sent to Japan in 1970 to assist in Jesuit educational work there. He practiced Zen under Yamada Koun Roshi of the Sanbokyodan lineage. Leaving the Jesuits in 1989, he moved to Dallas, Texas, to teach at Perkins School of Theology, Southern Methodist University. He also serves as spiritual guide at Maria Kannon Zen Center. He is married to Maria Reis Habito, and they have two sons, Florian and Benjamin. His books include *Healing Breath: Zen for Christians and Buddhists in a Wounded World* (Wisdom, 2006) and *Experiencing Buddhism: Ways of Wisdom and Compassion* (Orbis, 2005).

Hurmon Hamilton is the president of the greater Boston Interfaith Organization (GBIO) and the senior pastor of the Historic Roxbury Presbyterian Church in Boston, Massachusetts. He has been featured as a regular speaker, lecturer, and preacher at Harvard University, Boston University, and Princeton University. The Reverend Hamilton, along with his church (RPC), created a groundbreaking Adopt-a-School Program, which organized a coalition of community and faith-based organizations to adopt struggling schools in the local Roxbury neighborhood.

S. Mark Heim is the Samuel Abbot Professor of Christian Theology at Andover Newton Theological School. A graduate of Amherst College, Andover Newton Theological School (MDiv) and the Boston College-Andover Newton doctoral program (PhD), he has been deeply involved in issues of religious pluralism. He is the author of *Salvations: Truth and Difference in Religion* (Orbis, 1995), *The Depth of the Riches: A Trinitarian Theology of Religious Ends* (Eerdmans, 2001) and *Saved from Sacrifice: A Theology of the Cross* (Eerdmans, 2006). An ordained American Baptist minister, Heim represents his denomination on the Faith and Order Commission of the National Council and World Council of Churches.

Bradley Hirschfield is the president of the National Jewish Center for Learning and Leadership (CLAL). He conceived and hosted a landmark interfaith TV series titled *Building Bridges: Abrahamic Perspectives on the World Today*, airing on Bridges TV (American Muslim TV Network). Rabbi Hirschfield was featured in the acclaimed film *Freaks Like Me*, where he explores our fear of the "other." In 2007, under the auspices of the U.S. State Department, he joined a mission to the Middle East to build global citizenship. Hirschfield is a co-author of *Embracing Life and Facing Death: A Jewish Guide to Palliative Care* (CLAL, 2003) and author of *You Don't Have to Be Wrong for Me to Be Right: Finding Faith without Fanaticism* (Three Rivers Press, 2009). An Orthodox rabbi, he received his MA and MPhil from the Jewish Theological Seminary, and his BA from the University of Chicago.

Sherman A. Jackson holds the *King Faisal Chair in Islamic Thought and Culture and Professor of Religion, and American Studies and Ethnicity* at the University of Southern California. His areas of expertise are Islamic and Near Eastern studies, along with American law and African American studies. The hallmark of his research is his attempt to bring the classical tradition of Islamic learning into more serious and fruitful conversations with modern and most particularly American reality and to venture beyond the boundaries imposed upon Islamic studies by the area studies paradigm out of which it has traditionally operated. He was recognized in 2009 as one of the 500 most influential Muslims in the world by the Royal Islamic Strategic Studies Center in Amman, Jordan, and the Prince Alwaleed Bin Talal Center for Muslim-Christian Understanding. He is author of several books including the forthcoming *Sufism for Non-Sufis: Ibn 'Ata' Allah's Tāj al-'Arûs* (Oxford University Press, 2012).

Rodger Kamenetz is the author of ten books, most recently, *Burnt Books: Rabbi Nachman of Bratslav and Franz Kafka* (Schocken/Nextbook, 2010). He's best known for *The Jew in the Lotus*, his classic groundbreaking account of Jewish-Buddhist dialogue. A professor emeritus at Louisiana State University, he lives in New Orleans and teaches spiritual direction using dreams.

Valarie Kaur is an award-winning filmmaker, writer, advocate, and public speaker. A third-generation Sikh American, she uses strategic storytelling to advance social action campaigns on racial justice, immigration reform, religious pluralism, and gender equality. Her critically acclaimed documentary film *Divided We Fall: Americans in the Aftermath* (http://www.dwf-film.com) (2008) on hate crimes after September 11 has inspired national grassroots dialogue. Valarie earned bachelor's degrees in religion and international relations at Stanford University, a master's in theological studies at Harvard Divinity School, and a law degree at Yale Law School, where she teaches visual advocacy as founding director of the Yale Visual Law Project. In 2011, she joined Auburn Theological Seminary as the director of Groundswell, a broad-based initiative to spark and empower the multifaith movement for justice.

Paul F. Knitter is the Paul Tillich Professor of Theology, World Religions, and Culture at Union Theological Seminary, New York. Previously, for some thirty years, he taught theology at Xavier University in Cincinnati, Ohio. He received a licentiate in theology from the Pontifical Gregorian University in Rome (1966) and a doctorate from the University of Marburg, Germany (1972). Most of his research and publications have dealt with religious pluralism and interreligious dialogue. Since his groundbreaking 1985 book, *No Other Name?* (Orbis Books), he has been exploring how the religious communities of the world can cooperate in promoting human and ecological well-being.

Nancy Fuchs Kreimer is the director of the Department of Multifaith Studies of the Reconstructionist Rabbinical College. A graduate of the Reconstructionist Rabbinical College, she holds a PhD in Jewish-Christian relations from Temple University. For more than thirty years, Rabbi Fuchs Kreimer has explored what joins and separates religions in their practice and approach to holy texts. She has designed and led innovative workshops and retreats that bring emerging religious leaders together, in part thanks to two major grants from the Henry R. Luce Foundation. She writes her own blog, http://www.multifaithworld.org, and is published regularly on the *Huffington Post*.

Ramdas Lamb is associate professor of religion at the University of Hawaii and the president and founder of the Sahayog Foundation, a nonprofit organization that helps educate poor rural youth in Central India. He continues to be a member of the Ramananda Sampraday, the Hindu order in which he was a monk in the 1970s, although now he is a layman.

Bill J. Leonard is James and Marilyn Dunn Professor of Church History and Religion at Wake Forest University, where he was founding dean of the School of Divinity, 1996–2010. He holds a PhD from Boston University and has held teaching positions at the Southern Baptist Seminary, Louisville, and as chair of the Department of Religion at Samford University, Birmingham. He is the author or editor of some eighteen books, including *The Challenge of Being Baptist* (Baylor University Press, 2010).

Michael Lerner is editor of *Tikkun* (http://www.tikkun.org) and chair of the interfaith Network of Spiritual Progressives (http://www.spiritualprogressives.org). He is rabbi of Beyt Tikkun synagogue-without-walls in San Francisco and Berkeley, California, and the author of eleven books, most recently, *Embracing Israel/Palestine: A Strategy for Middle East Peace* (North Atlantic Books, 2012). He gives lectures and serves as scholar-in-residence at universities, synagogues, and churches throughout the United States, Canada, the United Kingdom, and Israel. He can be reached at RabbiLerner.tikkun@gmail.com.

Jeffery D. Long is associate professor and chair of religious studies and co-director of Asian studies at Elizabethtown College in Elizabethtown, Pennsylvania. He received his PhD from the University of Chicago Divinity School in 2000. He is the author of *A Vision for Hinduism: Beyond Hindu Nationalism* (2007), *Jainism: An Introduction* (2009), and the *Historical Dictionary of Hinduism* (2011). Dr. Long's religious affiliation is with Hinduism. He is an active member of his local Hindu temple, the Hindu American Religious Institute, near Harrisburg, Pennsylvania (where he teaches Sunday school), and an active member of the Ramakrishna Vedanta Society.

John Makransky is a professor of Buddhism and comparative theology at Boston College, senior adviser to Chokyi Nyima Rinpoche's

Centre for Buddhist Studies in Nepal, and board member of the Society of Buddhist-Christian Studies. He is the guiding teacher of the Foundation for Active Compassion, a socially engaged Buddhist organization. In 2000, John was ordained a Tibetan Buddhist lama in the lineage of Nyoshul Khen Rinpoche. His books include *Awakening through Love* (2007) and *Buddhist Theology* (2000, co-edited with Roger Jackson). John's research focuses on doctrines and practices of Indian and Tibetan Buddhism, and the adaptation of such teachings in new contexts in response to contemporary social needs.

Brian D. McLaren (http://www.brianmclaren.net) is an author, speaker, and activist. For twenty-four years, he served as the founding pastor of a nondenominational Christian church in the Washington, D.C., area. His books include *A Generous Orthodoxy* (Zondervan, 2004), *Everything Must Change* (Nelson, 2007), *Naked Spirituality* (Harper, 2011), and *Jesus, Moses, the Buddha, and Mohammed Walk Into a Bar: Christian Identity in a Multi-Faith World* (Jericho, 2012). He lives with his wife Grace in southwest Florida, where he enjoys kayaking in the Everglades and observing wildlife. They have four adult children.

Gregory Mobley is professor of Christian Bible at Andover Newton. Mobley is the author of *The Return of the Chaos Monsters—and Other Backstories of the Bible* (2012), *The Empty Men: The Heroic Tradition of Ancient Israel* (2005), *Samson and the Liminal Hero in the Ancient Near East* (2006), and with co-author T. J. Wray, *The Birth of Satan: Tracing the Devil's Biblical Roots* (2005). Mobley is an ordained American Baptist minister and is active in Jewish-Christian dialogue in the Boston area.

Richard J. Mouw is president and professor of Christian philosophy at Fuller Theological Seminary. He has been active in various interfaith dialogues, serving with Robert Millet of Brigham Young University as co-convenor of an ongoing Evangelical-Mormon dialogue, as well as working with the Board of Rabbis of South California in planning Jewish-Evangelical conversations. Representing the Presbyterian Church (USA), he co-chaired the official dialogue between Reformed and Roman Catholic theologians for six years, focusing on Baptism and the Eucharist. An editor of *Books and Culture*, he has authored sixteen books, including *Uncommon Decency: Christian Civility in an Uncivil World.*

Janet M. Cooper Nelson is an ordained UCC minister and director of the Office of Chaplains and Religious Life (OCRL) at Brown University. Joining the Brown faculty in 1990 after posts at Vassar, Mount Holyoke, and Dartmouth, she leads Brown's associate chaplains and religious affiliates endeavoring to increase religious literacy and deepen piety within the university community. With degrees from Wellesley, Tufts, and Harvard Divinity School, she advises undergraduates, teaches at Brown's Alpert School of Medicine, serves on the ethics committee of Home and Hospice Care of Rhode Island, and works on the twin concerns of America's religious illiteracy and robust religious history.

Ji Hyang Padma serves as director of Spirituality and Education Programs and as the Buddhist chaplain at Wellesley College. Ji Hyang also teaches at Babson College, Omega Institute, and Esalen Institute. She has done intensive Zen training and teaching in Asia and North America for twenty years. She has also served as Abbot of Cambridge Zen Center, as well as serving as a meditation teacher at Harvard University and Boston University. She is currently completing a PhD in transpersonal psychology. Her book, *Zen Practices for Transformative Times*, is being released by Hampton Roads Press in 2012.

Rebecca Ann Parker is president and professor of theology at Starr King School for the Ministry, the Unitarian Universalist and multireligious member school of the Graduate Theological Union in Berkeley, California. She is the co-author, with Rita Nakashima Brock, of *Saving Paradise: How Christianity Traded Love of This World for Crucifixion and Empire*, and with John Buehrens of *A House for Hope: The Promise of Progressive Religion*. Her conversation partner for this essay, Ibrahim Abdurrahman Farajajé, is provost and professor of cultural and Islamic studies at Starr King School and senior research analyst at the Center for Islamic Studies in Berkeley.

Eboo Patel is a founder and president of Interfaith Youth Core (IFYC), a Chicago-based organization building the global interfaith youth movement. Author of the award-winning book *Acts of Faith:*

The Story of an American Muslim, the Struggle for the Soul of a Generation, Eboo is also a regular contributor to the *Washington Post, USA Today,* and CNN. He served on President Obama's inaugural Advisory Council of the White House Office of Faith-based and Neighborhood Partnerships and holds a doctorate in the sociology of religion from Oxford University, where he studied on a Rhodes scholarship. Dr. Patel was named by *US News and World Report* as one of America's Best Leaders of 2009.

Laurie L. Patton is the dean of the faculty of arts and sciences at Duke University. Formerly, she was the Charles Howard Candler Professor of Religions at Emory University and director of Emory's Center for Faculty Development and Excellence. Patton is the author or editor of eight books on South Asian history, culture, and religion. She translated the classical Sanskrit text, the Bhagavad Gita, for the Penguin Classics Series and has written two books of poetry. Her current research for two forthcoming books focuses on religion in the public sphere and on women and Sanskrit in contemporary India. Patton has lectured widely on religious pluralism and religion in the public sphere and is the founder and co-convener of a Religion, Conflict, and Peacebuilding Initiative at Emory.

Jennifer Howe Peace is assistant professor of interfaith studies at Andover Newton Theological School in Newton, Massachusetts. Dr. Peace co-directs the Center for Interreligious and Communal Leadership Education (CIRCLE), a joint program between Andover Newton and the Rabbinical School at Hebrew College. Author of numerous articles and essays on interfaith cooperation, Dr. Peace has been an interfaith organizer and educator since the 1990s. She served as a founding board member of the United Religions Initiative, a founding leader of the Interfaith Youth Core, and a founding member of the Daughters of Abraham—a movement of book groups for Jewish, Christian, and Muslim women that was initiated by her mother-in-law, Edie Howe.

Jonah Pesner is the founding director of Just Congregations. He works with synagogues pursuing social justice across the country and teaches on all three campuses of the Hebrew Union College-Jewish Institute of Religion. As a congregational rabbi at Temple Israel in

Boston, he pioneered the Fain Award-winning Ohel Tzedek / Tent of Justice social action initiative. He has led efforts to engage thousands of members of congregations to join together in successful campaigns for health care access, affordable housing, public education, gay and lesbian rights, nursing care workers' rights, and the living wage. As a leader of the Greater Boston Interfaith Organization, Rabbi Pesner was the chair of the GBIO effort in the Massachusetts Affordable Care Today! coalition that successfully secured health care for more than half a million uninsured residents of the Commonwealth.

Rodney L. Petersen, PhD, is executive director of the Boston Theological Institute (BTI), an ecumenical and interfaith consortium of theological schools in the Greater Boston area. He teaches in the member schools and overseas, serving also as co-director of the Religion and Conflict Transformation program at Boston University School of Theology. Petersen has participated in reconciliation workshops throughout the world, most recently in Nagaland. He is an ordained minister in the Presbyterian Church, U.S.A., where he serves on several committees. He also works with a variety of nonprofit organizations. Petersen is author or editor and contributor of articles and books on reconciliation, most recently *Overcoming Violence: Religion, Conflict and Peace-building* (BTI, 2011) and *The Changing Contours of World Mission and Christianity* (Wipf and Stock, 2011).

Wendy Peterson is a Jesus-following Métis ("mixed blood") woman from the original Red River Settlement of Manitoba, Canada. She is a founding board member of NAIITS (North American Institute for Indigenous Theological Studies) and edits the *NAIITS Journal*. She is adjunct faculty at Providence Theological Seminary in Manitoba and is writing her PhD dissertation on reclamation of Indigenous culture for Asbury Theological Seminary (Kentucky). She is married and has three children and ten grandchildren.

Judith Plaskow is a professor of religious studies at Manhattan College and a Jewish feminist theologian who has been teaching, writing, and speaking about Jewish feminism and feminist studies in religion for over forty years. Co-founder and for ten years co-editor of the *Journal of Feminist Studies in Religion,* she is author or editor of several works in feminist theology, including *Standing Again at Sinai: Judaism* *from a Feminist Perspective* and *The Coming of Lilith: Essays on Feminism, Judaism, and Sexual Ethics, 1972–2003.*

Zeenat Rahman is the co-founder of *The Hijabi Monologues,* a play that presents the true life experiences of Muslim American women. Zeenat is passionate about advancing positive narratives of Muslims in the West and advancing interfaith dialogue. She previously built and managed international programs for the Interfaith Youth Core (IFYC) and also served as the director of policy, in which role she was a strategic adviser to the White House and various federal agencies on issues related to youth, religious identity, interreligious engagement, and interfaith service. She travels abroad frequently to speak about American Muslim civic engagement. Most recently, she served as Acting Director of the Center for Faith-Based and Neighborhood Initiatives at USAID.

Anantanand Rambachan is professor and chair of religion at Saint Olaf College, Minnesota. Professor Rambachan is the author of several books, book chapters, and numerous journal articles. His books include *Accomplishing the Accomplished: The Vedas as a Source of Valid Knowledge in Shankara, The Limits of Scripture: Vivekananda's Reinterpretation of the Authority of the Vedas, The Advaita Worldview: God, World and Humanity,* and *Not-Two: The Liberating Teachings of Advaita* (State University of New York Press, forthcoming). His scholarly interests include the Advaita (Nondual) Vedanta tradition, Hindu ethics, Hinduism in the contemporary world, and interreligious dialogue.

Paul Brandeis Raushenbush is the senior religion editor of the *Huffington Post.* From 2003 to 2011 he was the associate dean of religious life and the chapel at Princeton University. An ordained American Baptist minister, Reverend Raushenbush speaks and preaches at colleges, churches, and institutes around the country. He has appeared on ABC *World News Tonight* and is a repeated guest on CNN and NPR. His first book, *Teen Spirit: One World, Many Faiths* (HCI), was released in the fall of 2004. He is the editor of the 100th anniversary edition of Walter Rauschenbusch's book, *Christianity and the Social Crisis—In the 21st Century* (HarperOne, 2007).

Or N. Rose is founding director of the Center for Global Judaism at the Hebrew College. He also serves as co-director of the Center for Inter-Religious and Communal Leadership Education (CIRCLE), a joint venture of Hebrew College and Andover Newton Theological School. The author or editor of several articles and books on Jewish spirituality, social justice, and interfaith cooperation, Rabbi Rose recently co-edited *Jewish Mysticism and the Spiritual Life: Classical Texts, Contemporary Reflections* (Jewish Lights, 2010).

Zalman Schachter-Shalomi is widely recognized as one of the most important Jewish spiritual teachers of our time. Reb Zalman's teachings incorporate wide-ranging knowledge of the spiritual technology developed by peoples all over the planet. He is committed to a post-triumphalist, ecumenical, and Gaian approach. His many published works include *Jewish with Feeling: Guide to a Meaningful Jewish Practice* (Riverhead Trade, 2006) and co-authoring of *A Heart Afire: Stories and Teachings of the Early Hasidic Masters* (Jewish Publication Society, 2009).

Samir Selmanovic, PhD, is author of *It's Really All about God: How Islam, Atheism, and Judaism Made Me a Better Christian* (Jossey-Bass/ Wiley, 2009) and a founder and Christian co-leader of Faith House Manhattan (http://www.faithhousemanhattan.org), an interfaith "community of communities" that brings together forward-looking Christians, Muslims, Jews, atheists, and others who seek to thrive interdependently. Samir is also the director of a Christian community in New York City called Citylights and serves on the Interfaith Relations Commission of the National Council of Churches and speaks nationally and internationally. See http://www.samirselmanovic.com.

Judith Simmer-Brown, PhD, is professor of religious studies at Naropa University in Boulder, Colorado, where she has been on the faculty since 1978. She is an Acharya (senior dharma teacher) in the Shambhala Buddhist lineage of Chogyam Trungpa and Sakyong Mipham Rinpoches. She served as an officer in the Society of Buddhist-Christian Studies from 1985 to 2005 and was a member of the Cobb-Abe Theological Encounter (Buddhist and Christian) from 1984 to 2004. She participated in the Gethsemani Dialogues in 1996 and 2002. She lectures and writes on Tibetan Buddhism, American Buddhism, women and Buddhism, and interreligious dialogue. Her books are *Dakini's*

Warm Breath: The Feminine Principle in Tibetan Buddhism (Shambhala, 2001) and *Meditation and the Classroom: Contemplative Pedagogy in Religious Studies* (State University of New York Press, 2011). She is married to Richard Brown and has two college-aged children.

Varun Soni is the dean of religious life at the University of Southern California (USC), where he oversees ninety student religious groups and forty campus religious directors. He is also a University Fellow at USC Annenberg's Center on Public Diplomacy and a member of the State Bar of California, the American Academy of Religion, and the Association for College and University Religious Affairs. He serves on the advisory board for the Center for Muslim-Jewish Engagement, the Music Preservation Project, CrossCurrents, Hindu American Seva Charities, and the Parliament of the World's Religions.

Najeeba Syeed-Miller is a practitioner and educator in the area of conflict resolution among communities of ethnic and religious diversity. Her involvements include conducting gang interventions, implementing diversity training in universities and public agencies, conflict resolution in public schools, interreligious dialogue among the Abrahamic traditions, and environmental conflict resolution. Syeed-Miller's mediation work has taken her to India, Latin America, Guam, Afghanistan, Israel, and Palestine. Her model of intervention is to build the capacity of those closest to the conflict. In particular her research and community activist efforts have focused on the role of women as agents of peacemaking.

Richard Twiss is a Native American educator and author. He is a member of the Sicangu Lakota Oyate from the Rosebud Lakota Sioux Reservation in South Dakota. Co-founder and president of Wiconi International (Wee-choe'-nee is Lakota for "life"), Twiss is also a Christian minister, author, and public speaker. He and his wife, Katherine, have four grown sons and live in Vancouver, Washington.

Burton L. Visotzky serves as Appleman Professor of Midrash and Interreligious Studies as well as director of the Milstein Center for Interreligious Dialogue at the Jewish Theological Seminary. Rabbi Visotzky is the author of ten books; the most recent is *Sage Tales: Wisdom and Wonder from the Rabbis of the Talmud* (Jewish Lights, 2011).

Pravrajika Vrajaprana has been a nun at the Sarada Convent of the Vedanta Society of Southern California since 1977, taking her final vows of monasticism, or *sannyasa,* in 1988. Vrajaprana is the author of *Vedanta: A Simple Introduction* as well as other books on Hinduism and Vedanta. Most recently, Vrajaprana co-authored with Swami Tyagananda *Interpreting Ramakrishna: Kali's Child Revisited.* Vrajaprana's books and articles have been translated into a number of European and Indic languages. Vrajaprana was the Hindu representative at both the Dalai Lama's 2006 Gathering of Hearts / Illuminating Compassion conference and the Dalai Lama and Desmond Tutu's 2008 Seeds of Compassion conference. She has presented papers on topics relating to the Hindu traditions at the American Academy of Religion and at the East/West Philosophers' Conference.

Jim Wallis is CEO of Sojourners. He is a best-selling author, public theologian, speaker, and international commentator on ethics and public life. He recently served on the President's Advisory Council on Faith-based and Neighborhood Partnerships and currently serves as the chair of the Global Agenda Council on Faith for the World Economic Forum. His latest book is *Rediscovering Values: On Wall Street, Main Street, and Your Street—A Moral Compass for the New Economy.* His two previous books, *The Great Awakening: Reviving Faith and Politics in a Post-Religious Right America* and *God's Politics: Why the Right Gets It Wrong and the Left Doesn't Get It* were both *New York Times* best sellers.

Arthur Waskow is the founder (1983) and director of the Shalom Center, a prophetic voice in Jewish, multireligious, and American life. He is the author of the *Freedom Seder, Seasons of Our Joy, Godwrestling—Round 2,* and *Down-to-Earth Judaism.* He and Rabbi Phyllis Berman are co-authors of *A Time for Every Purpose under Heaven: The Jewish Life-Spiral as a Spiritual Journey* (Farrar, Straus and Giroux) and of *Freedom Journeys: The Tale of Exodus and Wilderness across Millennia* (Jewish Lights, 2011).

Homayra Ziad is assistant professor of religion (Islam) at Trinity College. After receiving her first degree from Bryn Mawr, she earned a doctorate in Islamic Studies from Yale. Her scholarly interests include

Sufi traditions, theologies of pluralism, Quranic hermeneutics, and religion and humor. She has published on the Sufi pluralism of the eighteenth-century Delhi theologian and poet Khwajah Mir Dard, Urdu literature and qawwali, women and Islam, chaplaincy and scriptural reasoning, and Muslim liberation theology. She is deeply involved in interfaith initiatives and educational outreach on faith, and finds a home in scriptural reasoning and Jewish-Muslim dialogue. Homayra is inspired in her work by spiritual and pluralist traditions within Islam.